Inter-American Politics Series

SPONSORED BY THE

Center for Inter-American Relations/New York

GENERAL EDITOR: RONALD G. HELLMAN

VOLUME 1
Terms of Conflict:
Ideology in Latin American Politics
editors: Morris J. Blachman & Ronald G. Hellman

VOLUME 2
Authoritarianism in Mexico
editors: José Luis Reyna & Richard S. Weinert

AUTHORITARIANISM
IN MEXICO

editors:

José Luis Reyna & Richard S. Weinert

ISHI A Publication of the
Institute for the Study of Human Issues
Philadelphia

Manufactured in the United States of America

Library of Congress Cataloging in Publication Data:

Main entry under title:

Authoritarianism in Mexico.

    (Inter-American politics series; v. 2)
    Includes bibliographical references and index.
    1. Mexico—Politics and government—1910–1946—Addresses, essays, lectures. 2. Mexico—Politics and government—1946–   —Addresses, essays, lectures. 3. Mexico—Economic policy—Addresses, essays, lectures. 4. Mexico—Social policy—Addresses, essays, lectures. 5. Authoritarianism—Addresses, essays, lectures. I. Reyna, José Luis, 1941–   II. Weinert, Richard S. III. Series.
JL1281.A77   320.9'72'082   77–339
ISBN 0–915980–64–9
ISBN 0–89727–002–9 pbk.

For information, write:

Director of Publications
ISHI
3401 Science Center
Philadelphia, Pennsylvania 19104
U.S.A.

Preface

The Center for Inter-American Relations has worked, since it began operations in 1967, to build in the United States an understanding of the other nations in the Western hemisphere. Through its Literature, Visual, and Performing Arts programs, the Center promotes a broader awareness in the U.S. of the cultural achievements of the Americas. In numerous meetings scheduled each year by the Center's Public Affairs program, political, social, and economic subjects of inter-American interest are discussed and debated. The Center offers an unofficial platform from which public and private leaders, scholars, and social critics can make their thoughts known to diverse international audiences.

The purpose of this publication is to expand the Center's efforts by reaching those interested in inter-American affairs who are not able to participate personally in the Center's activities. We hope that this work, along with previous and forthcoming volumes sponsored by the Public Affairs program, will contribute significantly to the permanent body of research and commentary.

RONALD G. HELLMAN
CENTER FOR INTER-AMERICAN RELATIONS

Editors' Acknowledgments

We wish to acknowledge the invaluable contributions of many who attended the seminars at which the essays in this volume were first presented. Though they made no written contribution to this volume, their critical comments helped to improve the essays and shape them into their final form. They are David Barkin, Douglas Bennett, Marvin Bernstein, Hjordis Bierman, David Burks, Ricardo Cinta, David Collier, Abraham Lowenthal, Aurora Loyo, Donald Mabry, Guillermo O'Donnell, Ricardo Pozas, Kenneth Sharpe, Beatrice Treat, Frederick Turner, Lois Wasserspring, and Martin Weinstein.

We also wish to acknowledge the role of Ronald G. Hellman of the Center for Inter-American Relations. The original conception was his, and he provided the initial stimuli, discreetly retreating into the background once things were underway, but always remaining to provide support and encouragement whenever needed.

We would like to thank the Center for Inter-American Relations itself for sponsoring the seminars, and the Tinker and Ford Foundations for their financial support.

Finally, we wish to express appreciation to several people whose help was vital. Victoria Garcia helped plan and organize the four seminars. Felipe Gorostiza provided written minutes of each session. Anna Ivan generously lent her efficient administrative and secretarial skills. Ellen Seiler helped to edit the original manuscript.

JOSÉ LUIS REYNA AND RICHARD S. WEINERT

Contents

Introduction

RICHARD S. WEINERT

Mexico has long posed a challenge for political analysts and students of development. Many of the criteria indicate that contemporary Mexico is one of the most successful nations in the Third World. First, she has enjoyed and has consistently maintained for thirty years one of the highest rates of economic growth in the world. Second, she possesses a stable political system, dominated by civilian politicians who govern and change office in accordance with constitutional norms and procedures established more than forty years ago. And, third, Mexico's social structure has managed to withstand the shocks conveyed by rapid industrialization and urbanization despite the fact that recent developments in the social infrastructure—transportation, communication, and education—have disturbed much of the traditional coherence of society.

But in contrast to this positive picture of the achievements of modern Mexico, there are major blemishes which, at the least, serve to cloud the image. Rapid economic growth, far from eradicating poverty, has been accompanied by a worsening of the distribution of income. The net result is that large segments of the population have been bypassed by the growth process, and certain groups may have been left even worse off than before. The much-vaunted stable political structure has also been bought at considerable cost. It is upheld by the heavy-handed authoritarianism of a single-party system which has honored the forms of democratic process more than its substance. Mexican society suffers from autocratic control and rigidity. Potentially disruptive forces, such as pressures for change, protests, and alternative movements, have been repressed, suppressed, or forcibly altered by cooptation and other forms of manipulation. In short, a surface stability has been purchased at the cost of stifled expression.

The paradoxes may be multiplied. Mexico experienced the world's first violent social revolution of this century, antedating the Russian revolution by seven years, and the only successful revolution in the hemisphere until Cuba's. Yet Mexico today is a preeminent example of capitalist development, in which all the achievements, flaws, and distortions of that economic system are on prominent display. Again except for Cuba, Mexico is the most nationalist and independent nation in the hemisphere, recognizing Cuba in defiance of the United States, and providing a haven for Allende's widow and numerous other exiles of the left. Yet no nation's economy is more closely linked to and dependent on the United States than Mexico's.

As one probes further, the mystery deepens. Consider the question of leadership and institutionalization. On the one hand, the immense social and economic changes since the 1910 Revolution have occurred without the commanding leadership of a single charismatic figure. Mexico boasts no Mao, Ataturk, Nasser, or Perón—figures who, in their respective countries, dominated political and cultural affairs while presiding over radical economic transformation. Instead, Mexico seems to have developed strong and sophisticated institutions which have spawned a succession of competent leaders who have each contributed to the evolution and strengthening of the institutional base of society. Thus one can argue that Mexico today has the richest store of political and administrative talent of any Latin country. It has the largest and most competent body of public servants who manage the most efficient and complex web of autonomous and semiautonomous government economic agencies in Latin America. Even in private life, Mexico meets an unusually high standard of management among banks and corporations, of sophistication among lawyers, doctors, and accountants, of excellence in crafts, dance, and the arts.

On the other hand, one would strain to find a political leader with greater personal power than a Mexican President. When his six-year term ends, he leaves office, but during that term he rules with nearly total authority. The government bureaucracy over which he presides, moreover, is riddled with systematic and thorough-going corruption, which belies the sophisticated institutionalization mentioned above.

How then to understand Mexico? Where to place Mexico in some rough conceptual framework? In the late 1950s and early 1960s American social scientists saw Mexico as a developing democracy. The essence of the vision was the constitutional framework and democratic procedures which were so evident in Mexican politics. Mexico held regular elections, with a national campaign reminiscent of more developed democracies. It had political parties with both national and regional structures, and while these structures were weak by European standards, they compared favorably with American parties. There was a relatively free press, with at least no obvious censorship; and there were no blatant interferences with other civil liberties.

Imperfections were recognized. Elections were regular but not truly competitive. Thus the campaigns, party organizations, and other paraphernalia of democratic politics may have been more formalistic than substantive—or may have served different purposes than in truly democratic systems. There were disturbing signs that civil liberties were tolerated more in principle than in practice. Yet these and other imperfections were viewed as flaws which would be eradicated over time. Continued economic growth, urbanization, literacy, and so forth would produce an increasingly democratic society, with improving income distribution, more vital pluralism, and more zealously guarded civil liberties. Mexico, in short, was firmly on the road to a free and open democratic society.

In the late 1960s, this view of the inherent virtue and self-perfecting character of Mexican society gave way to a more critical view in which flaws took on the character of essential rather than accidental features. Instead of a nascent and emerging democracy, Mexico was seen as a special and successful kind of authoritarianism, in which democratic forms masked a stern executive branch which orchestrated Mexican life to serve the interests of a narrow elite. The "imperfections" of the earlier view became structural necessities, and the direction and tendencies of Mexican society began to be viewed in a wholly different context.

Simultaneously with this shift in the view of Mexico, a group of scholars concerned primarily with Brazil and Argentina began developing a new conception of Latin American politics. Fernando Henrique Cardoso, Guillermo O'Donnell, Alfred Stepan, and Philippe Schmitter in different essays worked out a concept variously referred to as *associated dependent development*, *corporatist politics*, and *bureaucratic-authoritarian government*. Some salient features of the political structures to which these terms applied were an expanding state role, an increased reliance on foreign capital, and a prominent role for technocrats in place of traditional civilian politicians. These features in turn promoted strong authoritarian governments which manipulated popular sectors to facilitate capital accumulation and achieve a higher economic growth rate. Such governments were led to impose measures which usually worsened income distribution and sometimes lowered absolute income levels for the working classes.

Although there were good intellectual grounds for considering Mexico in the formulation of these new concepts, in fact the country was overlooked. The oversight was not deliberate, but can be explained on a very practical plane: the theorists were not sufficiently familiar with Mexico to incorporate it in their initial theorizing.

In retrospect it seems obvious that there are points of convergence between the more recent view of Mexicanists described above and the conceptual frameworks developed to analyze countries to the south. This volume seeks to explore these parallels and promote this convergence.

This task is important in two ways. First, it enriches understanding of Mexico by utilizing a broader conceptual framework than has been considered to date. Second, it helps refine the concepts by seeing how they apply to a country to which they should be relevant but which was not prominent in their formulation.

The essays that follow grew out of four meetings of scholars during 1975, under the aegis of the Center for Inter-American Relations, and supported by grants from the Tinker Foundation and the Ford Foundation. The meetings were a part of the Center's ongoing series of "country studies" seminars. In this case the sessions brought together Mexican and United States scholars from several of the social sciences to consider the broad question of how to understand the workings of Mexican authoritarianism. To orient subsequent discussions, the first meeting was largely devoted to consideration of the nature of bureaucratic-authoritarian regimes in Latin America, and was centered on a presentation by Guillermo O'Donnell growing out of his work on Argentina. Thus, most of the first meeting did not touch directly on Mexico. However, since almost all present were Mexicanists, Mexico was never far from view.

This initial session served two valuable purposes. First, it oriented our individual thinking along certain lines so that later discussions of different aspects of Mexican life returned to the same themes. Second, it demonstrated the need for concreteness to overcome what threatened to become rarified abstractions which gratified the speaker but communicated little to listeners. This guaranteed an empirical foundation to each of the essays; as the reader will see, each one in this volume contains some hard information on an aspect of Mexican life, as well as shedding light on one or more conceptual themes.

Subsequent meetings were devoted to presentation and discussion of the essays that comprise this volume, as well as some other written contributions which have not been included but which enriched the discussions. Each author substantially revised his essay following the discussions. Moreover, each author participated in discussions of other papers and so could gain additional insights to incorporate explicitly or implicitly in his own work. This also permitted a great deal of cross-referencing among the essays, which contributes to their conceptual coherence.

While the major themes will emerge as the essays are read, it may be useful to attempt a brief formulation of them in this introduction. The starting point for all of the authors is that there is a proliferation of organizations within the structure of the Mexican state. The state therefore becomes bureaucratized. But contrary to the view of traditional pluralism and interest group theory, this bureaucratic structure serves as the basis not for democracy, but rather for authoritarian rule. Specifically, it is indispensable for four aspects of political domination: the regulation of class conflict, the rationalization of political procedures, the implementation of political and economic decisions, and the effective execution of political control to assure the continued functioning of the state.

An essential aspect of this *corporatist* form of authoritarianism is that it depends on a degree of popular participation and mobilization. Hence there is a beguiling similarity to democratic politics. However, the participation and mobilization are carefully controlled and manipulated for nondemocratic ends. This implies that the government is versatile in responding to popular pressures; its reactions range from granting of popular demands to overt repression. The dominant mode of response is at neither extreme, but rather consists of a subtle combination of cooptation and token responsiveness which diverts popular pressures into harmless outlets.

The end result of this complex process is the promotion of capitalist growth. This implies the familiar pattern of capital accumulation, skewed income distribution, foreign debt and investment, and the enrichment of a small elite. The process occurs, however, not in an ideological context of laissez-faire capitalism, but in one of revolutionary and populist idealism which presents today's evils as a transitory phase in the progress toward tomorrow's paradise.

The essays explore the workings of this system from different points of view by examining various aspects of Mexican society. They fall into three rough groupings. The first three chapters treat the relationship of the state to the masses. Lorenzo Meyer, a Mexican historian, compares certain aspects of the Porfirian state with contemporary Mexico to examine the basis of political control. He argues that the 1910 revolution did not destroy significant aspects of Mexican historical continuity, and he finds some striking similarities in means of control before and after the Revolution. The major difference, he suggests, lies in the significantly greater degree of institutionalization and bureaucratization of modern Mexico. Susan Eckstein, an American sociologist, and Rosa Elena Montes de Oca, a Mexican economist, explore in greater detail how the state has dealt with popular pressures emanating from the urban poor and poor peasants. Drawing on first-hand experience in urban slums, Eckstein explores how the state is able to control and manipulate the disadvantaged sector with a minimum of repression. She argues that the key is token responsiveness to demands combined with a complex web of organizations which diffuse potential protest and offer participation without representation in the system. Montes de Oca surveys the growth of peasant organizations and land invasions to demonstrate how the state has successfully diffused pressure from the rural sector primarily by controlling most peasant organizations and manipulating their leadership and programs. This has permitted isolation and repression of the few truculent organizations.

The second group of essays examines the state and the economy.

René Villarreal, a Mexican economist, surveys the strategy of Mexican economic development and its implications for social policy. He focuses particularly on the period of rapid growth from the end of World War II to 1970, a period characterized by import-substituting industrialization. The economic policy of these years, he argues, neglected social development and produced an increasing dependence on foreign financing. Mexico thus fell into a vicious cycle of balance-of-payments deficits aggravated by an increasing burden of debt service and an exchange rate policy which subsidized imports and penalized exports. Villarreal concludes by recommending a new course of economic policy for the López Portillo administration, one that would reorient the economy and provide the foundation for economic growth and social development. In my essay, I examine Mexico's policy toward foreign capital, and note a coexistence of permissive and restrictive practices. I argue that the underlying rationale may be found in a toleration of social and economic distortions while an attempt is made to meet the challenge to sovereignty posed by foreign capital. Peter H. Smith, a U.S. historian, examines Mexico's political and economic elites to see to what extent they are identical or similar. Challenging the popular wisdom, he finds them to be significantly different, thereby verifying in an unexpected way the independence and autonomy of the state bureaucratic structure.

A final group of essays pulls together the themes of the preceding chapters, looks to the future, and offers a comparative perspective. José Luis Reyna, a Mexican sociologist, synthesizes the discussion and offers an overview of Mexican authoritarianism. Building on the previous essays, he develops the concept of "populist corporatism" to describe the Mexican system. Drawing then on the theoretical literature on corporatism, he relates the manipulation of popular sectors and the social costs incurred to the development model, and demonstrates how the state has struggled to build and maintain legitimacy. Susan Kaufman Purcell, a U.S. political scientist, accepts the difficult task of peering into the future. She identifies points of stress and foresees increasing mobilization and politicization which will necessitate a hard choice between greater distribution of benefits and more repression. Finally, Robert R. Kaufman, a U.S. political scientist, places this work in a comparative perspective. He notes many points of similarity between Mexico and other countries with bureaucratic-authoritarian regimes, and addresses the question of why Mexican authoritarianism has functioned so much more smoothly than that of Brazil or Argentina. He argues that the key factor was that, in Mexico, institutionalization occurred prior to the maturation of industrialization and thus made it possible for the Mexican state to confront and control the popular pressures which accompany capital accumulation.

1

_____

The State and the Masses

Historical Roots of the Authoritarian State in Mexico

LORENZO MEYER

On February 5, 1975, Jesus Reyes Heroles, the President of the National Executive Committee of the Partido Revolucionario Institucional (PRI) and a historian, made this statement: "Mexico arrived late to the twentieth century. The Porfirian dictatorship not only interrupted the ascent of our social liberalism, but initiated a regression and led Mexico into the path of false development and economic dependency for the benefit of a privileged few." The fact that such a statement was made before the President of the Republic on the anniversary of the adoption of the Constitution of 1917 gave an official character to its view of Mexico's recent political history.

It has long been commonplace to use the Porfirian system as the background of any analysis of Mexico's present political system. For those committed to the official view, the Porfiriato, as Reyes Heroles stated, was only an unfortunate parenthesis in the democratic progress of the country. The alleged march toward a modern and mature democracy supposedly began in the early nineteenth century with the achievement of independence from Europe and was consolidated half a century later with the triumph of the liberal party over foreign invaders, the Church, and other reactionary forces. Historians of the left also consider the struggles of the nineteenth century and the 1910 Revolution as positive contributions. Although they did not result in liberal democracy, they did destroy the feudal structures that had inhibited the development of Mexican capitalism and therefore subsequent socialism and they did give to the masses a limited place in the political arena. Both traditional and leftist historians, then, have viewed modern Mexico as the negation of its past. Only a few marginal spokesmen of the old right dare to question the

3

importance of the change brought by the Revolution to the political life of the country.

It is time to submit this orthodoxy to a more rigorous examination, time to ask: To what extent have the years since the promulgation of the Plan de San Luis in 1910 represented a negation of the old system of political control? No one can deny that important changes have taken place, but of what nature? By now, there is more than enough distance and historiographical material to reappraise the Mexican Revolution. The light that we can cast on these questions has more than historical interest, because with its help we can arrive at a better understanding of the nature of the present political structure and process of Mexico, as well as the possibilities for change. It is the theme of this chapter that the changes were less significant than the continuities. The Mexican Revolution did not destroy the authoritarian nature of Mexican political life, it modernized it.

Political Control in the Old System

Among the most important means of political control during the Porfiriato, the first and most obvious was the removal of content from the electoral process. Elections were not held to give those who had the right to vote a chance to choose between two or more political organizations of the elite. By the time General Porfirio Díaz presented his nomination for a third term to the presidency in 1888, the meaning of the electoral contest was completely lost: there was no contest. The last remnants of parliamentary opposition had disappeared and Díaz won the election with 98 percent of the votes. From that moment on, no governor, representative, or senator came to power without the authorization of the President. For a long time, cooptation, fraud, and a limited use of force inhibited the formation of a political organization that could offer a real alternative to Díaz's hegemony. When, in spite of everything, such an alternative appeared, first in the form of the Partido Liberal Mexicano and later in that of the Maderista movement, the central and local governments made it impossible for them to show their strength at the ballot box and they had to resort to rebellion.

It would be wrong, however, to conclude that the electoral ritual during the Porfiriato served no purpose. It performed a very different but important function from its role in Western democracies. The aim of the campaign was not to confront Díaz or Díaz's followers with their political opponents but to renew the loyalty of the people to their leader, and to affirm the fidelity of the leader to the ideals of material progress, order, and independence.[1]

The lack of content in the electoral process facilitated the emergence of a second important characteristic of the system of political control: centralization. Since independence, fragmentation had been one of the main characteristics of Mexico's political life. After Díaz's seizure of power, however, a rapid process of political centralization began. At the national level, Congress and the Supreme Court lost all capacity to act as checks on executive power, especially after 1888. Instead, they became mere appendages of it, always giving their seal of approval to decisions previously taken by the President. At the same time, they were useful to Díaz as a means to reward the services of many local loyal *porfiristas* without giving them any real participation in the shaping of political events at the national level. The other side of the coin was centralization in Mexico City, no matter what the Constitution of 1857 may have intended to the contrary. The net effect of these tendencies were the emergence of a very powerful presidency whose great capacity to control political events was to a certain extent the result of an expropriation of the powers of the legislative, judiciary, and local government. The only limits to presidential power were socioeconomic and geopolitical realities—the geographical isolation of many communities, the backwardness of the economic system, and the dependency of the country on the United States and Europe. Legal limits were almost nonexistent.

The gradual elimination of the old local "strong men," a product of the long period of civil war after independence, was an important step in this process of concentration of power. The most important obstacle for Díaz was the presence of General Manuel González, who had been his loyal collaborator at the time of the 1876 coup. Once González was discredited after his presidency from 1880 to 1884, Díaz's followers had little trouble neutralizing his bid for re-election. The elimination of such strong first followers of the Plan de Tuxtepec as generals Jerónimo Treviño and Francisco Naranjo was a little easier and unavoidable. After this, the remains of federalism presented almost no problem to Díaz.

Side by side with elimination of political opposition and the centralization of power in the hands of the President, a third characteristic of the system began to emerge: the cult of personality. By the end of his third presidency, General Díaz had became the "irreplaceable leader of the nation" and the embodiment of its destiny. Internal stability and the continuity of the modernization process were guaranteed by the sheer presence of Díaz. The constant pitting of one group of political followers against another helped the President in his quest for irreplaceability. After a while, there was no other political leader of national importance. But if this practice gave Díaz much room for political maneuvering, it also prevented the institutionalization of the system and the peaceful transmission of power. This personalization of political power was very useful at its beginning, when it facilitated the concentration of power, but at the end it constituted the most vulnerable aspect of the system. Mexico's political stability became linked to the survival of the charismatic leader.

The personalization of power brought with it a certain kind of paternalism. This was not new; its roots were in the relationship established between the Spanish Viceroy and the Indian population during the colonial period. For all practical purposes, the President could dispose of all public resources at will, and to some extent he could do the same with the lives and fortunes of individual citizens. The real discretionary powers of the President were formidable, notwithstanding the formal limits specified by the Constitution. Of course, the closer the individual to the upper levels of the social structure, the less he had to fear those powers, but no one—except, perhaps, some foreign entrepreneurs—was outside their reach. Díaz could undo the fortunes of even the very powerful, as he certainly did from time to time to those of some of his associates. The power of the State was his power.

The use of this power, however, was far from irrational. As a matter of fact, Díaz tried to be predictable to the point that, for the first time in independent Mexico, public expenditure was programmed and became the tool of the regime's policies.[2] Díaz himself cannot be accused of illicit enrichment or capricious acts, but the same cannot be said of many of his collaborators—the *científicos* for example. To a great extent, it became functional for Díaz's purposes to permit a certain amount of corruption among his inner circle. It was a simple but effective means to ensure their loyalty; to fail the President would have meant to endanger a very attractive political as well as economic position.[3] There is, for example, little doubt that at the beginning of the century Olegario Molina was in control of the political and economic destiny of Yucatán. Molina made his great fortune by using his position as governor of the state first and Minister of Fomento later to ensure his monopoly of the henequen trade, the main product of Yucatán and very much sought after by American agriculture. Molina had been able to monopolize this and other collateral activities because Díaz permitted it and for no other reason. Therefore, when the President ordered Molina to cut away Quintana Roo from Yucatán and let the federal government administer it directly, the governor obeyed without hesitation. All the protests and riots in Mérida had little effect on Molina because his interests lay in complying with the President's will and not his state's. It is possible to find other examples like this all over the country.

A fourth characteristic of the Porfirian system, and to a certain extent a product of the previous ones, was that with the passing of time the political elite became an integral part of the economic elite.[4] Because of the presence of a foreign entrepreneurial group, it is not possible to state categorically that the politically and economically dominant groups were identical, but if foreigners are taken out of the picture we can state that there *was* a power elite, as the concept was defined by C. Wright Mills. The equivalence of political and economic hegemony emerged in a context in which almost all the rest of society was excluded from meaningful political participation. The landless peasantry had no political representation and very little capacity to make successful demands on the government. A typical example is provided by the useless efforts of the communities and towns of Morelos to defend themselves against the encroachment of the big haciendas of the Escandón, the García Pimentel, the Amor, the Araoz, and some other families. The same encroachment affected the Yaqui and Mayo tribes in Sonora, among other examples. If whole towns had no rights, even less did individual peasants and workers; politically they were nonentities. The industrial worker had no right of association to defend his interests; at the most, he could enlist the benevolent intercession of the authorities on his behalf. What help he received was a grace, not a right.

While even the middle class was without proper channels of representation, in contrast to the other sectors it had a much wider capacity to formulate demands, and after a while its resentment began to show in political terms. The growth of its frustration was related to the way in which economic development began to increase its ranks. A sizable proportion of the 15,000 lawyers, 5,000 medical doctors and civil engineers, and even more numerous schoolteachers and agronomists who existed by 1910 felt very little loyalty toward a system that had kept them outside the decision-making process. Social mobility was very difficult in the Porfirian system and, as a result, a good many leaders of the Revolution were to rise from the middle class.[5]

The dominant position of President Díaz was not maintained by the use of force or corruption alone. Equally important was the ability of the President to remain the ultimate arbiter of all political contests of the establishment. He did this by creating and maintaining in every state two or more rival political groups who were loyal to him. The everyday political struggle took place among these small cliques and in this way was kept within very clearly defined boundaries. Díaz was the final arbiter of such struggles and his decisions could not be appealed. For instance, at the beginning of the century in Yucatán, Olegario Molina, in spite of his immense local power, had to live with several enemies. Conspicuous among them were the former governor, Colonel Francisco Cantón, Joaquín Baranda, a member of the Supreme Court, and General Guillermo Palomino; even the governor of the state of Veracruz, Teodoro Dehesa, was among his enemies. All had credentials as good *porfiristas* and for that reason had to accept the leadership of Molina, but their displeasure with him was well known. If for some reason Díaz had wanted to destroy Molina's position, he could always have counted on these people. In Jalisco in the 1880s, Díaz at first supported General Francisco Tolentino as governor of the state in order to end the *cacicazgo* of Ignacio Vallarta, but later on he decided to give his blessing to General Ramón Corona, an enemy of Tolentino, to succeed him as governor. In this way, the President created two parties and divided the political elite of Jalisco, but this was not all. He also created a desire for power in the military commander, Pedro Galván, the governor of Mexico City, José Cevallos, and a local politician, Luis Curiel. They served as a kind of "third force" in Jalisco. These examples of "divide and rule" could be repeated in all the other states and at the national level. Such was the case of Bernardo Reyes, the strong man of Nuevo León and Minister of War, and José Yves Limantour, the aristocratic minister of the treasury and leader of the *científico* group. In the first decade of this century, the struggle among them to succeed Díaz almost got out of hand, and a high political price was paid for it. The very overthrow of Díaz can be linked to the fragmentation of the elite produced by the Reyes-Limantour struggle. Control through the systematic fragmentation of the elite was very successful while the *caudillo* was in complete command of his mental and political faculties. However, when signs of old age began to emerge, the struggle among the several *porfirista* factions began to rip the system apart, so that the regime was in a poor position to confront the Maderista revolt successfully.

According to the historical school that prevailed after the victory of the Revolution of 1910, the single most important element of political control in the old regime was the use of force, and it is true that violence was a very common response of the Porfirian system to opposition from the lower levels of the social structure. The stories of the rebellion of the Yaqui Indians in Sonora, the Mayan Indians in Yucatán, the textile workers of Río Blanco in Veracruz, and the miners of Cananea are too well known to be retold here. However, when the opposition came from groups such as students, the intelligentsia, and the middle class in general, the response was much less violent and repressive. With the upper classes, cooptation and negotiation were the most common responses, not force.

The Porfirian army had about 20,000 men. The most professional and mobile security force was the *rurales*, numbering about 3,000. This would hardly have been an impressive force had it been the main basis of support of a bloody dictatorship. But, through cooptation and compromise in the 1870s and 1880s, Díaz was able to overcome the old antagonism of the members of the clerical party as well as that of former followers of Lerdo and Iglesias. These methods of confronting political opposition brought good results with some ambitious young professionals and politicians. The constant criticism from the press, which was a permanent headache of the regime, was met not only by an enormous number of arrests but also by hiring sympathetic writers and generously supporting friendly newspapers. When Camilo Arriaga began to form the radical Liberal Party, Díaz's response to this very well-known member of the old liberal elite was mild indeed. For a long time, Madero, too, was free to agitate, and after his arrest in San Luis Potosí in 1910 he was permitted to escape to the United States. But if the old regime was not particularly prone to use force against the opposition, when force *was* used no legal or political barrier could protect the victim. The State was supreme.

The main political problem of the old system was not so much its authoritarian character as its resistance to depersonalization, and depersonalization would have been the only way to handle the transmission of power in an orderly fashion. The presence of Díaz as the charismatic leader was necessary at the beginning, but his resistance to leaving or sharing power inhibited the formation of structures that could have ensured the maintenance of the system after Díaz. The constant re-election of the President, as well as many of the governors, made it difficult to renew political personnel and closed off the careers of many young and ambitious people. The aging of the leadership and the systematic exclusion of the majority of the population, the middle class included, was the result of the inability to transform an authoritarian situation into an authoritarian system.

The New Regime

The structure of political control that replaced the one destroyed by the Revolution took form slowly through a process of trial and error. Only after ten years from the start of the Revolution did politics begin to substitute for mere force as a means to gain and retain power; the movement of Agua Prieta in 1920 was the last successful military revolt. After the civil wars between Villa and Zapata on the one hand and Carranza on the other, the increasing power of the central government was able to handle the rebellious actions of De la Huerta, Serrano, Gómez, Escobar, and Cedillo in the 1920s and 1930s. By the 1930s local strong men did not even attempt direct action. Adalberto Tejeda, Joaquín Amaro. Garrido Canabal, and Juan Andreu Almazán knew quite well when their causes were lost and accepted almost without resistance the destruction of their local bases of power by the central government. Even Calles, the "Jefe Máximo," did not try very hard to confront President Cárdenas with a military upheaval in 1935. The most important political struggle of the 1930s—the confrontation of the *agraristas* and *veteranos* with opposing agrarian reform policies—was resolved mainly by political means. The new regime was entering a new stage of its development. Discipline arose from the chaos of the Revolution.

By about 1940, the central government had enough control over political forces that a minimal set of rules institutionalizing the exercise and transmission of power superseded the period of turmoil and uncertainty in the political arena. From the Presidency of Ávila Camacho (1940–46) to the present day, the system of political control in Mexico has changed very little and has proved its ability to maintain the political discipline necessary to encourage economic growth. Mexico has become a unique case in Latin America of stability and development.[6] We can thus return to our original question: To what extent is the new system different from the old one?

In socioeconomic terms, Mexico today is very different from the Mexico Díaz left in 1911. The country is now almost an urban society in the process of industrialization. The State, grown stronger, has many more responsibilities than in the past. More important, all the former political outsiders—peasants, workers, and middle class—have their own political organizations and have rights guaranteed by the 1917 Constitution. But is the manner in which political control is exerted very different from the past? In order to give a satisfactory answer, let us examine each of the central elements of the Porfirian system and see if they are still present today, if they have been modified, and if new ones have been added.[7]

In theory, the system through which today's leadership is selected is democratic, but the reality is very different. Since the creation of the Partido Nacional Revolucionario (PNR) in 1929, the Mexican party system has had a purpose that is not democratic. The official party—the PNR and its successors, the Partido de la Revolución Mexicana (PRM) and the Partido Revolucionario Institucional (PRI)—was not created to win elections but to maintain a permanent campaign of propaganda in favor of the revolutionary leadership and to enforce the necessary amount of discipline among the "revolutionary family" and the organizations that support it. According to Moreno Sánchez, the PRI is only a branch of the government, its electoral agency.[8] In the new regime the opposition parties have never been able to win a governorship or a place in the Senate, to say nothing of the presidency. Their only victories have been very modest, a few representatives at the National Congress and in a few municipal governments. In order to receive the *registro* that enables them to appear on the ballot and to use free time on radio and television, opposition parties have to prove that they will behave more or less as a "loyal opposition." They must shy away from attacking the bases of legitimacy of the system, they must not endanger the hegemony of the PRI, and they must not represent a real alternative.

The electoral campaign is still a formality. In some places, the electoral triumphs of the PRI are in the 90 percent range, not very different from those of the Porfirian era. In several states, PRI candidates do not even have a symbolic opposition. Because electoral campaigns are only a period in which the official rhetoric gets more inflated but nothing important is in question, urban voters are becoming more rebellious. During the federal elections of 1973, 36 percent of all registered voters did not bother to register their vote in spite of specific sanctions against abstention. (In Mexico, voting is at the same time a right and an obligation.[9])

Electoral fraud and manipulation of the vote have been difficult to prove but are nevertheless facts since the beginning of the dominant party system. Vasconcelos was said to receive only 5.32 percent of the national vote in 1929 and Almazán, 5.72 percent in 1940. These figures are suspiciously low for two movements that were obviously popular, at least in the urban areas. With the passing of time, the government has been more generous with the opposition; in 1946 Esequiel Padilla was assigned 19.33 percent of the vote, and General Miguel Henríquez Guzmán, 15.87 percent in 1952. The new electoral law permits the opposition parties to oversee the voting process, but they do their job only in the most populated areas.[10] Suspicious figures are still coming from the marginal areas. In 1973, the PRI's victory in Chetumal was an extraordinary 98.2 percent of the vote, and in Comitan, Chiapas, 98.6 percent. The weakness of the organized opposition thus makes the electoral process meaningless.

Let us examine another characteristic of the present system, political centralization. The predominance of the executive power over the judicial and legislative did not change with the Revolution. In order to avoid being alone in Congress, the government has given a few places to the official opposition parties according to the total vote they received at the national level. They are not there as a result of a direct victory at the ballot box, however, but because they are *diputados de partido*.[11] In spite of the presence of this limited opposition, the great majority of the resolutions passed by the Legislature are still presented by the executive branch and the day that one of them is voted down is still in the future. Even PRI legislators have places in Congress not because they won an election but because they have the confidence of the President. They are his extremely loyal collaborators. As Pablo González Casanova has demonstrated, the Supreme Court has contradicted the President only in a few instances, always in areas related to the defense of private economic interests.[12] This opposition has been functional to the system, because it recognizes the real power of wealth without forcing the President to bow before it.

The geographical division of powers is similar to the functional. For many reasons, federalism is still as weak as in the past. The federal government has control of about 80 percent of all public resources (as compared with about 60 percent at the end of the Porfiriato). All important investment projects at the state level are dependent on federal support. However, the strong men of the past, the *caciques*, are still with us. Examples of the recent past are Leobardo Reynoso of Tamaulipas, Gonzálo N. Santos of San Luis Potosí, and Manuel Sánchez Vite of Hidalgo. But the fates of these men demonstrate that when the federal government considers their presence a problem they cannot survive.

Generally speaking, the state governors are the center of the local political system, but all their important decisions are made in consultation with the President and some of his ministers. The entire political life of a governor is controlled by the center, from his nomination by the Party to the selection of his successor.[13] On the few occasions when local power has clashed with the central government, there is no "federal pact" that can protect a state governor from a decree of the National Congress dissolving the local government. The presence of the federal army is a guarantee that such a decree will always be effective. President Cárdenas used this procedure ten times to eliminate governors still loyal to Calles; as recently as 1975, Echeverría used it against the governors of Guerrero and Hidalgo when they showed a lack of discipline.[14]

The personalization of power is very different from that of the Porfiriato. For a time, the Revolution reinforced the *caudillista* nature of Mexican political life—Obregón is a case in point—but after the PNR and especially after Cárdenas, the charisma of the leader was transferred to the office.[15] This was a help to, as well as a result of, institutionalization. Today, after a very well-organized public relations campaign, the presidency always seems to be occupied by a person who, like Don Porfirio, has all the best qualities of leadership: wisdom, intelligence, honesty, patriotism, and magnanimity. He is the very incarnation of the national interest, and for that reason he is almost infallible. However, after six years his term in office is over, and it is then possible to admit some of his shortcomings. In this way, the head of the new government always represents a step forward in the path of the Revolution.

These changes in the charismatic character of the presidency, however, have had very little impact on the paternalistic way in which the incumbent uses his power. There is no national plan or institutional check that can control the decisions of the President in regard to the use of government resources. No matter how irrational a project may be in the eyes of specialists, if the President approves it, it must be carried out. Outside the public sector the tremendous power of the President can also still be felt. If, for some reason, he decides to act against a group or an individual citizen, there is little they can do to protect their position and, in some instances, their lives. There is still truth in the popular view that the President can do as he wishes.[16] The President's enormous freedom of action—Díaz Ordaz admitted only history as a judge after the violent and bloody suppression of opposition in 1968—is also the source of the great discretionary powers of his ministers.

One of the most notorious effects of this power is corruption. Corruption has many faces in Mexico. Perhaps the least important is the direct use of public funds for private purposes. More important are useless projects, inflated costs in their execution, the unwillingness of the government to act on vital matters because special interests are affected, and so on. From the political point of view, perhaps the most difficult problem is the limitless corruption of the judicial process. Corruption of everyday justice produces more frustration and alienation in the common citizen than the waste and irrational use of public resources.[17] Nevertheless, as Peter H. Smith demonstrates in his essay in this volume, it is precisely this illicit enrichment that makes it possible for many members of the political elite to leave power without causing any problem to their successors. This renewal of the elite, so vital to the maintenance of the system, is something the old regime was unable to achieve.[18]

It has been argued that it is time to put an end to corruption, that it is becoming dysfunctional. One of the chief complaints in official technocratic circles is that special interests have often impeded the implementation of government orders. One suggested solution is the creation of a true civil service and the elimination of the spoils system. However, the sexennial reward in the form of thousands of public jobs to the faithful militants of the PRI is one of the most powerful glues that keeps the Party—and the political machinery as a whole—in one piece. Besides, the fact that a great many of the top politicians and administrators have indulged in corrupt practices gives the President an additional weapon to keep them in place. To expose a dishonest politician is not a common practice, but everyone knows that if the President considers it necessary someone will present the mass media with adequate information. The spectacular avalanche of accusations of corruption that preceded the fall of governors Israel Nogueda of Guerrero and Otonial Miranda of Hidalgo in early 1975 is a case in point. In a clash with the President, politicians and administrators have a lot to lose and very little to gain.

In the final years of the Porfiriato, the "political class" and the economically powerful became almost undistinguishable. At a first glance, it appears that the Revolution put an end to this. Its first task was to eliminate completely the old upper class from all positions of power, and in due time, through agrarian reform, they lost their economic privileges too. Government became the dominion of the middle classes. Generally speaking, those who make a career out of politics today are not members of the upper class. As a result, some analysts of the Mexican political system have talked a great deal about the division between the politicians and *técnicos*, on the one hand, and the entrepreneurial class, on the other. According to them, the divergence in their origins and interests constitutes one of the main characteristics of the system.[19] Spokesmen of the government have accepted this view because much of the regime's legitimacy derives from its claim that since the Revolution it has represented the interests of the so-called "popular classes," first against the reactionary *hacendados* and, these days, against unidentified but powerful capitalists associated with large foreign enterprises. According to this view, a revolution made in favor of peasants and workers cannot be led by capitalists.

The real situation is a bit different. From the very beginning of the Revolution, such important leaders of the movement as Alvaro Obregón, Abelardo Rodríguez, Aarón Saenz, and Juan Andreu Almazán, to mention only a few, joined the ranks of the entrepreneurs. Today the case of Miguel Alemán is paradigmatic. Thousands of politicians and upper-level administrators know that if, in the next presidential term, their political career is finished, they can switch from the public to the private sphere. Therefore, even if the top political personnel have no capital and no family connections with the business community, they cannot regard their interests as opposed to those of private enterprise; they need a strong business community as a personal safeguard for their own business. This fact blurs to a great extent the difference between the political and the economic elites.

Exclusion was a daily reality for the great majority of Mexicans during the Porfiriato, in politics as well as in many other things. One of the most striking changes from the old system to the new regime was the admission into the political arena of a vast number of people from the lower and middle classes. This incorporation occurred first in the overthrow of Díaz and in the civil war that followed. After Cárdenas, these masses were admitted as organized members of the dominant party. Their political rights were recognized and guaranteed by the Revolution. In theory, even if some groups find the PRI unsatisfactory they can take some action, such as forming their own parties. Therefore, political exclusion is not inherent in the new system. It might seem that we have here, at last, the real difference between the two systems, but the facts are not as clear as they seem. PRI's organizations have a membership of about 9 million, or about 56 percent of the adult population of Mexico. The other three registered parties are not mass parties, and their membership is very small. Around 40 percent of the voting population does not belong to any party or formal political organization. At the same time, this 40 percent has no other institutional channel through which to transmit its demands to the system. Even those who belong to organizations that are part of the PRI, such as CNC, CTM, or CNOP, can act politically only within limits. Their leadership represents the interests of the government as much as the interests of the rank and file; when the two are in conflict, the interests of the government almost always prevail. Given the lack of substance in the electoral process, we must conclude that in Mexico today the majority of the population have no political representation. Their alternatives are resignation or violence.[20] It is no wonder that Almond and Verba have insisted on the parochial character of the great majority of the Mexican public.[21]

The systematic division of the political elite into antagonistic factions loyal only to the person of the President—as in the Porfirian system—is not entirely absent today. However, this is not the main form of political control over the elites. Here we have one of the most important differences between the Porfirian and the Revolutionary regimes: the formation of the official (and dominant) party. President Díaz rejected the idea of encouraging the institutionalization of his system of government through the creation of a real political party. The Unión Liberal, created in the last decade of the nineteenth century, could have been the beginning of such institutionalization, but Díaz rejected the idea because every step in this direction was a diminution of his personal power. Thus, when the time came to replace the head of the system, the institutions to permit a peaceful transition were not there. When the head of the "revolutionary family," General Alvaro Obregón, was assassinated in 1928, the Party was hurriedly created; the alternative was an internal struggle similar to the one that preceded the downfall of Díaz. The PNR was created at the beginning of 1929—in addition to all the small political parties then operating (there were several hundred)—and was able to conduct the presidential campaign of Pascual Ortiz Rubio the same year. By 1933, the old parties had disappeared and the PRM, a new and very powerful mechanism to keep all the members of the "Revolutionary family" in line, was born. In 1938, with the formation of the PRI, direct membership was replaced by affiliation through a national organization belonging to any of the four functional sectors: army, labor, the peasantry, and the so-called "popular," or bureaucratic, sector.

Since 1938, the most important political struggles have taken place within the Party and its organizational network. The problem of succession at any level of government—municipal, state, or national—or within the organizations that form the Party was finally institutionalized. The struggle within the establishment has very definite rules, and after it is over party discipline requires that everyone support the winner. The most important and decisive political battle takes place before the presidential nomination. The struggle between two or three factions—almost always headed by members of the Cabinet—involves the whole political class. To a large extent, this competition is conducted beyond the view of the general public, and all sorts of dirty tricks are used by the contestants to discredit each other before the President and the general public. But once the President announces through the Party his choice of a successor, the entire leadership of the coalition that constitutes the dominant party—and even some of those outside it, such as the entrepreneurs—back the candidate. The exceptions are few, and in principle the divisions caused by the struggle are all but forgotten. Of course, the closest competitors of the candidate are relegated to political limbo, but six years later they may make a comeback.[22] The main difference between the old system and the new regime, therefore, lies not in the internal struggle of the elite but in the facts that this struggle does not destroy the governing coalition and that the divisions created by the infighting do not last. The depersonalization of the political process makes the persistence of old divisions unprofitable; the only path available to the losers is to join the winner. The motto of the dominant party is "Unity, Discipline."

Institutionalization, continual renewal of the leadership, and the acceptance of new actors in the political arena have made it possible for cooptation to become one of the central elements of Mexico's present political system. Almost any person with a political vocation can be accepted by the regime and given a chance within the Party or the administration.[23] Failure to coopt political leaders of the middle and lower classes was one of the reasons for Díaz's downfall. An example may be found in the so-called "Sonora group." The main link between rich *hacendados* like José María Maytorena, a small rancher like Benjamin Hill, and a small businessman like Plutarco Elías Calles was their political exclusion at the end of the Porfiriato. The closeness of the political group in Sonora, headed by such big landholders as Ramón Corral, Luis Torres, and Rafael Izábal, convinced these otherwise law-abiding citizens that their only chance to gain power was through revolution. In contemporary Mexico, the situation is quite different. The Party is open to all classes and ideologies; only the extreme right and left are excluded, not necessarily by the Party but by themselves. PRI has room for both Marxists and classical liberals who believe that a strict observance of the doctrines of Adam Smith or Milton Friedman is the only way out of underdevelopment. The thousands of jobs available—at national and local levels—in government agencies every six years provide adequate rewards for those coopted.[24] An example of this process is the way in which the intelligentsia—a possible source of conflict in any authoritarian regime—was neutralized after the governments of the Revolution made their peace with the universities in the 1940s. From its support of the Marxist "Mexican School of Painting" to its support of the universities, the State has provided a living for thousands of intellectuals, and its embassies are full of writers and social scientists.

Cooptation is not completely independent of the social structure. It is obvious that those who benefit most by it are the middle and upper classes. Young people from the laboring classes still have a much more difficult time achieving success. As a group, workers and peasants are underrepresented in PRI. This is one of the several reasons their demands are taken into consideration less frequently than they are ignored.[25]

The Mexican Revolution is frequently described as an anti-imperialist struggle. To a great extent this is true, but, in the final analysis, the nature of the relationship between Mexico and the outside world has changed very little. The weight of the American presence at all levels of Mexican life, from the economic to the cultural, is as great or even greater now than in the past. Mexico is now an undisputed part of the U.S. zone of influence, a fact that was not clear during the Porfiriato. The recent efforts of the Mexican government to neutralize this dependency with overtures toward Latin America, Europe, China, and Japan are even more useless than those of Díaz. In modern Mexico, it is the State and not foreign enterprise which controls such basic industries as oil, power, and railroads, and the financial sector is entirely Mexican. Foreigners have no agricultural land, and the mining industry is now mostly in Mexican hands. However, the most dynamic economic sector—the manufacturing industry that emerged from the economic conditions created by World War II—is becoming increasingly dependent on foreign capital and technology.[26] In general terms, foreign capital accounts for less than 10 percent of the gross national product, but if we look at key sectors the situation is different. In 1970, about 70 percent of total manufacturing output came from the approximately 800 enterprises in which foreign capital was present. In sectors such as the automobile industry, the capital-goods industry, or the chemical industry, foreign participation is around 100 percent. The rate of growth of foreign vis-à-vis national enterprise is astonishing—60 percent higher or more. The picture is completed when we consider that a good part of the investment made by the public sector is financed by capital borrowed from abroad.[27] It is now obvious that the struggle to lessen Mexico's economic dependency reached its height during the 1938 oil expropriation but was not a definitive victory; there was a regression after World War II.

The return of foreign influence stems to a great extent from the fact that the type of development sponsored by Díaz and his minister, Limantour, is not very different from that favored by Miguel Alemán and all his predecessors. To construct a "modern" capitalist society, Mexico had to be linked to the goods and capital markets of the United States. There is, however, a difference: in Díaz's time the participation of the State in the economy was mostly indirect. Since the Revolution, the new "active

State" has created a mixed economy in which public funds and enterprises have been used to support the very rapid development of private enterprise—both foreign and national—shielded behind a protective tariff barrier. Around 40 percent of federal expenditures since 1940 have been devoted to this type of direct support to economic development. As a result, industry has been growing at an average annual rate of 9 percent.[28]

The Porfirian type of development caused agricultural production to lag behind the rest of the economy. The same is true today, because the nature of Mexico's development is not very different. In the 1960s, the annual rate of growth of farm production was 3.6 percent; at some point in recent years, the increase in population became greater than the increase in food production.

One of the most frequent accusations against the Díaz regime was that it permitted the concentration of private wealth in very few hands. According to the industrial census of 1965, about 0.3 percent of all enterprises accounted for about 46 percent of the capital invested in the manufacturing sector. In the agrarian sector, about 0.5 percent of all private landholdings produced about 30 percent of the agricultural output. If we add income-distribution figures, the picture is not particularly bright. In 1968, the upper 5 percent of families were in possession of about 28 percent of disposable income. On the other hand, the 50 percent of families with the lowest income had only 18 percent of the total, a situation not very different from, say, the United States or Argentina, countries which have had no "social revolution" in this century.[29]

In spite of all the similarities between the old and new types of development, the Mexico of today is a country quite different from Mexico at the beginning of the century. Its social structure has undergone several dramatic changes as a result of economic and demographic growth. Modern Mexico now has more than 60 million inhabitants, in contrast with 16 million in 1910. The population explosion is linked in many ways to the social policies of the Revolution. The rural character of the old Mexico is disappearing very rapidly; today almost half the inhabitants are living in towns with populations of 15,000 or more. Urbanization and industrialization have increased the ranks of a social group that was very small during Díaz's days, the so-called "middle sector." The same thing can be said about workers; for the first time there is in Mexico a real urban proletariat. The emergence of these two classes plus the emergence of a native industrial entrepreneurial sector gives the political life of the country a much more complex structure than in the past. The political actors are more numerous, as are the demands channeled into the system.[30]

The creation of the official Party made it possible to confront the new political complexities of Mexico's economic and social life more or less successfully, to handle them in a better way than the old regime. Through the Party, the actors created by economic growth initiated in the Porfiriato and accelerated by the Revolution could be incorporated permanently into the decision-making process. Large enterprise was left outside the discipline of the Party (but not of the system), and because peasants, workers, and the middle class were subject to it, rapid capitalist development of the Mexican economy took place in an environment of political tranquility. The authoritarian political system of the Porfiriato was not changed by the Revolution but given a new life that made its modernization possible.

A Final Consideration

If our analysis is correct, the Mexican Revolution is not a negation of the political past but rather an impressive step forward in the modernization of the Mexican authoritarian state. Nevertheless, the new regime has some weaknesses. Potential sources of instability can be found in the increasing demand for effective participation by some social and interest groups. Indeed, the process of economic growth encourages such demands. The fragmentation of the governing elite is therefore not impossible.[31]

Any consideration of the present political system of Mexico must take into account that authoritarianism in Mexico has deep roots that have proved very difficult to extirpate. The pre-Hispanic past and three centuries of Spanish colonial domination were not an ideal preparation for democracy. When the Mexican State was born, the Mexican nation was still in the making. The social environment left by the eighteenth century as its heritage to the new republic was extremely hostile to the installation of a liberal democracy. The nineteenth century was the century of liberalism, and it was at this crucial moment that democracy failed to take hold in Mexico. About 80 percent of the population at that time were Indians and *mestizos*, who had no political significance. The liberal institutions created by Juárez and his followers in the second half of the nineteenth century had no citizens to give them flesh and blood. The Porfirian dictatorship signified the recognition of this fact. Institutional exclusion was again accepted as the main ingredient of political control. The Mexican Revolution confronted this situation and, in 1917, Mexico gave itself one of the most advanced sets of political rules at that time, but the raw material for democracy was still absent. Perhaps the time lost could not be regained. The Revolution, struggling for survival, had no time to create the necessary social and political preconditions for democracy. Expediency and social inertia led to the adaptation of the authoritarian system of the past to the conditions of the present. President Calles made the crucial decision in this respect.[32] After a while, privileges and a powerful set of vested interests flourished in a system hostile to democracy, and the beneficiaries are now its most dedicated supporters.

Has democracy—any kind of democracy—a place in Mexico's present political system? The answer is at best uncertain.

Notes

1. The bibliography on the Porfirian period is considerable. Among the general works that can be useful are: Daniel Cosío Villegas, *El Porfiriato: vida política interior*, published in two volumes as part of the larger work *Historia moderna de México* (Mexico, D.F.: Editorial Hermes, 1972); Ralph Roeder, *Hacia el México moderno: Porfirio Díaz*, 2 vols. (Mexico, D.F.: Fondo de Cultura Económica, 1973). An interesting case study of the relationship between the federal government and the states is Gerald D. Barber, "Horizon of Thorns: Yucatán at the Turn of the Century" (unpublished manuscript).

2. For a brief but interesting discussion of the nature of the Porfirian administration, see the second section of Wendell K. G. Schaeffer, "La administración pública en México," *Problemas agrícolas e industriales de México*, vol. 7, no. 1 (January–March 1955).

3. Francisco Bulnes gave first-hand testimony in regard to the enrichment of the Porfirian political elite in *The Whole Truth about Mexico: President Wilson's Responsibility* (New York: M. Bulnes Book Company, 1916).

4. A useful case study of the relationship between the political and economic elites of this period is contained in James Cockcroft, *Precursores intelectuales de la Revolución Mexicana* (Mexico, D.F.: Siglo Veintiuno Editores, 1971; there is also an English version).

5. Besides Cockcroft's work, this lack of social mobility and the political marginality of the middle class are very well presented in Hector Aguila Camín, "La revolución sonorense, 1910–1914" (tesis doctoral, El Colegio de México, 1975).

6. The role of the foreign enterprise in Mexico during the Díaz era can be examined in Cosío Villegas, chapter ten of *La vida económica*, which is part of *Historia moderna de México*. See also José Luis Ceceña, *México en la órbita imperial* (Mexico, D.F.: Ediciones "El Caballito," 1970), pp. 49–101; Gerald Theisen, "La Mexicanización de la industria en la época de Porfirio Díaz," *Foro internacional*, vol. 12, no. 4 (April–June 1972): 497–506.

7. Among the most important studies of the contemporary political system of Mexico are: Pablo González Casanova, *La democracia en México* (Mexico, D.F.: Ediciones Era, 1965); Daniel Cosío Villegas, *El sistema político mexicano* (Mexico, D.F.: Cuadernos de Joaquín Mortiz, 1972); Arnaldo Córdova, *La formación del poder político en México* (Mexico, D.F.: Ediciones Era, 1972); Robert E. Scott, *Mexican Government in Transition* (Urbana: University of Illinois Press, 1964); Vincent Padgett, *The Mexican Political System* (Boston: Houghton Mifflin, 1966); Roger D. Hansen, *The Politics of Mexican Development* (Baltimore: Johns Hopkins University Press, 1971); Martin C. Needler, *Politics and Society in Mexico* (Albuquerque: University of New Mexico Press, 1971).

8. José Luis Reyna briefly discusses political control in modern Mexico in "Control político, estabilidad y desarrollo en México," *Cuadernos del CES*, no. 3 (1974).

9. Manuel Moreno Sánchez, *La crisis política de México* (Mexico, D.F.: Editorial Extemporáneos, 1970), pp. 51–63 and 136–65.

10. An interesting analysis of opposition parties in Mexico is Antonio Delhumeau et al., *México: realidad política de sus partidos* (Mexico, D.F.: Instituto Mexicano de Estudios Políticos, 1970); see also Soledad Loaeza, "El Partido Acción Nacional: la oposición leal en México," in Luis Medina et al., *La vida política en México, 1970–1974* (Mexico, D.F.: El Colegio de México, 1974), pp. 101–26.

11. A good study on the nature of Mexico's electoral system is Rafael Segovia's "La reforma política: el ejecutivo federal, el PRI y las elecciones de 1973," in Luis Medina et al., *La vida política*, pp. 49–76.

12. González Casanova, *La democracia*.

13. An interesting analysis of the control of the federal government over state governors can be found in Sánchez, *La crisis política*, pp. 160–65.

14. See the reports on the dissolution of the local powers of the state of Guerrero in *Excelsior*, February 1 and 2, 1975.

15. An example of the institutionalization of charisma in the case of Luis Echeverría can be found in Daniel Cosío Villegas, *El estilo personal de gobernar* (Mexico, D.F.: Joaquín Mortiz, 1974).

16. Such a view of the presidency is presented in Cosío Villegas, *El sistema político mexicano*, pp. 22–35. The apparently limitless power of the President to deal with the opposition is well illustrated in Carlos Fuentes, *Tiempo mexicano* (Mexico, D.F.: Joaquín Mortiz, 1971), pp. 109–22.

17. There is not a single good work that explores the problem of political and administrative corruption, but some insights can be found in Rosario Castellanos et al., *La corrupción* (Mexico, D.F.: Editorial Nuestro Tiempo, 1969). In regard to political alienation, see the chapter on Mexico in Gabriel Almond and Sidney Verba, *The Civic Culture* (Princeton, N.J.: Princeton University Press, 1963).

18. Peter Smith, "La movilidad política en el México contemporáneo," *Foro internacional*, vol. 15, no. 3 (January–March 1975): 379–413.

19. Raymond Vernon, *The Dilemma of Mexico's Development* (Cambridge, Mass.: Harvard University Press, 1968), pp. 123–53.

20. There are very few studies on violence, but some facts are presented by Jaime López in *10 años de guerrillas en México (1964–1974)* (Mexico, D.F.: Editorial Posada, 1974).

21. See Almond and Verba, *The Civic Culture*, chap. 14.

22. Interesting views about the cliques within the establishment are found in Kenneth F. Johnson's *Mexican Democracy: A Critical View* (Boston: Allyn and Bacon, 1971), pp. 59–84, and Daniel Cosío Villegas, *La sucesión presidencial* (Mexico, D.F.: Joaquín Mortiz, 1975).

23. Bo Anderson and James D. Cockcroft, "Control and Cooptation in Mexican Politics," in Irving Louis Horowitz, Josué de Castro, and John Gerassi (eds.), *Latin American Radicalism* (New York: Vintage Books, 1969), pp. 366–89.

24. The nature of rotation among the Mexican political elite is well described in the work of Peter Smith, "La movilidad política." See also Frank R. Brandenburg, *The Making of Modern Mexico* (Englewood Cliffs, N.J.: Prentice-Hall, 1964), pp. 156–62.

25. Political exclusion is analyzed by González Casanova, *La democracia*, pp. 89–126. See also Arturo Warman, *Los campesinos, hijos predilectos del régimen* (Mexico, D.F.: Editorial Nuestro Tiempo, 1972); Roger Bartra et al., *Caciquismo y poder político en el México rural* (Mexico, D.F.: Siglo Veintiuno Editores, 1975).

26. The nature of the foreign presence in modern Mexico is explored in Lorenzo Meyer et al., *La política exterior de México: realidad y perspectivas* (Mexico, D.F.: El

Colegio de México, 1972). See also Bernardo Sepúlveda et al., *Las empresas transnacionales en México* (Mexico, D.F.: El Colegio de México, 1974).

27. A good analysis of the expansionist nature of transnational enterprises in Mexico is the work of Fernando Fajnzylber and Trinidad Martinez Tarragó, "Las empresas transnacionales: expansión a nivel mundial y proyección en la industria mexicana" (unpublished manuscript circulated by COMACYT and CIDE, 1974).

28. An analysis of the economic model of Mexico's development since the Revolution is presented by William Glade, Jr., and Charles W. Anderson, *The Political Economy of Mexico* (Madison: University of Wisconsin Press, 1968). See also Leopoldo Solís, *La realidad económica mexicana: retrovisión y perspectivas* (Mexico, D.F.: Siglo Veintiuno Editores, 1973); Clark Reynolds, *The Mexican Economy: Twentieth-Century Structure and Growth* (New Haven: Yale University Press, 1970); Timothy King, *Mexico: Industrialization and Trade Policies since 1940* (London: Oxford University Press, 1970).

29. Banco de México, *La distribución del ingreso en México* (Mexico, D.F.: Fondo de Cultura Económica, 1974), p. 17.

30. A general view of Mexico's social structure is presented in Joseph A. Khal (ed.), *Comparative Perspectives on Stratification: Mexico, Great Britain, Japan* (Boston: Little, Brown, 1968), pp. 1–82.

31. Samuel P. Huntington, "Social and Institutional Dynamics of One-Party Systems," in Clement H. Moore (ed.), *Authoritarian Politics in Modern Society* (New York: Basic Books, 1970), pp. 32–40.

32. This relationship between revolution and the increase of State power had been presented by Marx. A non-Marxist formulation is to be found in Bertrand De Jouvenel, *Du pouvoir* (Geneva: Constant Bourquin, Editeur, 1974), pp. 263–88.

The State and the Urban Poor

SUSAN ECKSTEIN

A capitalist state needs capital to generate production and to provide resources for the administrative apparatus.[1] It must also maintain legitimacy, which depends on the support of all major socioeconomic groups. To obtain and maintain the support of the poor, the State must either rely on repression and ideological control or respond to their concerns.

Mexico's post-World War II economic expansion reflects both the play of market forces and direct and indirect government initiatives. While the country's rate of growth is impressive, certain negative aspects should be noted. (1) Production is highly concentrated in capital-intensive enterprises.[2] This is largely the result of government policies that encourage the substitution of capital for labor, the bias of the nation's businessmen toward "modern" technology, and direct foreign investments in Mexico that import mechanized production methods. (2) The distribution of the newly generated wealth is extremely inegalitarian. According to rough estimates, the poorest 80 percent of the population receive only slightly more than 40 percent of the national income.[3] This situation can be traced to a variety of factors, among them regressive fiscal policies, protection of oligopolistic enterprises, spotty enforcement of existing tax laws, and inflationary government policies. (3) Social and economic opportunity is to be found mainly in the cities, particularly Mexico City.[4] Agriculture is becoming increasingly mechanized and no longer absorbs the rural population. Nonagricultural opportunities are located in metropolitan centers, and the provincial people have been migrating to the cities, but industry has not

---

For a longer treatment of the subject of this essay, see Susan Eckstein's *The Poverty of Revolution: The State and the Urban Poor in Mexico* (Princeton, N.J.: Princeton University Press, 1977).

expanded rapidly enough to absorb the growing urban population. As a result, the absolute and relative number of city dwellers with low and unstable incomes has increased over the years.

To protect the interests of capital (and, to a lesser extent, the interests of the salaried "middle class"[5] and workers in the capital-intensive sector) while regional and class inequalities increase, the Mexican state, particularly since the 1930s, has centralized power and formed the Institutional Revolutionary Party (PRI). With its populist, Revolution-linked ideology and sectoral organization, the Party conveys the impression that it represents its affiliated peasant, labor, and "middle class" groups. However, while formally autonomous, the PRI enjoys no decision-making or budgetary authority. It is run oligarchically, has a nominating procedure that assures elite control, exercises little power except for putting people into office, and is ultimately subservient to the President, since the President appoints and removes the Party head at his discretion.[6] Because the PRI lacks power, the interests of capitalists have not been undermined despite their exclusion from the Party: their interests are represented in the informal deliberations central to decision-making.

In addition to the Party apparatus, the legislature, the military, and regional political forces, though formally autonomous, are all subordinate to the President and the interests he serves. The legislature exercises negligible control over the federal budget, and it ratifies almost all laws backed by the President. Thus, the laws passed in the 1960s and early 1970s entitling minority parties to limited numbers of congressional seats provide opposition parties with no institutionalized base from which to influence the decision-making process. Thus, also, the recent creation of two new political parties, in line with the government's proclaimed concern with *apertura democrática* (democratic opening), reflects the further expansion of formal, not real, democracy. Regional politics, in turn, have been subordinated to the President through his control over patronage, political recruitment, and budgetary allotments. This is especially true in the capital, where the municipal government is a national ministry. As a result of these political developments, the Mexican state manages to resolve conflicting economic and political demands above all in the interest of capital.

This essay focuses on the way state-linked forces regulate the urban poor even when the poor secure certain goods and services from the regime. It illustrates how residents in newly formed low-income neighborhoods become associated with groups which, in effect, extend the regime's legitimacy where political order had not previously existed. The state gains the support of the inhabitants largely by extending social, economic, and political benefits. It appears to be responsive to and protective of their interests, but the benefits it allots tend to reinforce the established stratification system. Moreover, to gain access to these resources, the resident poor affiliate with groups that provide them with formal power but no institutionalized access to decision-making authority or budgetary discretion; that is, they gain symbolic power but no means to make the government act in their interest. In the process, residents are subjected to social and political controls. They expand the regime's support base, regardless of the intentions of *políticos* and residents when they established the political and administrative ties. Thus the State facilitates the impingement of the social forces that dominate society at large, even though the grass-roots organizations, with their populist objectives, give the impression that they are operating in opposition to these forces.

The data derive from a 1967–1968 multi-method study I made of two low-income areas—a now-legalized squatter settlement formed by an organized land invasion in 1954 and a government-financed housing development that opened in 1964 on the periphery of Mexico City. Most residents of the legalized squatter settlement live in one- or two-room houses of differing quality, depending largely on the homeowners' financial resources. In comparison to the land-invaded area, the development contains better-constructed and more uniform housing, is more spacious, and is better serviced. While neither community was ever economically homogeneous, the majority of the original residents of both settlements were employed in low-paying service and commercial activities. Most of the residents moved there from other sections of the city, although the majority were born in the provinces. The areas therefore provide housing for the city's burgeoning migrant population.

Statements about leaders and group activities are based on "semi-structured" interviews with the heads of all locally operating, formally chartered groups and agencies; participant observations; and written documents. I found the leaders by visiting all visible local agencies and organization headquarters, asking those in charge of the operations the names and addresses of other agencies, institutions, and organizations in the areas, speaking to the persons in charge of the places so named, and asking them, in turn, the same question. I continued this procedure until I could find no new groups. Where a group had city and national divisions, I interviewed not only the heads of the local affiliations but also the nonlocal persons to whom they were formally responsible in their organizational hierarchy, since they too shaped relations within the communities. I asked questions about the groups they headed, their personal backgrounds, the history of their local communities, and relations between local and nonlocal groups. I supplemented and cross-checked the information I obtained in these interviews with observations I made in the communities, including observations at local group meetings held during the time I did my field research, and with information from newspapers,

government files, and such documents as correspondence between local individuals and groups, on the one hand, and district, city-wide, and national political and administrative government agencies, on the other.

I will describe the types of benefits extended to residents and the nature of local government and political operations, and then delineate the formal and informal processes through which local residents have been incorporated into the political-administrative apparatus and exposed to forces that subordinate their interests to those of well-to-do Mexicans. Next, I will analyze processes limiting the political power of organized residents and inducing local leaders to collaborate with higher-ranking functionaries even when they are denied institutionalized access to power. Finally, the relationship between the State and the urban poor in Mexico will briefly be contrasted with the situation in other capitalist countries and in socialist Cuba.

Benefits Extended to Local Residents

In 1954, when the squatters invaded what is now a legalized settlement, the area was muddy and partially covered with water. It contained no urban or social services. After 1958, the area was recognized officially by the municipal government as a *colonia proletaria* (proletarian colony), and *colonos* (residents of *colonias proletarias*) obtained two public primary schools and a kindergarten for their children, as well as paved streets, police protection, a government-administered social center and medical clinic, and legal rights to their land.

The Law of the Colonias Proletarias technically protects the interests of the urban poor. When the land it covers is sold to the residents, it becomes inalienable (*patrimonio familiar*). The law also stipulates that the land may not be absentee-owned and must be inhabited by lower- and working-class persons. In this way, it prohibits land speculation and land grabbing by wealthy persons who can afford housing in the nonsubsidized market. Although the *colonos* had to finance their own housing, the government sold the property to them for the nominal fee of 80 cents a square meter, payable in monthly installments over a 10-year period.

The housing development, in contrast, was built by the government of the Federal District, a ministry of the national government. Recipients of houses buy the property from the government at cost, in monthly installments ranging from $9.60 to $28.00 over a period of 15 years. While the cost is high for low-income Mexicans, the development offers recipients a unique opportunity to own fairly well-constructed homes and to enjoy many urban and social services. The development is divided into several distinct neighborhoods, each of which contains a government-constructed primary school, a market, and public land. In addition, the community has a park with a zoo and lake, sports centers, a government-run children's hospital, a funeral parlor, a social center with a swimming pool, public technical and academic secondary schools, and a post office.

Besides material benefits, residents of both areas now have access locally to formally recognized social, economic, and political associations.[7] The groups include territorial units of the municipal government and the PRI; union locals (and factions within the locals) of market vendors and school teachers; lay groups associated with parish churches; independent, government, and PRI-linked social groups, including athletic groups; and groups formed to promote government social-athletic centers. Through divisions of the electoral organ of the PRI and the municipal administrative apparatus, residents enjoy formal power; through economic associations, residents ostensibly "articulate" and "aggregate" their class interests; through social groups, they nominally satisfy their nonpolitical, noneconomic interests. However, most of the groups are formally affiliated with national PRI or government-linked organizations, and even the nominally independent ones are subject to PRI and government influence because the leaders overtly or covertly associate with PRI or government groups or persons associated with such groups. The affiliated groups provide residents with no institutionalized authority or budgetary discretion.[8] While the formally autonomous groups do have authority, they are constrained by their limited financial resources.

Rank-and-file participation in community groups has declined since the areas were first settled. In any case, participation in the housing development never was as extensive as in the squatter settlement, largely because the first settlers in the development were not faced with the problem of securing legal land rights and basic social and urban facilities.[9] Participation varies according to local conditions, not merely according to formal organizational affiliation. In this respect, the organizations are adaptive to the interests of their members.

Residents wield political power not merely through such groups but also through the vote. They elect legislators and the President, *políticos* who in theory have institutionalized power and are responsive to their constituents. Accordingly, district *políticos* in the squatter settlement appear to have petitioned government offices successfully for schools, roads, pavement, markets, and public transportation. However, they generally no not exercise their constitutional power on behalf of residents. They do not view as their main task representing their constituents' interests in the legislature. They spend little time in their districts, and they contribute to the near-unanimous support congressmen give to all legislation brought to a vote. Local PRI congressmen identify more with the functional occupational groups with which they are affiliated than with residents in the districts who elected them to office.[10] Thus, institutionalized access to power provides residents with no guarantee that their interests are protected.

The Political-Administrative Apparatus

The PRI is the only party with a grass-roots organization and local social-service agencies. District PRI offices offer classes in sewing, cooking, hairdressing, and typing, and medical and barber services. PRI functionaries also write job recommendations for residents and periodically distribute to residents such gifts as rice, *frijoles*, and candy. Furthermore, the PRI is the only party which regularly solicits the government for social and urban facilities on behalf of residents. It thereby serves as an intermediary between the local communities and the municipal government.

Although formally autonomous, the PRI and PRI-affiliated groups help promote and organize administrative activities by directly collaborating with government functionaries, by complementing the work of the government, and by serving as intermediaries between residents and the government. Members of PRI-affiliated youth and market associations collaborate with the government through their participation in civil activities, and PRI functionaries collaborate with local and district-level government functionaries in the annual festivities commemorating the anniversary of the squatter settlement and in the inauguration of government-financed projects in both areas. Accordingly, the head of a PRI youth group in one of the local districts commented to me, "We call a political meeting whenever there's an urgent need to prepare for a civic act—for example, for national *fiestas* and patriotic celebrations."

PRI-affiliated groups also assist the government by sponsoring services, such as medical care, which supplement those provided by the government, and by helping to avert the development of local opposition to the regime. They even offer services which according to law are supposed to be provided by the government. For instance, a PRI district office houses an officially recognized closed-circuit educational program.

Local-government and PRI agencies at times use the same personnel and stress the same concerns. Persons on occasion are deliberately selected for posts in one of the two institutions because of their affiliation with the other. In the housing development, the heads of the PRI-affiliated Federation of Lower Class Areas and two government-linked groups—the promotion committee for the new social center and one of the territorial-based administrative organs—agreed to share the same personnel for their block representatives. Moreover, on one occasion a government functionary organized a group that subsequently affiliated with the PRI. In the legalized squatter settlement, government functionaries claimed that they secured administrative posts because of their prior involvement in the PRI and PRI-affiliated groups. The highest-ranking local functionary headed the district youth division of the PRI, and his predecessor had been secretary-general of the local PRI-affiliated association of market vendors and a local coordinator for the PRI. As a result, leaders of government and government-affiliated groups involve members in PRI-related activities, even though such groups are supposed to be politically neutral. By claiming that they involve groups members individually, not the group collectively, they technically avoid the legal restriction.

The PRI and the government also are linked through informal ties among leaders of groups affiliated with the two institutions. Personal bonds, which frequently cut across institutional lines, generally have a more decisive bearing on patterns of interaction than formal institutional affiliation. For instance, one of the district government officers in 1968 had daily contact with the head of the city-wide division of the Federation of Lower Class Areas, yet he had contact with the other district government bureaucrats of his rank at most only once a month. Similarly, a government officer in one of the areas reported having daily contact with PRI functionaries at the district office but only weekly contact with his government superior. Through such ties, leaders of PRI and government groups influence one another's point of view and plan activities which they consider mutually beneficial.

Furthermore, government agents help subsidize the PRI and publicly associate with PRI politicians. They do not subsidize other political parties locally, even though the government reputedly does so on the national level. According to district PRI functionaries, some of the medicine for the PRI clinics is provided by government agencies. During the campaigns, government functionaries tacitly lend their support to the PRI even if they do not directly engage in political activities. Government functionaries, for instance, welcomed PRI candidates at local political rallies and praised the candidates.

At times, the political involvement of groups affiliated with the government is less explicit and direct. For instance, at the request of congressmen and other PRI district functionaries, school directors allow students to participate in inaugurations of public-works projects, manifestations in commemoration of national holidays, the President's departures from and returns to Mexico, and other civic activities in which the PRI also is active. Educated residents in the two areas were probably involved in similar activities when they were in school.

In general, there is little difference between the government and the PRI in the two areas, largely because local groups affiliated with both institutions are formally powerless and subject to similar hierarchical constraints. Overlapping leadership, informal ties, and common and complementary concerns among leaders of groups affiliated with the two institutions link the PRI with the government despite their formal separation. Consequently, groups affiliated with the two institutions reinforce each other even when the leaders of these groups do not do so intentionally.

Consequences of State Involvement in Local Communities

While local residents unquestionably now enjoy benefits from the government, including legally defined ones, state concern with the interests of inhabitants is limited. Laws protecting lower-class interests are not strictly enforced. Moreover, the groups to which residents have access shape the demands that residents make on the regime, and incorporation into official national organizations automatically helps extend the legitimacy of the mainly pro-capital regime.

Several stipulations of the Law of Colonias Proletarias, for example, are violated. Contrary to the law, the sponsors of the land invasion never provided the area with urban services or set aside 15 percent of the land for public facilities. The government therefore charged the squatters two to three times the cost of the land for sidewalks, street paving, and drainage facilities. Many of the poorest squatters were forced to move away when the government began to collect money for urban services. Also in violation of the law, professionals and other "middle-class" people are moving to the area now that it is fully urbanized, for only they can afford the "going" price of local property: $3,200 for an average-sized house, $8,000 to $16,000 for the largest homes. As a result, according to early leaders of local organizations, at most 25 percent to 50 percent of the original squatters still live in the area. Furthermore, the law notwithstanding, by the late 1960s one-third of the residents were tenants and the largest *vecindades* (one-story tenements) generally were illegally owned by persons who had never lived there. Thus, while the government publicly claims to protect the lower classes, it allows market forces to assert themselves to the disadvantage of the poor.

The housing development also increasingly serves the interests of "middle class" Mexicans. Although it was officially built for families displaced by public-works projects and for families living in unsanitary squatter settlements and slums, abandoned women in the areas destined for demolition could not legally qualify for housing in the development. Moreover, the government allocated a large proportion of the homes to organized working- and "middle-class" groups—for example, to divisions of the police, industrial unions, journalists, municipal government functionaries, the army, and political parties which, in turn, distributed their allotments to select members. Although property here is technically inalienable, as in the squatter settlement, according to residents and local leaders, by 1971 approximately one-third to one-half of the homes no longer were occupied by the families who originally were allotted homes. In the main, the poorest beneficiaries left. Current residents and the housing administrator claim that poor families moved because (1) they never fully adjusted to the area; (2) they preferred living closer to where they worked; (3) they could not afford the monthly payments; or (4) they were tempted by the money others were willing to pay them to give up their property. Their successors are mainly "middle-class" families who can afford the cost of the housing and consider the area a desirable place to live.

The benefits enjoyed by the residents cost wealthy Mexicans little. First, the land that residents in both areas occupy formerly belonged to *ejidos*. Hence, the property was obtained at the expense of *ejidatarios*, beneficiaries of Mexico's revolutionary-linked peasant land reform. Wealthy Mexican proprietors have not been compelled to rescind land rights. Second, although government revenues are used to provide the local communities with such social services as schools and clinics, local residents pay for urban services. Consequently, the government needs to tax well-to-do Mexicans only minimally to make goods and services available to local inhabitants.

The material benefits that residents receive from the Party and the government rarely serve to reduce inequalities in urban income. According to persons in charge of district PRI offices, only about two dozen people make use of most of the services offered at their headquarters. The PRI only intermittently allocates gifts locally, and a small proportion of the residents actually receive them. By contrast, capitalists and organized working- and "middle-class" groups (through partially financed government social security programs) get more and better-quality services. Such benefits as infrastructure facilities and tax write-offs indirectly generate more income than the land and other benefits extended to the local poor. Moreover, the availability of inexpensive land encourages rural-urban migration, providing a large supply of inexpensive labor in the competitive sector of the urban economy. Since property ownership in general makes people conservative, the government's tacit urban land policy indirectly benefits capital, economically and politically.

The extension of political as well as social and economic resources to resident poor serves to reinforce the stratification system prevailing in the society at large. While the extension of the franchise and the incorporation of local residents into a mass-based party convey the impression that the state is democratic and representative of the numerical majority, these measures extend symbolic, not effective, institutionalized power, because the formal political apparatus has no power.

Moreover, formal incorporation of local groups into national organizations, like the overt and covert cooptation of leaders, serves as a mechanism through which the state, in effect, regulates residents. Residents are immobilized so that they impose limited demands on the regime. Upon affiliation with national groups, associations that once had large and highly active memberships became largely inactive, and members increasingly came to deal with their group leaders on an individual basis about individual problems.[11] Whereas initially the groups focused on local concerns, now collective participation centers mainly around civic and political rallies. Affiliates who continue to participate in group-sponsored activities generally do so in return for, or in anticipation of, personal favors from the leaders. Participation has become ritualized; it is no longer an effective form of collective power.

Even groups that are still formally autonomous urge members to attend civic and political manifestations, and expose members to political-administrative matters. The leaders feel that they thereby may be able to secure services for their constituents which they themselves cannot provide. Some leaders also feel that such collaboration with *políticos* may help them secure political patronage. Although these groups, unlike the PRI and government-affiliated groups, technically have some authority, they have few resources with which to satisfy members' concerns. Therefore, they too turn to *políticos* for help. Leaders operate their groups almost as if they were PRI- or administratively-linked affiliations, either because they are formally affiliated with the PRI- and government-linked organizations as individuals or because they anticipate political patronage. As a good example, the head of a deliberately apolitical lay group became privately affiliated with the PRI-linked Federation of Lower Class Areas. Afterward, political and civic matters assumed high priority in his association. Although he maintained that his affiliation with the PRI-linked group was purely as a private citizen and not as a representative of his group, he subsequently reported regularly on the activities of the PRI group, and allowed the leader of the PRI-affiliated group to monopolize a number of rallies held by the social group. The head of the PRI-affiliated group used the opportunity largely to talk about his own group, his own leadership credentials, and the various benefits that residents of the housing development enjoyed as a result of his efforts. He even claimed credit for the same improvements that the head of the social group previously had said were his doing. Above all, in the process this group was diverted from its original social and economic goals.

Hence, formal incorporation of established groups into national organizations and overt and covert cooptation of leadership have similar effects on group members. They serve as mechanisms of social and political control. Residents' difficulties in securing benefits from the government stem not from any "organizational incapacity" or "political incompetence," as some commentators on Mexico claim. Inhabitants' organized efforts have met with limited success because most of their groups have no institutionalized access to power and because affiliation with PRI- and government-linked groups has undermined their organizational effectiveness. Covert as well as overt cooptation have left local groups without effective power. Residents are not as successful at securing goods and services from the government as they were initially. Residents in the squatter settlement and the poorest section of the development have been particularly ineffectual. For example, the government has not responded to the petitions of *colonos* for schools for the 2,000 children for whom there was no space in the existing school.

Structures and Processes Limiting the Political Power of Organized Residents

Why have residents not been able to use their formal power to pressure the government for more benefits? Their efforts have met with limited success because membership in most groups has not entitled them to institutionalized access to power, because affiliation with the PRI- and government-linked groups undermined their political effectiveness and because informal class and political forces dominating in the society at large constrained them from using formal power for their own ends.

The informal forces rooted in the national political economy which inhibit the political effectiveness of organized residents include the hierarchial nature of national inter- and intragroup relations, the class structure, the personalized style of Mexican politics, the multiplicity of competing groups operating in the society, and the government's threat to apply force. They reflect social structural forces closely associated with the state, but generally not deliberate efforts of functionaries to regulate the local poor. For these reasons, political stability can be maintained at minimal financial cost to the government, and the state can advance the interests of capital nationally without using repression against a major base of political support.

The hierarchical way in which *políticos* are appointed and removed from office and the hierarchical channels through which urban and community services are obtained limit residents' ability to use local groups to advance their own interests, because local leaders are constrained to conform to "rules of the game" that they themselves do not establish. Otherwise they can neither personally advance politically nor secure benefits for their constituents. The prospect of removal from office also compels local subordinates to conform with the expectations, or perceived expectations, of higher-ranking functionaries. In this way "appropriate" local concerns are delimited and heads of local groups are encouraged to be subservient, even though they are not necessarily rewarded for it. As a politically ambitious head of a local division of a government agency noted, "If you do more than your boss, you're in real trouble."

Higher-ranking national functionaries also prevent the consolidation of power within local branch organizations by appointing and removing local functionaries at their own discretion. Periodic reassignments keep local officeholders from identifying with local interests. One market administrator explained to me that the head of the Division of Markets regularly reassigns administrators to different markets so that "no administrator gets entrenched in local politics to the extent that he becomes subservient to local interests and fails to fulfill his obligations." As this case suggests, higher-ranking functionaries may restrict the activities of local groups because they are concerned with the overall effectiveness of their organization, not because they are conspiring against local residents.

In addition, the hierarchical promotion system drains local divisions of their best leaders. In the squatter settlement, the most charismatic leader was promoted to higher-level political and administrative posts outside the area. His successor was less popular and effective in defending local interests. Even when functionaries remain at their local posts, the hierarchical system weakens their groups' political effectiveness; ambitious local leaders recognize that their prospects for political advancement are enhanced if they collaborate with higher-ranking functionaries outside their areas rather than restrict their activities to the local communities. Thus, during the last two national campaigns the leading local *políticos*, especially in the development, engaged almost exclusively in political activities in electoral districts in other parts of the capital. One of them even worked outside Mexico City.

The hierarchical system also limits the ability of local groups to organize collectively. At times, individual divisions are isolated from, and in competition with, other branches of the same parent organization for favors from higher-ranking functionaries. For example, such a local PRI-affiliated social group as the Federation of Lower Class Areas had to compete with other divisions for favors from municipal offices. Similarly, the largest locally operating economic group involving local residents—the association of local market vendors—divides members' loyalty. Almost all markets have at least one "union" leader. Yet the only contact "union" heads in each of the markets have with one another is through the regional offices of the union. There is no horizontal communication or collaboration. Even within any one market, the loyalty of the small-scale tradesmen is divided when there is more than one local "union" leader. As a result, local leaders tend to be subservient to commands from their superiors. For example, they encourage vendors to be acquiescent and to participate in civic and political rallies. As one administrator proudly noted: "*Comerciantes* [petty merchants] have become more docile and responsive since I've been working here. If I ask them to do something, they do it. Now they want and accept us as representatives of the 'authorities'." The leaders do not organize protests to pressure the government for better working conditions, fringe benefits, or social and political justice.

Because of hierarchical constraints, the various local functionaries feel pressured to give residents the impression that higher officials are concerned with local problems and at the same time to convince residents that they should obey orders from authorities. When government functionaries raided homes in the poorest section of the housing development to confiscate animals that inhabitants were illegally raising to supplement their incomes, the local head of a PRI-affiliated group made no attempt to retrieve the animals. He expressed outrage over the incident at one of his weekly meetings, but he simultaneously led residents to believe that the intruders were thieves, in order to avert resentment of the government. Similarly, the housing administrator who commanded the men to raid the homes confided to me that he intentionally dissociated himself publicly from the men "for fear of making local enemies."

In addition to the hierarchical structure of political and administrative groups, class biases that permeate relations within the areas constrict the political effectiveness of local groups. Access to local leadership posts, opportunities for political advancement, and the ability of local groups to secure benefits for members—particularly once relations within the groups are routinized—depend largely on the socioeconomic status of group members and leaders.

While resident functionaries are not the local economic elite, they tend to be among the most economically successful residents. In 1968, the top functionaries in the squatter settlement were a market vendor, a shopowner, and a factory worker, and in the development they were white-collar employees in the wealthiest sections and a factory worker in the poorest section. Actually, leadership in the areas has become increasingly "middle class" over the years as the socioeconomic composition of the areas has improved. Whereas the first government functionaries in the squatter settlement were poorly-educated persons holding low-prestige jobs, in 1971 the highest-ranking local officer was a bureaucrat with a secondary (military) school education. He said to me, "Now we need people who are more skilled than we did before. My predecessor didn't have enough technical skills. He did things in his own way—not the way he was asked."

Furthermore, local leaders' prospects of political mobility increasingly have come to depend on class standing and contacts outside the local areas. Leaders of humble class origin stood the greatest chance of promotion when members of their groups were highly mobilized, a rare situation once relations within the areas were routinized. The most successful lower-class *político* the two areas produced was the previously mentioned charismatic leader of the squatters, who gained preeminence immediately after the land invasion. He received several higher-level political and administrative posts, some of which have given him access to so many payoffs that he is now reputedly a "millionaire" and a recipient of a house in the housing development.

Economic groups provide greater prospects for advancement than territorial groups, reflecting the general post-revolutionary importance of economic over geographic-based power. The head of the Federation of Lower Class Areas in the housing development exemplifies the opportunities unions hold for faithful workers. Originally a railroad worker in the northern state of Sinaloa, he rose to several posts in the local and national division of the union of railroad workers. He now holds a salaried white-collar job in a government office and entertains the idea of becoming a congressman. His social, economic, political, and even geographical mobility derived from his initial union affiliation. Similarly, the congressman in the section of the development controlled by a labor confederation began his career as a rank-and-file factory-hand. He subsequently became a textile engineer and active member of a textile union. After successive union posts, he finally obtained the highest position in the union and, thereby, one of the highest political posts in the country, although one that rarely promises further political advancement. These men both gained political status on the basis of their work status.

Functionaries might serve the interests of the local poor without themselves being of low socioeconomic status, but because they are primarily interested in their own advancement they tend to be hierarchically, rather than community oriented. Rarely do local leaders collaborate to promote programs for the benefit of residents. They have much more contact with persons of higher rank in their own organizations outside the local communities than they do with one another.

Class constraints also limited most local *políticos'* ability to secure guidance and useful political contacts, as a leader of a local group in the housing development explained to me. "We go to the PRI office to try to establish friendships with persons who can help orient us, and to find out what PRI can do for us. We also can learn from them, because we lack friends who can help us resolve our problems quickly. We suffer because we personally aren't known in the high levels of the government."[12]

The government in general has rewarded residents inversely to their economic "need" ever since organizational life in the areas has been institutionalized. As a result, residents of the more "middle class" of the two areas, the housing development, receive the most social services, even though they had better facilities from the start. Moreover, within the development the sections with the largest number of "middle-class" residents and leaders receive the largest share of government assistance. Their effectiveness stems not from formal group affiliations which they alone have, for local divisions of the same PRI and government-affiliated groups in the other area have not been equally effective. Rather, their good fortune derives from the fact that high-ranking functionaries generally favor their "middle-class" constituency.

The personal manner in which *políticos* are appointed and removed from office, goods and services are distributed, and local demands and conflicts are articulated and resolved further limits residents' ability to use local groups to serve their own ends. The groups operate in a highly personalized manner because the structure of power induces politicians to adopt personalized strategies. Thus, the head of the local branch of a PRI-affiliated group in the housing development regularly reassured followers that he served their interests before the authorities. At a meeting he announced, "We are like your family, in permanent struggle. Our duty is to see that you have few problems, to personally take your problems to the Treasury and other government dependencies. We are at your orders. We do not feel distant or indifferent. We realize that there is misery in many places, but we hope that this will change. That's our preoccupation." Similarly, a former government functionary in the legalized squatter settlement worked hard to become a "broker" between local residents and higher authorities. "I help *colonos,*" he explained to me. "If they can't afford fines or taxes I connect them with people who can help them for little money. I am lucky. Whenever I used to go to government offices I spoke with people there. I asked them their occupation. If I thought they could help people here in the *colonos* I became friendly with them. I told them that I'm from here and that I have X number of people behind me. Out of friendship they charged *colonos* less than their usual fee. *Colonos* who know that I have such contacts come to me."

The structurally induced personalized style of Mexican politics makes residents feel dependent on and indebted to the government for the material benefits they receive, including the land and pavement for which they pay. These "gifts" are officially "given" to them at public rallies attended by such high-ranking dignitaries as the President of the country and the mayor of the city. Local leaders also periodically distribute material benefits which they acquire through contacts, to entice residents to attend their meetings. The head of the Federation of Lower Class Areas in the development, for example, distributed dinner plates and used clothing at gatherings I attended. Above all, he gave those attending the impression that he might get them houses in the section of the development under construction. Thus, even a nonresident regularly attended the meetings because the head of the organization led him to believe that he would get a house if he used his connections at the phone company where he worked to get telephones installed in the area.

Anticipation of favors from specific functionaries induces residents to be subservient. For example, a number of residents in the development helped a local government functionary organize local civic festivities in the hope that the *político* in turn would help them get legal title to their homes.

In the very process of securing personal favors from the government, the collective effectiveness of residents was undermined. Particularly when legalizing illegal land claims, local functionaries collaborated with higher functionaries to establish social order and routinize local organizational life. Group members were instructed to personally request, not demand, goods and services, and to petition for benefits either individually or in small groups, not en masse as the squatters initially did. Local *políticos* conform because they believe that the government otherwise may not be responsive to their concerns. In the process, though, the government is less pressured to provide residents with goods and services.

Because politics is personalized, conflict is also. Competition for political and economic spoils pits local leaders against one another, weakening the potential collective strength of local inhabitants. Local leaders accuse each other of being self-serving and corrupt. Such division directs residents' energies toward local personalities rather than toward those national institutions which, on the one hand, generate the conditions giving rise to local conflicts and, on the other hand, have the resources to help improve the level of local well-being. Furthermore, when conflicts are personalized, residents never criticize political and administrative institutions in ways which might undermine the legitimacy of those institutions and the regime itself.

The multiplicity of groups operating locally further weakens the political power that residents might achieve through collective organization. This multiplicity is a by-product of the fact that numerous vertically structured groups operate nationally in affiliation with the PRI and the government and that higher-ranking functionaries tacitly encourage such an array of organizations by periodically distributing gifts to them, by attending their group meetings, and by seeking their support for civic and political events. Divisions within the state thereby seem to strengthen executive power and the interests it protects.[13]

The hierarchical system of appointments induces the various leaders to compete for local support and influence even when the groups they head are affiliated with the same parent institution and are concerned with the same issues. In the process, residents obtain some personal benefits through leaders but their potential collective strength is undermined. For example, when "middle-class" residents of the development wished private telephones, they did not collectively pressure the phone company. Though ostensibly a nonpolitical demand, it became a political issue. A leader of a local group told me, "There were three groups which collected petitions for phones. The heads of the group competed to get the most signatures. One of them even lied about the cost of phones so that people would be most apt to sign his petition." After collecting signatures, the leaders individually spoke to people they knew at the phone company. One leader promised to help persons in the phone company get homes in the area in return for their assistance. Yet, as he admitted privately to me, "It really would have been better if we had formed one big group, because we would have been a much larger force."

Nonetheless, competition among leaders of the diverse groups does not by itself account for the limited political effectiveness of the groups. When members are highly mobilized and nonlocal functionaries want to capture local support, residents succeed in securing benefits from the government even though they are divided. The squatters' initial success in acquiring public facilities and private property, even though they were not all united behind a single leader, is a case in point.

At the same time that the government encourages groups, it in fact regulates and restricts them. The government requires all groups to be officially registered, and the law of "social dissolution" gives it the right to intervene in local groups.[14] The very existence of these laws and the government's monopoly of the legitimate use of force inhibit residents both from forming groups and from engaging in activities which challenge the government's authority. The government rarely repressed local groups by force, although some residents of the squatter settlement did have difficulty organizing during the first years the area was inhabited. The laws served as a useful device by which controversial local leaders were repressed even when they espoused the same objectives and concerns as leaders of officially recognized groups.

The State and the Urban Poor in Comparative Perspective: A Brief Overview

While Mexico's dominant mass-based party and formal political stability contrast with the recurrent political shake-ups and military coups in most other leading Latin American capitalist countries today, social and economic benefits are no more equitably distributed in Mexico than in these other countries. The apparently less democratic regimes similarly subordinate the interests of the urban poor to capital, although regimes with less effective revolutionary-linked formal political apparati have had to use more repressive means to maintain political order. The other regimes generate similar social and economic effects, partly because, there too, real political power is not vested in formal political institutions. Additionally, inter- and intragroup relations are hierarchically structured and the governments are highly centralized, regardless of whether military men or civilians publicly rule.[15] Specific institutions which help regulate the urban poor, such as the PRI, are unique to Mexico. However, other Latin American countries also have clientelistic, class-biased regimes which allocate benefits to the urban poor that mainly serve to reinforce a capitalist order.

The organized urban poor portrayed here share common experiences not merely with the urban poor in other dependent capitalist countries but also with the urban poor in advanced capitalist countries. Although the class is proportionately larger in the less-developed countries, the urban poor in advanced capitalist economies also are handicapped by their class background: politically, they have limited means to exert influence through legitimate channels. Even in the United States, where political power is officially more decentralized than in Mexico, the urban poor are unable to exert effective pressure to reduce income inequality through the ostensibly pluralistic and democratic party apparatus. As in Mexico, most initiatives in the United States for eliminating poverty and improving the conditions associated with it come from the federal government, and initiative has been negligible except when the government has been threatened by major domestic economic and political crises.[16]

Despite these similarities, the Mexican and U.S. urban poor differ in important ways, owing to differences in the structures of the Mexican and U.S. capitalist economies. In the United States, the urban poor enjoy a higher standard of living, and the percentage of the population living at a subsistence level is smaller. Even the nature and location of housing available to the urban poor in the two countries differ: Instead of the centrifugal "invasion and succession" pattern of tenant residency found in many early industrial cities in the United States, in Mexico the urban poor increasingly live in small owner-occupied and constructed homes in vertically-integrated new areas on the periphery of the city. The Mexican state formally or tacitly recognizes and at times encourages such housing.

Furthermore, the economic subsidies extended to the urban poor and the manner in which the benefits are distributed are different in the two countries. Mexico offers its urban poor no direct economic assistance. It extends no direct income benefits comparable to those provided in the United States through the Aid to Families with Dependent Children Program, and no work-incentive schemes. In Mexico, economic assistance at best is indirect, through state protection of market commerce and other labor-absorbing economic activities, and through *de jure* recognition of *de facto* illegal land claims by the urban poor.

While benefits in the United States are allocated through impersonal bureaucratic channels, in Mexico they are allocated through paternalistic institutions. The different distributive methods reflect the more rational-legal government administration in the United States and Mexico's more paternalistic-populist government administration. Since Mexico's paternalistic system is deliberately recreated in new areas as they emerge, the cross-national differences reflect the different principles upon which the authority of the two governments is premised, not merely the persistence of long-established political institutions. Its continued paternalism helps Mexico's government gain and maintain the support of the ever-increasing urban poor population. The urban poor, in turn, contribute to the government's stability and its modicum of independence of capital.

The level of well-being of the Mexican urban poor differs not only from that of urban poor in the United States and other advanced capitalist countries but also from that of the urban poor in such socialist countries as Cuba. The differences in the two types of underdeveloped societies are rooted, above all, in the differing structures of their economies and government policies.[17] To the extent that the Cuban government regulates its urban poor in the process of extending benefits to them, it does so for different ends: to institute a contrasting type of political economy. Schooling and health-care facilities are more available to Cuban than to Mexican urban poor. Furthermore, income is more equitably distributed in Cuba than in Mexico, and the poorest city dwellers in Cuba are not faced with the same housing problems as are the urban poor in Mexico and other dependent capitalist countries. Although there is still a shortage of housing in Cuba, rent there never exceeds 10 percent of workers' salaries. New housing is planned and distributed through work groups on the basis of need and work contributions, not market forces and manipulation of private property by corrupt *políticos*. Moreover, because the Cuban government is deliberately expanding social and economic opportunities in the provinces, urbanization—and associated urban blight—is not increasing as rapidly in Cuba as in Latin American capitalist countries. Above all, Cuban men, unlike their counterparts in capitalist economies, have guaranteed employment. Consequently, the Cuban lower socioeconomic stratum is not subject to the same degradation, unstable income, and job insecurity as poor people in market economies. In addition, participation in mass-based groups—the geographically organized Committees for Defense of the Revolution, the Federation of Cuban Women, and unions—is more extensive in Cuba than in other Latin American countries. Mainly because the Cuban state above all identifies with proletarian interests, state power is used for different ends there than in capitalist countries, where the state above all protects the interests of capital.

Conclusions and Implications

Residents in my study had limited individual and community benefits, but not because of a lack of will or ability to organize. To a certain extent, organization even contributes to their low material level. Because of collective efforts and persevering leaders, residents secured certain improvements and property rights which they otherwise might not have attained. This happened chiefly at an early period when they were least acquiescent, but not antagonistic, toward the government, and when their organization was still largely informal. Formal organization has proved of limited help.

Cooptation of leaders and incorporation of local groups have served to establish and maintain the status quo. Residents have affiliated with groups which reinforce and extend the legitimacy of the regime, provide little institutionalized access to power, and subordinate their interests to those of other classes despite the groups' declared populist objectives. Above all, informal constraints inhibit residents from using the groups in ways which might significantly alter their position in the urban social and economic hierarchy. Control of the one channel for institutionalized access to official decision-making, Congress, is monopolized by nonlocal residents primarily concerned with their own personal interests and those of the corporate occupational groups with which they are associated. The effectiveness of this channel of influence is further circumscribed by the fact that Congress actually does not act independently of the President.

Local organizations contribute to the formal democratization of the society, for through them the people of the areas are transformed from an "unreliable" citizenry into an "accessible" public. Yet the local groups which legitimate themselves in the name of the Revolution are democratic more in theory than in practice. They give residents access to the public symbols of power but only limited, informal, and indirect access to government resources and decision-making.

Viewed from the local level, cooptation of leaders and the incorporation of groups into the political-administrative apparatus occur primarily because the opportunity structure encourages local leaders to affiliate with PRI and government groups either individually or together with other members of their groups. The populist or grass-roots doctrine and organization facilitate acceptance of the government and enable the government to stand as the champion of local residents, while the cooptative processes contribute to the stability of the pro-capital regime.[18]

It should not be forgotten, though, that cooptation *has* resulted on occasion in a government commitment of resources to local residents. The coopting and the coopted groups, and the leaders affiliated with each, generally all benefit from cooptation, even though unequally. The difference in the living standards between local residents and those who coopt them suggests that the local poor benefit least.

While one cannot generalize with assurance from relations within these two areas to relations between the State and the urban poor in general in Mexico City, under similar conditions the State is likely to regulate the organized poor in comparable ways. To the extent that this is true, propertied urban poor are likely to provide a conservative base of support for the government. The overwhelming electoral support the regime gets in these and other lower-class districts of the city and the fact that processes operating locally are linked to national institutions suggest that the processes probably are not unique to the two areas.

The State's support of its urban poor seems to enhance its ability to allocate certain material resources to other interests besides capital, while informal forces enable the government to act against the basic interests of the urban poor. The State thereby is able to generate production while maintaining and extending its bases of legitimacy as the urban population expands. The Mexican State resembles Bonaparte's in the aftermath of the French Revolution, but it is more modern and institutionalized, and more suited to Mexico's contemporary political economy. Small propertied peasants were a critical support base for Bonaparte, and as the Mexican population has become predominantly urban, small propertied urban poor in peripheral sections of Mexico City are becoming an important social base for the conservative, pro-capital regime.

Ultimately these and other urban poor in Mexico may withdraw their support from the regime, but this is likely to occur only under certain circumstances: when competition among higher-ranking functionaries induces political elites to mobilize lower-class clientele in ways which disrupt the existing structure of formal and informal controls, when residents feel they have more to gain by withdrawing than by continuing their support of the regime, or when urban guerrilla or other activities delegitimate the regime.

Notes

1. Two expressions used in this essay need to be explained: By "state" I mean "public" as distinct from "private" organizations, institutions, and relations. Politi-

cal institutions that form part of a state apparatus include government bureaucracies, the military, the executive, the judiciary, and the legislature. By defining the state as a specifically political set of institutions, we can study its relationship to society, the economy, and class power under specific historical conditions. Mexico is a middle-level "dependent, capitalist society" in terms of economic productivity, diversification, and dependence on foreign capital and technology. Its economy is less autonomous and more vulnerable than the economies of advanced capitalist countries, but more autonomous and less vulnerable than subsistence- and export-oriented mono-crop and extractive-oriented economies. In the terminology of I. Wallerstein, "The Rise and Future Demise of the World Capitalist System: Concepts for Comparative Analysis," *Comparative Studies in Society and History*, vol. 16 (September 1974): 387–415, Mexico represents a "semiperipheral" country within the world capitalist system, dependent on the "core" industrial countries but in different ways than are the "peripheral" countries.

2. The Law for New and Necessary Industries exempts industries importing capital goods from import taxes, and the overvaluation of the exchange rate (until September 1976) has implied a subsidy to imports of capital. For a discussion of Mexico's import and export substitution policies, see Villarreal's essay in this volume.

3. See I. Adelman and C. Morris, *An Anatomy of Patterns of Income Distribution in Developing Nations* (Washington, D.C.: Agency for International Development, Department of State, 1971), and Economic Commission for Latin America, *Economic Survey of Latin America*, 1970 (New York: United Nations, 1972), p. 65.

4. On regional inequality, see P. Lamartine Yates, *El desarrollo regional de México* (Mexico, D.F.: Banco de México, 1962); C. Reynolds, *The Mexican Economy: Twentieth Century Structure and Growth* (New Haven: Yale University Press, 1970); D. Barkin (ed.), *Los beneficiarios del desarrollo regional* (Mexico, D.F.: SEP/ SETENTAS, 1972); and *Economic Survey of Latin America*, 1970, p. 66. The government has encouraged industry to locate in the Federal District partly by subsidizing the distribution of wheat and corn, low-grade gasoline and diesel fuel, electricity and natural gas at prices favoring the city (see Lamartine Yates, *El desarrollo regional de México*, p. 127, and L. Randall, "The Process of Economic Development in Mexico from 1940 to 1959," Ph.D. dissertation, Columbia University, 1962). However, the government seems to be attempting to decentralize industry by extending tax breaks and eased-credit facilities for provincial enterprises.

5. I use the term "middle class" to refer to the consumer-oriented life style generally associated with salaried white-collar employees and professionals in the United States. Since the proportion of the Mexican population to whom this term can suitably be applied includes—according to most estimates—the top 15 percent to 30 percent of the population, it is not a statistically defined middle-class socioeconomic group. For a summary of different stratification profiles of Mexico, see C. Stern and J. Kahl, "Stratification since the Revolution," in J. Kahl (ed.), *Comparative Perspectives on Stratification* (Boston: Little, Brown, 1968).

6. In contrast, in *Mexican Government in Transition* (Urbana: University of Illinois Press, 1964), Scott generally attributes to the PRI decision-making power and balanced representation in policy formulation and outcome (see especially pp. 29, 32, 108, 145, 146). However, he, too, emphasizes the authoritarian elitist aspects of the political system in his "Mexico: The Established Revolution," in L. Pye and S. Verba (eds.), *Political Culture and Political Development* (Princeton, N.J.: Princeton University Press, 1965), pp. 39–95.

7. I use the terms "group," "organization," "association," and "agency" to refer to formal groups operating in the two areas. I specify whether these formal groups are nominally autonomous or affiliated with national or supralocal organizations or institutions.

8. Similarly, W. Cornelius, "Urbanization and Political Demand-Making: A Study of Political Participation among the Migrant Poor," *American Political Science Review*, vol. 68 (December 1974), found that residents in the low-income areas he studied did not influence government policy formation, although they did informally demand benefits from the government. Since the demand-making he describes is not a formally prescribed mode of political participation outlined in the statutes of political and administrative groups, his findings corroborate the point made here that the formal political apparatus provides the resident poor with no guaranteed, institutionalized means by which to influence the decision-making process.

9. When areas are formed gradually, community-based groups are apparently less likely to emerge than in either of the two areas under study; see L. Lomnitz, "The Social and Economic Organization of a Mexican Shantytown," *Latin American Urban Research*, vol. 4 (1974): 135–55. D. Goldrich, "Toward the Comparative Study of Politicization in Latin America," in D. Heath and R. Adams (eds.), *Contemporary Cultures and Societies in Latin America* (New York: Random House, 1965), also argues on the basis of his comparative analysis of the urban poor in Lima, Peru, and Santiago, Chile, that the initial experience with the authorities of residents of urban communities shapes subsequent political patterns. Residents who immediately face some government opposition but are not repressed are most likely to establish groups and initiate demands for community improvements. Since the Mexican government initially tried to prevent the land invasion, my findings support Goldrich's conclusions, except that differences between the areas I studied tended to diminish as relations within local groups became routinized.

10. While the regional office of the PRI ran some local PRI district offices, others were run by such "corporate functional" groups as the union of social security workers, the Revolutionary Confederation of Workers and Peasants (CROC), and the Mexican Workers Confederation (CTM). These groups paid for the maintenance of the district quarters and the salaries of group members who worked in the districts for the Party. They also provided some patronage to local residents and gave financial support to the Party. Interestingly, during the campaign the congressman in the district controlled by CROC gave away fabric that he obtained from the industries employing members of his union. This case illustrates a way in which industry is indirectly linked to the PRI through district-level politics, but in coordination with national political offices. Industry thereby helps support the Party even though it enjoys no formal power within the Party.

In contrast, the literature on social "mobilization," "political participation," and "marginality integration" assumes that participation is an ever-increasing phenomenon. See, for example, K. Deutsch, "Social Mobilization and Political Development," in J. Finkle and R. Gable (eds.), *Political Development and Social Change* (New York: John Wiley and Sons, 1966), and D. Lerner, *The Passing of Traditional Society* (Glencoe, Ill.: Free Press, 1958).

11. K. Johnson, *Mexican Democracy: A Critical View* (Boston: Allyn and Bacon, 1971), esp. pp. 59–84, argues that on the national level particular *caramilla* or political-clique memberships are generally of greater political consequence than formal political or administrative career patterns. The limited access residents have to such cliques informally limits their access to political power.

12. A case in point involves a government-sponsored program of forestation. The official purpose of the program was to combat pollution. While the tree planting did not purify the air, since factories and automobiles continued to pollute it, it served definite political functions. It gave local politicians the opportunity to petition higher-level functionaries for a community benefit and claim credit for obtaining the trees, even though the program was city-wide in scope. Because local leaders wanted to impress residents with their political effectiveness and because outside leaders wanted to gain, maintain, or expand chains of indebtedness and probable future support locally, the outside leaders led local leaders to believe that they were instrumental in securing the benefits. (Interestingly, pollution became a public issue in Mexico shortly after it did in the United States, despite the fact that Mexico City had highly polluted air long before.)

13. In countries where two or more parties compete for lower-class support, parties rather than groups affiliated with a single party often create divisions among the urban poor. On the divisive effect of political parties among the urban poor in other Latin American countries, see T. Ray, *The Politics of the Barrios of Venezuela* (Berkeley: University of California Press, 1969), pp. 98–127, and R. Pratt, "Parties, Neighborhood Associations, and the Politicization of the Urban Poor in Latin America," *Midwest Journal of Political Science*, vol. 15 (August 1971).

14. The government has applied the law of "social dissolution" against persons who allegedly diffused ideas or programs of foreign governments that disturbed public order or affected Mexico's sovereignty. Demetrio Vallejo and Valentin Campa, who led the 1958 railway workers' strike, and the Communist muralist, Alfaro Siqueiros, were imprisoned under this law. One of the six demands made by student protesters in 1968 was the repeal of this law, but all crimes covered by it now are covered in an amended Penal Code. See E. Stevens, *Protest and Response in Mexico* (Cambridge, Mass.: M.I.T. Press, 1974).

15. Similarly, P. Schmitter, *Interest Conflict and Political Change in Brazil* (Stanford: Stanford University Press, 1971), argues that Latin American regimes have much greater historical continuity than is apparent from the official forms of government. In particular, he discusses the underlying continuities in the Brazilian *sistema*, despite shifts from civilian to military rule.

16. For example, the U.S. "Great Society" programs of the 1960s were established under the initiative of the federal government, undercutting both state and local governments. A Rand Corporation study of St. Louis, Seattle, and San Jose, California, concluded that in all three cities federal policies had a greater impact on the cities than anything local authorities did (*New York Times*, October 18, 1973, p. 12). For an analysis of the impact of the 1960s effort to restore political order, see F. Piven and R. Cloward, *Regulating the Poor: The Functions of Public Welfare* (New York: Vintage Books, 1971).

17. For data on the expansion and distribution of goods and services and rural-urban trends since the Cuban revolution, see J. Dominguez, "The Performance of the Cuban Revolution," paper delivered at the American Society for International Law, Washington, D.C., April 1973; D. Barkin and N. Manitzas (eds.), *Cuba: The Logic of the Revolution* (Andover, Mass.: Warner Modular Publications, 1973); and R. Bonachea and N. Valdés (eds.), *Cuba in Revolution* (Garden City, N.Y.: Anchor Books, 1972).

18. In areas of Mexico such as Chihuahua, Villa Hermosa, and Durango, where local leaders have refused to be coopted, there is more opposition to the government.

The State and the Peasants

ROSA ELENA MONTES DE OCA

Although agrarian problems had been a matter of concern among intellectuals since the last part of the nineteenth century, it was not until the Mexican Revolution that the peasant masses made a dramatic entrance on to the political scene. Although peasant armies overthrew the old regime, in framing an agrarian reform program they could never advance beyond organizing the territories they occupied according to their conception of the "idyllic" traditional peasant community. This was the basis of Zapata's "Comuna de Morelos" and Villa's military colonies in Chihuahua. Zapata's agrarian program came from the traditional communities which had been destroyed by the aggressive advance of agricultural capitalism, represented by the sugar-cane haciendas and mills. Villa came from the north, where there were almost no traditional peasant communities. His army mainly consisted of *vaqueros*, or cowboys, and other agricultural workers, miners, and railroad workers. Villa never made his political program explicit. But whatever the judgment on Villa may be, it is certain that the class interests he represented were close to those confusedly expressed by Zapata's Plan de Ayala, which the Villistas explicitly adopted in 1914.[1] Although the peasant armies attempted to establish links with urban workers, these attempts were never successful.

Opposing the revolutionaries were Obregón and the Constitucionalistas, who had a plan for national political domination. They aspired to create a new state, and they knew what they wanted this state to be.

The military defeat of the peasant armies came after their political defeat, a defeat in which Carranza's agrarian law of January 6, 1915, was an important weapon. This law was extended by Article 27 of the 1917 Constitution, which stated that the nation has the right to give away

47

property or land, whichever most suits the public interest; that towns and villages have the right to their communal land and can ask for it; that land taken away from the communities under the Porfirio Díaz regime should be returned; and that only Mexican-born citizens may own land. This article did partially reflect the main demands of the popular movement during the armed struggle of the Revolution, but it did much more than that. It was one of the instruments that gave the state the power to set the rules of the game and helped define it as the promoter and regulator of economic development. Most important, through Article 27 the state was able to negotiate with and subordinate the peasant masses and their struggles.

The agrarian reforms instituted by the first revolutionary regimes were timid and slow. Carranza made it clear that land taken by peasants should be returned and that the peasants should wait until it was given to them legally by the government. The idea that predominated was expressed by Luis Cabrera, that land should be given to peasants only as an addition to income they obtained working as *peons* at the haciendas, so that they would take care of the land and stop being rebels. Obregón's idea of agrarian reform was to create a class of "farmers" like those in the United States. But the idea of really transforming the agrarian structure of the country was very far from the minds of those in power during the first revolutionary regimes. In fact, they even feared such a transformation, for they believed that it would do away with the main source of foreign trade, which at that time was the exportation of agricultural raw materials. In a speech delivered in Guadalajara, Obregón stated: "We must be very careful about the way we carry out agrarian reform, for an undiscriminating policy may lead us to destroy well-integrated production units, with very serious consequences to agricultural output and the national economy."[2] And that did happen where land reform took place. The big *haciendas* were divided into small parcels in order to give land to the peasant communities. Although legally it was given to the community as a whole, every peasant got his small parcel of land to work individually. The affected landowner, who could keep a hundred hectares of irrigated land or its equivalent in lower-quality land, could choose whatever part of the land he wanted to keep. Naturally, he always chose the highest-quality land and the land with important buildings on it. The land given to the peasants was mostly of very poor quality, and the parcels were very small. The peasants who got it turned to growing maize and beans, which gave them the assurance of surviving and needed no investment except their own labor. Obviously, with such procedures, agricultural output in the distributed land diminished. Circular No. 51, promulgated in 1922, tried to correct this situation by making the already existing *ejidos* into collective units. But this intention failed because the National Agrarian Commission did not have the technical means to carry out the plan, and the land that was distributed had been given to the traditional peasants, who no longer wanted to have anything to do with collective work.[3] There was also a plan to create local banks in every state of the republic to finance production in *ejidos*, but with the exception of those founded in Veracruz and Michoacán (which lasted only a few years), it remained a mere intention.[4]

By 1929, Calles declared that the agrarian reform was concluded, and that if the members of any community planned an application for land, they should make it within a few months. At that time, only ten million hectares had been given to 4,189 *ejidos* with 535,000 members. This agrarian reform was made mainly for political reasons. It took place wherever it was necessary to pacify a rebel group of peasants or where local political groups had great influence. It was mainly a weapon to threaten and negotiate with traditional landowners, who had already been defeated politically at the national level. Until 1934, the agrarian reform "did not give much to those it was supposed to give to and did not take much from those it was supposed to take from."[5]

But the world crisis in 1929 reduced agricultural exports, especially cotton and henequen, and weakened the economic importance of *latifundios*. Furthermore, the Cristero movement seriously affected the structure of the haciendas in the middle-western part of the country, which mainly produced grains for the internal market.[6] With this, the economic power of the traditional landowners diminished greatly.

Also as a consequence of the crisis, the United States sent back more than 200,000 migrant workers between 1929 and 1932. The number of unemployed grew, especially in the countryside. This development, coming at the same time as the announcement that the agrarian reform was concluded, produced restlessness among large groups of peasants and agricultural workers. This was evidenced in a number of small movements and agricultural workers' strikes, but chiefly in the creation of the agrarian leagues of Veracruz, Michoacán, and Tamaulipas. The agitating and organizing of the Mexican Communist Party, even of members of the official National Revolutionary Party (PNR), and also of ambitious local politicians, all played an important role in the creation of these agrarian leagues, but the reason they could flourish was that the grievances were real.

In 1920, Antonio Díaz Soto y Gama, who had been one of Zapata's advisors, together with Rodrigo Gómez and Felipe Santibañez, founded the Partido Nacional Agrarista (Agrarian National Party). They maintained that every peasant should belong to this party. In those parts of the country where it had influence it managed to get some land distributed, but its main objective was apparently to support Obregón.

In Yucatán, Salvador Alvarado organized unions of agricultural workers, and Felipe Carrillo Puerto (who became governor of that state and was murdered while still in office) successfully organized the peasants through resistance leagues affiliated to the Partido Socialista del Sureste (Socialist Party of the Southeast). Obregón, through the National Agrarian Commission, organized Leagues of Agrarian Communities, and Portes Gil did the same in Tamaulipas. Ursulo Galván, in close contact with the Communist Party and with militants from the workers' unions, some of them anarchists, did major organizing work in Veracruz, with the support of Governor Adalberto Tejeda (who, for this reason, had serious problems with Obregón). Primo Tapia and Issac Arriaga also organized a League of Agrarian Communities in Michoacán.

In this organizational "boom" (see the appendix to this chapter, which gives the dates on which the most important peasant organizations were founded), two tendencies were evident. First, the peasants themselves, led mostly by the Communists, intended to build independent organizations; second, the state tried to organize them from above to control them. Its own tactical errors and the repression it suffered made the Mexican Communist Party's efforts unsuccessful, although its organizations remained important until the Confederación Nacional Campesina (National Peasant Confederation) was founded. Several members of the Communist Party were in the upper hierarchy of the CNC for this reason, and many of the local peasant leaders, who had strong popular support even after the Cárdenas regime, were members of the Communist Party. On the other hand, the state could not have built a strong corporative peasant organization without true agrarian reform.

With the arrival of Cárdenas to the presidential office, the whole idea of agrarian reform and of agricultural organization changed. To Cárdenas, the *ejido* was to be the basis on which agriculture was organized and it was to be given the institutional and infrastructure and support from the state that it needed. Cárdenas not only distributed more land to the peasants than ever before or after (20,137,000 hectares to 776,000 *ejidatarios*), but he also amended the law so that *peones acasillados* (workers who lived permanently in the haciendas) could solicit to obtain land. He introduced a new way of organizing the *ejidos* as collective production units, especially in the case of highly productive and mechanized crops and those that were particularly important in the international market. He created the Banco de Crédito Ejidal to finance *ejidos*, especially the collective *ejidos*, and modified the corresponding law so that *ejidos* had preferential access to water resources. With these measures, the rural sector was pacified, there was some redistribution of income, the capital resources of traditional landowners were transferred to other sectors of the economy, and the road was opened for modern capitalist agriculture.

To carry out this agrarian reform, Cárdenas also organized the peasants by creating the Confederación Nacional Campesina (National Rural Confederation) in 1938. Cárdenas ordered the National Revolutionary Party (PNR) to organize a League of Agrarian Communities in every state of the republic. At the inaugural congress of the CNC, there were 37 local leagues and unions of agricultural workers. The unions had formerly been affiliated to the Confederation of Mexican Workers but were transferred to the CNC. The CNC's first general secretary was Graciano Sánchez, a former elementary school teacher and former head of the National Rural League of the PNR.

When Cárdenas was about to be elected, many observers thought that the unification of the peasants was almost impossible because there were so many peasant organizations, including the CROM (Confederación Regional de Obreros Mexicanos), PNA (Partido Nacional Agrarista), Liga Nacional Campesina Ursulo Galván, Federación Mexicana Unitaria Sindicalista, CGT (Confederación General de Trabajadores), Liga Nacional Campesina of the PNR, Liga Central de Comunidades Agrarias, Confederación Nacional de Obreros y Campesinos Mexicanos, and many local leagues and unions without defined programs. The National Rural League and the Mexican Rural Confederation had previously attempted to unify the peasant organizations with programs similar to those of Portes Gil and Cárdenas. They both failed, the former because it tried to do so against the will of the state, and the latter because it did not have the support of the state. The CNC was successful because it worked with the total support of the state.[7] And that could occur because the state was making real agrarian reforms.

The basic concept of the CNC is that everyone who is a peasant or who works in agriculture should belong to it. Once an *ejido* is formed, its members must elect a Comisariado Ejidal, who will legally represent them before agrarian authorities, and a Comite de Vigilancia (Supervision Committee). Both the Comisariado Ejidal and the Comite de Vigilancia automatically belong to the CNC. Even agronomists are supposed to be part of the CNC. During Cárdenas' time, that was significant because it meant that agronomists were not just technicians but also political agents of the agrarian reform.[8]

Cárdenas strongly opposed any interference of the Mexican Workers Confederation (CTM) in the peasant organizations. He made it very clear that it should be the state that organized and united the peasants. Technical reasons were given for this position—that the agrarian reform process was complex, and so forth. But Cárdenas also suggested that if the CTM competed with the government in organizing peasant organizations, it would introduce "the internal conflicts that have been so harmful among the industrial proletariat."[9] The President of the Partido de la Revolución

Mexicana (Mexican Revolutionary Party), Luis L. Rodríguez, added that industrial workers and peasants could not be united because workers would still depend on the capitalist entrepreneurs, while once the peasants received land, they would be independent. For this reason, he said, "It is necessary to remember that the CNC should not only have slogans and demands, but also be aware of the obligations it has. The Leagues and their central organizations should become the real allies of the agrarian powers and of the state in general."[10] Peasants, from then on, should back the state, for better or for worse.

The political language and the myths of the regimes of the Mexican Revolution was created with the idea that the state is above social classes. According to that myth, peasants are neither capitalists nor workers. Ever since the Red Batallions of the Casa del Obrero Mundial were formed to fight the peasant armies in 1915, the state has been very careful that workers and peasants never be united. This was especially important during the Cárdenas regime in order to keep the process of social reforms under the control of the state and not allow the mass movement to outgrow them.

Two principles have fundamentally guided the policy of the state with respect to peasant organizations: (1) to make any union with industrial workers impossible, and (2) to consider them a support and a part of the state. And for the state this has been an extremely effective policy of political control. For agricultural workers it has meant the lowest standard of living in the country.

Many of the so-called "peasant struggles" have really been struggles of an agricultural proletariat for proletarian, not peasant, demands. In the Laguna, at Lombardia and Nueva Italia, and in Soconusco (at the first two places, collective *ejidos* were formed by Cárdenas), the workers organized for proletarian goals to counteract capitalist exploitation. They wanted higher salaries, recognition of their unions, better living quarters, and supervision of piece labor. The government's response was to give this struggle a peasant solution. It gave the peasants agrarian reform and paid no attention to their proletarian demands.[11]

This solution struck at traditional landowners and neutralized the explosive struggle of the agricultural proletariat. From then on, all social conflicts in the rural areas were channeled through petition to the President of the Republic. The "principle of authority" and the paternalistic attitude of the government inaugurated by Carranza were thus strengthened and given permanent status.

Without the Cárdenas policy of agrarian reform and peasant organization, the development of modern capitalist agriculture would have been almost impossible. The policies pursued by subsequent regimes could not have been successful in an unpacified rural sector.

After Cárdenas

Agrarian reform virtually came to an end after Cárdenas left office. In fact, the rate of land-distribution decreased in the last two years of his administration. Significant changes in land-reform policy took place during the administrations of Ávila Camacho and Alemán. Some authors have referred to this period as the agrarian counter-reform; others think of it as a logical continuation, the reform of the reform.

Ávila Camacho's slogan was "National Unity," with all that that entailed. His agrarian policy was part of this "unity." During World War II, foreign demand for agricultural products rose, and there was fear that the *ejidos* could not cope with it. The slogan for Camacho's agrarian policy was "Security in the Countryside" *(seguridad en el campo).* Not only did the rate of land distribution decline but, in 1942, a new Agrarian Code was issued that greatly modified the one issued by Cárdenas in 1940.

From then on, support for the *ejidos* ceased and everything was done to favor large private properties. The collective *ejidos* were weakened through corruption, pressure from financing institutions, the creation of parallel local *ejidatario* organizations, and even by the assassination of their leaders, as happened in Valle del Yaquí. To many, the word "collective" brought to mind the collective farms of the U.S.S.R. and they saw collective *ejidos* as a dangerous Communist experiment. But I think that the real reason for their destruction was the strength the local *ejidatario* associations had attained in local politics.

During Alemán's regime, Article 27 of the Constitution was changed. With the new amendments, private land holdings dedicated to cotton growing could have a maximum of 150 hectares and those dedicated to crops such as sugar, vanilla, coffee, and cocoa crops—which require large investments and are important in the international market—could have a maximum of 300 hectares, instead of the 100 hectares originally permitted. The maximum amount of land permitted for cattle raising was also increased so that a "small property" dedicated to cattle raising could be as large as 30,000 hectares, depending on the quality of the land. Preference was given to private land holdings over the *ejidos* in the use of water resources. And, most important of all, the writ of habeas corpus *(amparo)* could again be used in matters concerning agrarian laws.[12]

The CNC had been the vehicle used to implement the agrarian reform in Cárdenas' administration, and it was as effective with Alemán. Gerrit Huitzer tells us:

Peasants were not given the opportunity to discuss the changes in the agrarian laws that undoubtedly have been of great importance in the process of change in the structure of land tenure from that time on. The changes in the legislation were submitted to the official party and the national Congress. Some legislators and some officials of the CNC openly said many times that it was not convenient that the peasants know the details of the new legislation, even if these were harmful [to their interests], so as to avoid any agitation in the countryside, which would be harmful to the entire economy of Mexico.... The publication of the Frente Zapatista, which is part of the CNC and the PRI, said that it was not the correct political moment to discuss the proposed amendments, because the mere announcement that the Agrarian Code would be changed to favor the creation of new "latifundios" would provoke disturbances among peasants, and if it were not suppressed, it would upset the great and patriotic plans that the government of President Alemán was putting forward.[13]

The CNC successfully suppressed discussion, even though only in the short run. The only dissident peasant voice was that of the Unión 40–46, the union of the collective *ejidos* in La Laguna, headed by Arturo Orona.[13] However, even the Unión 40–46 was no longer the combative organization it had been because its members had become part of an elite of *ejidatarios*. Still, the Unión denounced the corruption of the agrarian and Banco Ejidal authorities, as did the leaders of other unions of collective *ejidos* that had been founded by Cárdenas.

A peasant leader named Rubén Jaramillo in Morelos also denounced the corruption at a sugar mill in Zacatepec that was supposedly owned by the *ejidos*. This corruption diminished the income of the *ejidatarios*. Jaramillo tried to get a solution through legal channels, but without success, and in 1948 he took up arms. After he was given amnesty, he agitated in the Movimiento de Liberación Nacional (National Liberation Movement), an organization integrating most of the progressive groups and parties and headed by Cárdenas. During this time, Jaramillo fought within the legal framework, along with peasant groups demanding land. But again no attention was paid to these demands. In 1961, joined by 5,000 peasants, he invaded lands rented to a rich cattle raiser in Michapa and Guarin, in the state of Morelos. He was killed by the army in 1962.[14] Rubén Jaramillo became a symbol for groups of landless peasants. His assassination damaged the image of the regime of López Mateos, who had declared himself and his regime to be "on the left, within the Constitution."

When Vincente Lombardo Toledano was expelled from the Mexican Workers Confederation (CTM) in 1948, he created the Alianza de Obreros y Campesinos de México (Alliance of Mexican Workers and Peasants). In June 1948, the Partido Popular Socialista (Popular Socialist Party) was officially founded. Lombardo was its general secretary and Vidal Días Muñoz, peasant leader and head of the Alianza, its undersecretary. When several workers' unions decided to leave the CTM that same year, they joined the Alianza. After a massive Congress in June 1949, the Alianza became the Unión General de Obreros y Campesinos de México (General Union of Mexican Workers and Peasants) with 300,000 affiliated members, seventy percent of whom were peasants.[15] The Secretary of Labor's refusal to register the UGOCM, thus denying it the capacity to act in legal matters for workers affiliated with it, caused many of the unions that had joined it to leave. Only the peasants remained. Once again, the state prevented any kind of union between workers and peasants, at least in an independent organization.

The strongest independent peasant unions were those in the UGOCM from La Laguna, Valle del Yaquí, Taretan, and Michoacán. In 1957 and 1958, the UGOCM organized the most spectacular actions of the peasant movement during that period. In 1957 they invaded the lands of the Cananea Cattle Company. In 1958, thousands of peasants from Sonora, Sinaloa, and Baja California invaded simultaneously the *latifundios* in their regions, especially those owned by foreigners. A truck driver's union from Sonora helped to transport them to the *latifundios* they invaded and took them to other *latifundios* after they had been expelled by the army.

Finally, Jacinto López (the most important leader of the UGOCM until his death in 1971), after rejecting a large bribe, invaded again along with the peasants residing in Cananea. López and others were jailed in Hermosillo, and the Cananea land was expropriated and distributed to peasants.

When Jacinto López came out of jail, he said he would continue fighting for land reform, and until 1962 there were some invasions and hunger marches. With a program that went no further than asking for the original agrarian reform of the Mexican Revolution, nothing beyond what was granted in the Constitution, the UGOCM became a very serious threat to peace and stability in the Mexican countryside. The government managed to weaken the UGOCM by using its usual means of control: land petitions, applications for credit, requests for water-use preference, and so forth, were resolved favorably only if they had the backing of the CNC. In 1963, a group with a more radical program was expelled, and they later joined a peasant guerrilla group in Chihuahua. After Jacinto López died in 1971, the organization had serious internal conflicts, and finally in 1973 it split into two factions. Although one faction, the "Jacinto López" UGOCM, was more radical, both factions have lost their original combativeness and independence and have joined the official Congreso Permanente Agrario (Permanent Agrarian Congress).[16]

In April 1961, 300 delegates met in Zamora, Michoacán, representing 35,000 organized peasants. Some came from leagues that had separated from the CNC or from the UGOCM because they wanted a more radical program. They decided to form a large independent peasant movement and, in January 1963, the Confederación Campesina Independiente (Independent Rural Confederation) was constituted. For a time, the pressure the CCI exerted solved certain immediate problems. Then division arose between those who wanted a radical program and complete independence from the PRI and those who were closer to the CNC and the PRI. Since 1964 there have been two CCIs, a radical CCI led by Ramón Danzos Palomino, and one headed by Alfonso Garzón that later joined the PRI and the Congreso Permanente Agrario.[17]

Ramón Danzos Palomino, who has headed several marches and organized several invasions of *latifundios*, is constantly in and out of jail. During his last period in jail, there were several peasant marches from one town to another, particularly in Puebla, asking for his freedom.

Land Concentration

The emergence of an organized independent peasant movement stemmed mostly from the fact that, since the agrarian reforms of Cárdenas, there has been a reconcentration of the land and a concentration of resources. This is, of course, a natural tendency in the model of development followed by Mexico, but it was reinforced by the legislative changes made since 1940.

In 1940, 47.4 percent of the land belonged to *ejidos*, but by 1950, this figure had declined to 44 percent. This does not tell us very much about the trend in land and resource distribution, because all along the number of small holdings *(minifundios)* has been growing, while their average size has been getting smaller. The classification made by the Centro de Investigaciones Agrarias (CIDA) is more useful.[18] According to CIDA, by 1960, 0.5 percent of landowners owned 30 percent of all land, 40 percent of irrigated land, and 44 percent of machinery, and were responsible for 80 percent of the growth in the agricultural output from 1950 to 1960. At the other pole, 81 percent of holdings encompass 24 percent of all land, 2.7 percent of irrigated land, and 8 percent of machinery.[19]

This means that the very satisfactory growth rate of Mexican agriculture from 1940 until recently has benefited very few farmers. The income of those economically active in agriculture is less than half that of those employed in other sectors. In 1960, 29 percent of the families of those employed in agriculture had an income of US$24.00 a month, 35 percent an income from US$25.00 to US$48.00, 17 percent an income from US$48.00 to US$80.00, and only 19 percent received more than US$80.00 a month.[20]

Agricultural development programs, including the "Green Revolution," have widened the gap. Progress has been concentrated in the Irrigated Land Districts, especially for export crops. To be able to take advantage of the new seeds produced by the "Green Revolution," for instance, the farmers must have machinery, fertilizers, technical assistance, and so forth, and that means investments that 80 percent of the peasants cannot make. They are thus in a constantly worsening position compared with the large agricultural enterprises. Their cost of production, including salary, is higher than the market price. The small farm is progressively less capable of producing an income that supports the peasant family.

We have reported only data based on official statistics. Yet it is well known that disguised land concentration makes the situation even worse. For instance, a large proportion of the so-called "small properties" are really large properties that have been legally divided among the father, the mother, and the children, or just among false names. These are the so-called *latifundios simulados* (disguised *latifundios*), but there is nothing in the legislation prohibiting such simulated divisions. These are no longer the traditional *latifundios* that existed at the beginning of the century, but modern agricultural enterprises.

Another form of disguised land concentration is produced when the *ejidatario* who cannot survive on the income he makes by working in his land rents it to a large enterprise and then is hired as a *peon* by it. This practice is especially widespread in the Irrigated Land Districts, where competition is fierce for individual *ejidatarios*. In Valle del Yaquí, in 1971, 80 percent of the *ejidatarios'* land was rented to private agriculturists or to entrepreneurs who did not own land but just rented it.[21]

Until very recently, the *ejidatarios* never received credit from private banks. Government agricultural banks financed only about 13 percent of all *ejidatarios* and *minifundistas*, primarily those who produced crops for exportation. It should be mentioned here that official credit institutions have been another means of exerting political control. The granting of credit is done in a paternalistic manner often based on political rather than technical criteria.[22]

Most *ejidatarios* and *minifundistas* must therefore rely for financing on the local usurer, who is usually also a local *cacique*, and probably an intermediary. The commercial intermediation is such that, on the average, the peasant gets 10 percent of what his product costs in the city market, while products he buys from cities grow ever more expensive.[23]

To all this must be added that there are several hundred communities that have been waiting for 10, 20, or 30 years to obtain land which legally should be granted to them. Bureaucracy and corruption make the legal procedures eternal. When the land is finally granted to them by presidential resolution, the landowner receives a writ of *amparo*, after which the peasants must wait for Supreme Court decisions, and so forth. Through a sampling carried out by CIDA, it was discovered that, from 1915 to 1967, it took an average of 14 years from the time the community applied for the land until it received it.[24]

Under such circumstances, the CNC could act with much more energy in the defense of its members, or try to restrain their demands. But, as Gómez Jara tells us in his book published by the CNC, the role of this organization is (1) to organize the peasants under the control of the government, and (2) to be the social and political instrument for agrarian reform.[25] And, at this stage, "agrarian reform" should be understood to be directed toward higher productivity, not land distribution, as the declarations of public officials have suggested for several years now. Therefore, that is what the CNC has fought for. It has been acting mostly as an agent to obtain credit or to attend to small legal details for its members, the great majority of whom are already *ejidatarios* rather than those trying to obtain land.

The Present

During the last four or five years, almost everywhere in the country, thousands of peasants have invaded large private properties. It is not easy to say precisely how many invasions there have been. Only a very few of these movements have taken place within an organized framework. Most of those which have been organized were headed by the independent CCI, according to the local newspapers. In June 1973, the Secretary of Defense, General Cuenca Díaz, declared that the army had expelled 30 groups of invaders in one year in 7 states of the republic. From January 1972 to July 1973, there were 70 invasions about which something was published in the newspapers.[26] But in November 1973, in a series of articles published in *Excelsior*, Sánchez Navarro, spokesman for an important group of private entrepreneurs, said that during the last three years in the states of Tlaxcala, Guanajuato, and Michoacán, there had been 600 invasions.[27]

Most of these actions were carried out by groups of peasants who had gone through all the legal procedures to obtain the land and, though legally entitled to it, had never received it. Those groups of invading peasants that have made any declaration about their motivations for the invasions have made it clear that they are invading because they want to be included in the agrarian reform.[28] To them, invading is the logical continuation of ineffective legal procedures. The bureaucracy and promises of being given the title of *ejidatario con derechos a salvo* (which means they are included in the agrarian census of their community but do not receive any land and should wait for another occasion) no longer work as restraining mechanisms. These groups of peasants have virtually no organization, only the minimum required to invade.[29] When the army comes, they are completely helpless. Whether or not the properties invaded are of the size permitted by the law or are covered by a *certificado de inafectabilidad* (a certificate given by the agrarian authorities assuring the landowner that his property will not be subject to expropriation) matters neither to the invading peasants nor to the army.

Sometimes, during 1970 and 1971, the CNC and the Department of Agriculture viewed certain invasions with sympathy or even encouraged them. This was true particularly in parts of Tlaxcala and Guanajuato, where the invaders took over traditional *latifundios* that were obstacles to development or whose owners had local power against the government. But as the invasions spread throughout the country and became more threatening, the CNC completely disavowed them. When the Secretary of Defense announced that the army would allow no more invasions, the CNC declared itself in agreement because "*ejidatarios* and small private property owners should be able to work in peace." Nevertheless, the army cannot be a permanent and principal means of restraint by the state.

The agricultural crisis has been very serious. The highly satisfactory rate of growth of Mexican agriculture started to abate in the last half of the 1960s, and in 1972 it became negative. At the end of that year, products such as wheat that had previously been exported had to be imported to meet domestic demand. This agricultural crisis was in part the result of low public investment in this sector and in part the result of a crisis in confidence created by the invasions of private agricultural holdings. These problems were aggravated by droughts and floods. The crisis of production has been most serious for the domestic market. Production for the domestic market grew at the rate of 1.1 percent in 1971 and −5.1 percent in 1972, while production for export grew at the rate of 5.2 percent in 1971 and 5.0 percent in 1972. Negative growth in 1970 was due to a fall in foreign demand.

A new agrarian policy had to be designed. While the overall development model was being criticized officially, the CNC openly discussed reconcentration of land and resources. The members of the Cabinet who were concerned with agriculture considered the need to reorganize *ejidos* and to increase investment and credit for agriculture. Except in a very, very few cases, land distribution seems to be out of the question.

The government has created several new agencies and revitalized others that already existed to aid in marketing and technical assistance for certain specific products, such as coffee and tobacco.

The most significant changes started to occur in 1973. A very ambitious plan was put forward to collectivize by 1976 11,000 *ejidos*, or 50 percent of the total number, under state control. This plan, although it has advanced rapidly, is not going as well as was expected. According to Echeverría's fifth presidential address, 3,400 *ejidos* were already working collectively and 1,000 more were being organized in 1975. Therefore, it is improbable that the 11,000 goal will be reached by the end of 1976. In addition, an ambitious program of peasant training in new techniques, administration, and, of course, the official goals of the agrarian reform was planned.

The collective *ejido*, once seen as a dangerous socialist experiment, is now seen as a necessity for the capitalist development of Mexican agriculture. Now collective *ejidos* are openly referred to as "enterprises." The public agency or the financing institution makes all the decisions, not the *ejidatarios;* though the land is legally theirs, they are only employees. Collectivization will permit a substantial rise in productivity and probably a better income for the *ejidatarios,* as well as more employment in agriculture. This is the only way in which large investments can be made in *ejido* agriculture, especially by private banks and agribusiness enterprises. To expedite such investment, the financial system for the sector was reorganized. Three official banks were fused into one Banco Nacional de Crédito Rural, which it is hoped will bring about better coordination, lower administrative expenses, and new technical criteria. Most of the private investment in the *ejidos* will be through public agencies. The former Departamento de Asuntos Agrarios y Colonización has been renamed the Secretaria de la Reforma Agraria and effectively modernized. By all these measures, the Mexican state is becoming a powerful agricultural entrepreneur which will control a considerable amount of agricultural output.

To make this new agrarian policy function politically and to try to regain control of the peasants, the Congreso Permanente Agrario (CONPA) was formed in October 1973. It declared that one of its objectives was to "back firmly the internal and external policies of the President of the Republic."[30] CONPA was to be the peasant part of the "Alianza Popular Básica" which Echeverría had designed to cope with the conflict created by certain groups of conservative entrepreneurs in connection with salaries and fiscal policies.

But that was only the initial function of the CONPA. In its principal declaration, after admitting that the agrarian reform had failed to bring well being to the peasant masses and comparing Echeverría to Cárdenas, it disapproved anything that was done "outside the law," by which it meant invasions of private property. Its program is precisely the new agrarian policy, the collectivization of *ejidos.* What is most important is that in this Congreso Permanente Agrario are included the CNC, the CCI (headed by Garzón), the CAM (Congreso Agrario Mexicano), and the "Jacinto López" UGOCM. The latter organization that, as noted, was once independent, has now committed itself to follow the dictates of the state. The next step was the "Pacto de Ocampo," in which all these organizations decided to create one big peasant union around the CNC.

The state cannot distribute more land without affecting private agricultural enterprises, which it surely will not do, as has been very clearly stated. Therefore, whether or not this Central Única Campesina is successful in controlling the conflicts in rural areas depends on several things. The principal factor is its ability to create a mediating group within the *ejidatarios* in collective units and to control the agricultural proletariat, perhaps by creating and controlling labor unions. That depends on how willing or how able the agricultural bourgeoisie is to support such an apparatus and to give small concessions that will allow it to work.

Appendix: Dates on Which the Most Important Peasant Organizations Were Founded[31]

1920   Foundation of the Partido Nacional Agrarista (PNA).

1922   Foundation of the Liga de Comunidades Agrarias y Sindicatos Agrarios de Michoacán.

1923   First "Congreso Nacional Agrarista."

Foundation of the Confederación Nacional Agraria by a group that separated from the PNA.

Foundation of the Liga de Comunidades Agrarias de Veracruz.

1926   Foundation of the Liga Nacional Campesina.

1929   The Liga Nacional Campesina is divided into (1) Liga Nacional Campesina "Ursulo Galván," (2) Liga Nacional Campesina (affiliated with the PNR, led by Graciano Sánchez), and (3) Confederación Sindical Unitaria.

1931   Foundation of the Confederación Campesina Mexicana which later that same year joins the PNR.

1937   Foundation of the Unión Nacional Sinarquista.

1938   Foundation of the Confederación Nacional Campesina (CNC).

1949   Foundation of the Unión General de Obreros y Campesinos de México (UGOCM).

1951   Foundation of the Unión de Federaciones Campesinas.

1961   Peasant Congress in Zamora, Michoacán, out of which the Confederación Campesina Independiente (CCI) is founded.

1964   The Confederación Campesina Independiente is divided into (1) Central Independiente (led by Alfonso Garzón Santibáñez) which joins the PRI, and (2) Central Campesina Independiente (led by Ramón Danzos Palomino, a Communist leader).

1972   The UGOCM is divided into (1) UGOCM, and (2) UGOCM "Jacinto López."

1973   The Congreso Permanente Agrario is constituted by the CNC, the CAM, the CCI (the one directed by Garzón), the UGOCM, and the UGOCM "Jacinto López."

1974   The "Pacto de Ocampo" is signed by the above-mentioned organizations.

Notes

1. The Plan de Ayala was an agrarian program that maintained that the land the peasant communities had lost under the laws passed by the liberals and Porfirio Díaz should be given back to them.
2. Manuel Aguilera Gómez, *La reforma agraria en el desarrollo económico de México* (Mexico, D.F.: Instituto Mexicano de Investigaciones Económicas, 1969), p. 135.
3. *Ibid.*, p. 271.
4. *Ibid.*, p. 275.
5. Manuel Fabila Montes de Oca, *Cinco siglos de legislación agraria en México: exposición de motivos del Código Agrario, 1940* (Mexico, D.F.: Banco Nacional de Crédito Ejidal, 1941).
6. Jean Meyer, *La Cristiada* (Mexico, D.F.: Sobretiro de la Revista Historia Mexicana, El Colegio de México), p. 8.
7. Moises González Navarro, *La Confederación Nacional Campesina* (Mexico, D.F.: Costa-Amic Editores, 1967), pp. 82–85.
8. Arnaldo Cordova, *La política de masas del cardenismo* (mimeographed), p. 64. Also published by Editorial Era, Mexico, D.F., 1974.
9. González Navarro, *La Confederación*, pp. 145–55.
10. Anatol Shulgovsky, *México en la encrucijada de su historia* (Mexico, D.F.: Fondo de Cultura Popular, 1971), p. 265.
11. Gerardo Unzueta, "Relaciones de producción en el campo en México," *Nueva epoca*, no. 9 (1963): 27.
12. Aguilera Gómez, *La reforma*, p. 142.
13. Gerrit Huitzer, *La lucha campesina en México* (Mexico, D.F.: C.I.D.A., 1970), p. 85. My translation.
14. *Ibid.*, p. 86.
15. *Ibid.*, p. 89, and Francisco Gómez Jara, *El movimiento campesino en México* (Mexico, D.F.: Editorial Campesina, 1970), pp. 203–05.
16. Huitzer, *La lucha*, p. 91.
17. *Punto crítico*, no. 18, June–July 1973.
18. Gómez Jara, *El movimiento*, p. 219.
19. Reyes Osorio Stavenhagen et al., *Estructura agraria y desarrollo agrícola* (Mexico, D.F.: F.C.E., 1974), pp. 229 and 424.
20. *Ibid.*, p. 191.

21. Rosa Elena Montes de Oca, "Los ejidos colectivos del Valle del Yaquí, Sonora" (Tesis, Escuela Nacional de Economía, UNAM, 1971), p. 63.

22. Huitzer, *La lucha*, p. 80.

23. Unpublished investigation on the commercialization of agricultural products, Oficina de Investigaciones Económicas Especiales, Secretaría de la Presidencia, 1973.

24. Stavenhagen et al., *Estructura agraria*, p. 685.

25. Gómez Jara, *El movimiento*, p. 190.

26. *Punto crítico*, no. 18, June–July 1973.

27. *Ibid.*

28. *Ibid.*

29. *Ibid.*

30. *Punto crítico*, nos. 20/21, January 1974, and *Punto crítico*, no. 37, September 1975.

31. The source of this chronology is Daniel Molina, *Algunas consideraciones sobre los campesinos y la política* (Mexico, D.F.: Tase, 1973).

2

The State and the Economy

The Policy of
Import-Substituting
Industrialization, 1929–1975

RENÉ VILLARREAL

To understand the economic situation of contemporary Mexico, and to evaluate some policy alternatives for the 1970s, it is necessary to analyze and to evaluate the years 1940–70, a period of economic growth without development. We define economic growth as being a sustained increase in the per capita national product, while economic development incorporates growth and other policy goals: most notably, employment, income redistribution, and external independence.

The experiences of "underdeveloped" capitalistic countries in their evolution toward industrialization and "modern" economic growth have been marked by stages of transition more or less well-defined. Each stage has had a distinct mode of organization and operation of the economic system and can be described in terms of an economic "model" of transition toward modern growth.

The model of an enclave economy, or of a primary exporter economy ("outward-looking growth"), is the initial stage. The growth models that are presented as subsequent alternatives are those of industrialization via export promotion, via import substitution, and via export substitution.

Three types of economic policy have accompanied the process of change in the Mexican economy:

1. The Nationalist Project, which lasted from 1929 to 1939, and marked the breakdown of the enclave economy.
2. The phase of economic growth without development (1940–70), which was characterized by a long-run policy of industrialization via import substitution (replacing imports with locally manufac-

tured goods) and two short-run policies: that of growth with de-valuation and inflation (1940–58) and that of stabilized growth (1959–70).

3. The continuation of the import substitution model and the transition to stabilized growth (1970–75).

This essay will suggest that the next strategy might be a new phase based on industrialization via *export* substitution. This requires an economic policy of transition along the following lines: devaluation, stabilization of expenditure, and trade liberalization.

The Nationalist Project (1929–39) and the Breakdown of the Enclave Economy

The primary exporter or enclave-economy model has its roots in the colonial period, and attained its fullest expression in Mexican history during Porfirio Díaz's period of government. During this period the organization of the economic system was characterized by a model of outward-looking growth, in which the State played a passive role and the economy worked under the free interaction of the market forces, which were linked directly to the international market. In addition, the economy was characterized by the existence of a leading sector (the primary exporter sector) under the control of foreign concerns. Industrialization began under the enclave-export model, and became oriented toward the domestic market, but production tended to emphasize nondurable consumer goods and traditional inputs that were a necessary ingredient for the expansion of the primary exporter sector. That is, early industrialization was a function of the enclave economy and outward-looking growth.

By 1911 the main economic activities of the country were controlled by foreigners. The participation of foreign capital in mining was 97.5 percent, in petroleum 100 percent, in electricity 87.2 percent, in railroads 61.8 percent, in banking 76.7 percent, and in industry 85 percent.

The export promotion model under the enclave economy cannot be considered a viable strategy for sustained growth in the long run. Stagnation was, and still is, an inherent feature of this model, since the industrial sector that theoretically and historically should lead the economy toward sustained growth has little development potential. This is true for several reasons:

1. The orientation of the economy toward foreign markets implies that the industrial sector has to confront international competition, and the "infant" industries are not able to grow under such circumstances.

2. The processes of saving and accumulation of capital depend basically on the existence of rents, interests, and profits, which in these circumstances are under the control of foreigners and are consequently remitted abroad.

3. The terms of trade for primary products not only are unstable, but actually deteriorate in the long run.

It is therefore necessary to eradicate the enclave economy before industrialization and growth can be pursued in an effective manner.[1]

In Mexico the complete rupture with the enclave-economy model did not occur until the 1930s. This is in marked contrast to other Latin American countries such as Argentina and Brazil. However, the *beginning* of the breakdown can be traced back to 1929 and had its origins in two factors, one of an internal and political nature and the other based on external and economic events. The Partido Nacional Revolucionario (PNR) was created in that year; this put an end to the *caudillismo* period and gave birth to a "New State." On the external side, the Great Depression (1929–33) shrank the country's foreign trade to little more than half its previous volume.

Despite the balance of payments difficulties, Mexico did not at first make much progress in import substitution. The economy still exhibited the contradictions of the enclave model; that is to say, the level of economic activity depended on the swings in the world capitalistic markets and was a reflection of the international cycles of prosperity and depression.

The consolidation of a Nationalist Project and the final breakdown of the enclave model occurred during Cárdenas' government (1934–40). The structural reforms that were carried out by Cárdenas were oriented toward stimulating, in a decisive and effective way, the overall economic development (not just growth) and political maturity of Mexico, free from foreign influences. In the political sphere, the party under its new name (Partido de la Revolución Mexicana) incorporated the peasants as well as the labor and military sections of the population. In the economic sphere, the structural changes implied not only the execution of an agrarian reform and the nationalization of the oil industry and the railroads, but also, for the first time in the country's history, the State's active participation as an economic agent for promoting change and economic development. Federal expenditures began to be oriented more toward the attainment of goals of an economic and social character—the share of total expenditure in these areas rising from 23 percent and 13 percent respectively in 1929, to 42 percent and 18 percent by 1937. The creation of a Development Bank (Nacional Financiera), several agricultural credit banks, and the Central Bank (in 1925) formed the basis of an important financial system, while the establishment of the Comisión Federal de Electricidad jointly with the national petroleum industry allowed the energy sector to gear its productive capacity to the requirements of domestic growth.

However, it is necessary to point out that the Nationalist Project of Cárdenas meant the breakdown of the enclave model more than the emergence of an industrialization model via import substitution. Economic policy was directed toward the elimination of foreign control and the encouragement of agricultural development. Therefore the net effect was the consolidation of the New State as political entity and an economic agent. These were necessary if not sufficient conditions for accelerating the process of industrialization and growth over the next three decades.

Growth Without Development (1940–70): Industrialization via Import Substitution

THE ORGANIZATION OF THE ECONOMY
AND THE STAGES OF IMPORT SUBSTITUTION

An important explanatory variable in the relative success of Mexico's economic strategy as compared to that of other Latin American countries is that Mexico did not prematurely begin the process of industrialization via import substitution. The index of import substitution (ISI—the ratio of imports to aggregate supply on the basis of value added and in real terms) for the manufacturing sector decreased from a level of 0.52 in 1929 to a level of 0.45 in 1939.[2] This means that the share of imports in the total aggregate supply decreased a mere 10 percent during the decade of the Great Depression.

Several factors account for this phenomenon: (1) The State underwent political consolidation in 1929; consequently the government was not prepared to undertake the function of promoting an industrialization project during this early period; (2) the protectionist policy, even though it was modified in 1929, was based on specific tariffs; thus, as the international prices rose (in the period immediately following the Depression) the ad valorem tariffs decreased and so the effective protection of infant industries was reduced; (3) in the economic priorities of Cárdenas (1934–40), industrialization played a secondary role. It is interesting that this circumstance partially and paradoxically explains the "success" of the industrialization process during the 1940s, since agrarian reform and the orientation of economic policy toward the agricultural sector allowed agriculture to fulfill its role of supporting the growth process. That is to say, it was able to supply labor and raw materials to the industrial sector, food to the rural and urban populations, and foreign exchange (through exports) which allowed Mexico to finance the importation of intermediate and capital goods for industrial development.

During the 1940s Mexico effectively initiated the process of industrialization. World War II was the significant external factor that carried the economy to the threshold of such a process. In 1946 Alemán's government initiated an economic policy oriented toward accelerating industrialization and growth via import substitution. It was thought that the strategy of import substitution would automatically generate not only growth, but also economic development; that is to say, that it would increase employment and improve the standard of living of the masses (through income redistribution). All this would be accomplished with domestic autonomy, since inward-looking growth would permit the emergence of a national industry.

The first stage of import substitution, substitution of consumer goods, was practically completed during the 1940s. By 1950 the participation of consumer goods in total imports was only 17.6 percent, decreasing still more, to 12.7 percent in 1969. The index of import substitution for nondurable consumer goods was reduced by 68 percent, from 0.22 in 1939 to 0.07 in 1950, and remained at approximately that level until 1969. In short, for the manufacturing sector as a whole the participation of imports in the total supply decreased by 28 percent (the ISI declining from 0.45 to 0.31 during the period 1940–50; see Figure 1 and Table 1).

The reduction in the foreign supply of manufactured products during World War II automatically guaranteed the necessary protection for stimulating the growth of infant industries, which, having been oriented toward the domestic market at an early stage of development, could be expanded to meet the contemporary demand for manufactured consumer goods. It subsequently became necessary to give a new direction to the commercial and industrial policies in order to protect domestic industry from foreign competition. The strategy thus became one of self-conscious import substitution. The instruments of commercial policy—exchange rate, tariffs, and quantitative controls—were handled in different ways, with the general goal of providing domestic industry with a protectionist structure. The devaluations of 1948–49 (from 4.05 to 8.65 pesos per dollar) and 1954 (from 8.65 to 12.50 pesos per dollar) represented an increase of 200 percent in the nominal price of the dollar with respect to that prevalent in 1945.

During the period from 1954 to 1970 the exchange rate remained constant. The tariff and, more importantly, quantitative controls were the instruments used by the government. For the protection of new industries, the general tariffs for imports underwent some important changes in 1958 and changes of lesser magnitude during 1961–62 and 1965. In 1956, 25 percent of the total imports were controlled, but by 1970 almost 80

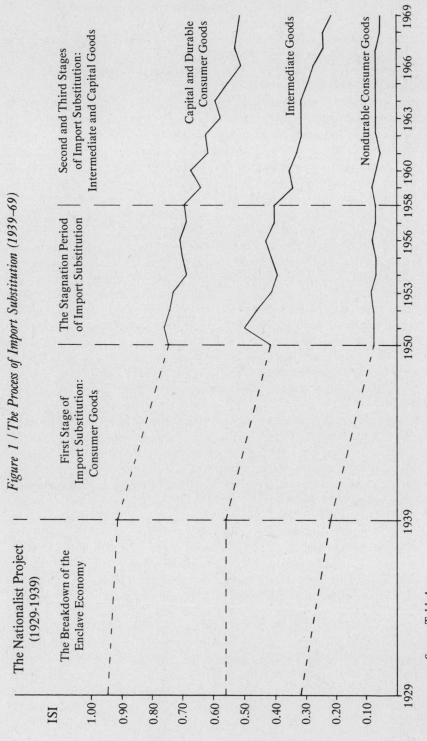

Figure 1 / *The Process of Import Substitution (1939–69)*

The Nationalist Project (1929-1939)

The Breakdown of the Enclave Economy

First Stage of Import Substitution: Consumer Goods

The Stagnation Period of Import Substitution

Second and Third Stages of Import Substitution: Intermediate and Capital Goods

Capital and Durable Consumer Goods

Intermediate Goods

Nondurable Consumer Goods

ISI

1.00
0.90
0.80
0.70
0.60
0.50
0.40
0.30
0.20
0.10

1929   1939   1950   1953   1956   1958 1960   1963   1966   1969

Source: Table 1

Table 1 / Import Substitution Index (ISI)

Year	Nondurable Consumer Goods	Intermediate Goods	Capital and Durable Consumer Goods
1929	.32	.56	.944
1939	.22	.56	.915
1950	.07	.42	.74
1951	.07	.50	.76
1952	.07	.46	.74
1953	.08	.42	.73
1954	.06	.39	.68
1955	.06	.41	.70
1956	.07	.43	.71
1957	.06	.40	.68
1958	.06	.40	.69
1959	.07	.34	.64
1960	.06	.35	.67
1961	.05	.33	.62
1962	.06	.31	.63
1963	.06	.31	.57
1964	.06	.31	.59
1965	.06	.29	.55
1966	.06	.27	.51
1967	.06	.24	.53
1968	.05	.24	.52
1969	.05	.22	.51

Source: René Villarreal, "External Disequilibrium, Growth Without Development: The Import Substitution Model. The Mexican Experience (1929–1975)," Ph.D. dissertation, 1975, Tables 12 and 19.

percent of all imports required a license before they could enter the country.

In summary, by 1960 a protectionist structure had been shaped in which the manufacturing sector received nominal protection (for the final product) of 35 percent and effective protection (for the factors of production) of 74 percent; these figures compared favorably with the level of protection of between 3.9 percent and 6.7 percent received by the agricultural sector. This guaranteed to domestic industry the elimination of external competition and provided the opportunity for profitable investment in other sectors of the economy, particularly the exporting sector.

Through the Law for New and Necessary Industries (Ley de Fomento de Industrias Nuevas y Necessarias) industrial policy also allowed partial or total exemption from several taxes (income tax up to 40 percent, stamp tax, and import tax). Rule XIV of the General Tariff granted a 65 percent subsidy toward the duties on machinery and equipment. These measures, together with a regressive fiscal policy, permitted a greater concentration of income and accumulation of capital.

In these ways the country developed a protectionist structure which can be described as excessive, permanent, and discriminatory. These characteristics, together with the smallness of the domestic market, promoted the consolidation of a monopolistic structure in which large national and international corporations acquired control of production and distribution in the industrial sector.

The new protectionist structure of economic policy; the role of the state as an economic agent; the strategy of industrialization and growth; the appearance of large corporations (national and multinational) in an oligopolistic market—all these factors allowed the Mexican economy to move forward into second and third stages of the import substitution process during the period 1950–70. In these years the substitution of imports took place in intermediate goods (second stage) and to a lesser extent in capital goods (third stage). This was despite the fact that the process of import substitution stagnated during the period from 1950 to 1958; that is, the import substitution index for the manufacturing sector as a whole stood at the same level in 1958 as it had in 1950 (0.31), which means that the share of imports in the total supply remained constant during these years. On the other hand, the figures for manufactured goods show that between 1958 and 1969 the participation of imports in total supply decreased by 25 percent, the import substitution index going from a value of 0.40 in 1958 to a value of 0.22 in 1969. At this stage the substitution of intermediate goods came to be the most significant feature of the process. The participation of imports in the total supply for this kind of goods decreased by 45 percent. In 1958 the ISI for capital and durable consumer goods had a value of 0.69 and by 1969 a value of 0.51, which means a reduction of 28 percent in the participation of imports in the total supply of durable consumer and capital goods. By 1969, for the sector of intermediate goods, imports represented only one-fifth of the total supply, while imports had been reduced to 50 percent of total supply in the case of consumer durable goods and capital goods. This indicates that the process of import substitution as an incentive for industrialization and growth had approached its upper limit—for a policy of substitution of capital goods is likely to imply increasing social costs.

PROLONGED IMPORT SUBSTITUTION: GROWTH WITHOUT DEVELOPMENT

Import substitution has undoubtedly been an effective (though not necessarily efficient) process for promoting industrialization and economic growth in Mexico. During the period 1940–70 the economy grew at a sustained rate, the rate of growth of GNP averaging 6.5 percent per annum and 3 percent per annum in per-capita terms. Manufacturing production grew at an average of 8 percent a year, while agricultural production grew at a similar rate during the 1940s, and at a rate of 4.1 percent per annum between 1950 and 1970.

However, the industrialization process has been inefficient. That is to say, the same goal of growth could have been attained with less sacrifice in terms of the resources of the country. The protectionist structure, as we said earlier, became permanent, excessive, and discriminatory. The tariff, working jointly with quantitative control, creates a captive market for industry; the individual firm can produce inefficiently, without worrying about utilizing all of its capacity and the most adequate techniques. This produces high costs and prices, which not only put a brake to the exports of manufactures but also hinder those exports of primary goods that constitute industrial inputs. Moreover, the terms of trade between agriculture and industry are biased in favor of the industrial sector, implying an inefficient allocation of the economy's resources among the different sectors. This phenomenon is also evident *within* the industrial sector, because of the discriminatory character of protection. It is also true that when the supposedly infant industry grows older, the perpetuation of protection allows the firm to obtain a "pure" rent (monopolistic or oligopolistic). The most extreme case is that of multinational corporations like Ford and General Electric, which came to Mexico with already standardized products (in terms of characteristics as well as production process) and are still considered "infant" industries that must be protected.

Just as the effectiveness of using import substitution to generate growth is evident, it is also obvious that this policy has implied a cost in terms of other objectives of economic development—employment, income redistribution, and external independence. Indeed, limits have been imposed on the process of growth itself during the 1970s, because of the continuous and permanent external disequilibrium (particularly the deficit in the balance of payments in current account) that has characterized the import substitution process.

EMPLOYMENT AND IMPORT SUBSTITUTION

Economic growth, as I said above, does not seem to have been a sufficient condition for solving the unemployment problem in Mexico. Estimates based on the 1970 census indicate that 5.8 million people were underemployed, which is equivalent to an unemployment level of 3 million, that is to say, 23 percent of the economically active population (EAP). This estimate plus that of open unemployment, which accounts for 485,000 people, amounts to an equivalent unemployment of 3.5 million or 26.8

percent of the EAP. The perspectives for the 1970s do not seem to be any more encouraging.

Fast demographic growth and the age structure of the population imply that the total EAP will be 20 million in 1980 and 28.1 million in 1990. Even if the levels of underemployment and unemployment remain constant, it will be necessary to create 6.8 million new jobs during the period 1970–80, and 8.4 million during the following decade. The most optimistic projections point out that the manufacturing sector, by growing at a rate of 8.9 percent during the period 1970–76, will have been able to absorb only 850,000 people, providing just 12.5 percent of the total of new jobs that will be necessary during the 1970s.[3]

The fast growth of population undoubtedly aggravates the unemployment problem. However, if the industrialization process were accompanied by an increasing use of labor-intensive technologies, the unemployment problem would decrease considerably. There is evidence to suggest that the import-substitution process has been characterized instead by an increased use of *capital*-intensive technologies. This is demonstrated by the fact that the manufacturing industry in Mexico involves production functions with a high elasticity of substitution.[4] That is to say, as the relative price of capital in terms of labor decreases, individual firms find it more profitable to use capital-intensive technologies. This helps to explain the inability of the manufacturing sector to provide a growing number of employment opportunities, even though its level of output is increasing.

The policy of import substitution has been consistently characterized by a cheapening of the price of capital with respect to that of labor. The overvaluation of the exchange rate until September 1976 implied a subsidy to the importation of capital goods as compared to the use of national capital and labor. The import tariffs that should have compensated for the exchange rate overvaluation have not played that role, since Rule XIV and the Law for New and Necessary Industries have allowed the industries importing capital goods to avoid paying import taxes. Moreover, Mexican businessmen are generally biased toward what is considered more "modern" equipment; this implies preferring capital to the use of labor. Machinery is considered to provoke fewer conflicts than labor unions and labor legislation. If to the foregoing we add the fact that the import substitution policy reduces the price of capital relative to labor in terms of its real opportunity cost for the economy, it can be seen that industry is encouraged to undertake a large capital investment for the use of each unit of labor.

Empirical evidence supports this conclusion. Ann D. Witte's estimates[5] show that relative capital cost (costs of capital/costs of labor) for the manufacturing sector in Mexico was reduced at an average annual rate of 5 percent in the period of 1945 to 1965. As compared to the 1945 level, relative capital cost had been reduced to 69 percent by 1950, to less than 50 percent by 1960, and to nearly one-third of the original level by 1964 (see Table 2). The effects of the lower relative price of capital made themselves felt through lower employment in the manufacturing sector. In 1945 this sector needed 9.6 man-years to produce 100,000 real pesos of value added per year; by 1965 only 2.8 man-years were required—that is, the coefficient decreased at an annual average rate of 6 percent in this period (see Table 3).

INCOME DISTRIBUTION AND IMPORT SUBSTITUTION

The economic growth of Mexico has been accompanied by a continuous trend toward a concentration of income. In 1950 about 50 percent of the families received only 19.1 percent of the national income, while at the upper range of the spectrum 10 percent of the families received 40 percent of the national income. By 1965 income was even more concentrated: in the upper range, 20 percent of the families received two-thirds of the national income, while, at the lower levels, 40 percent of the families received only one-tenth of the national income.

Income distribution is one of the problems that have been neglected both theoretically and in empirical research. In general terms, it can be argued that the use of capital-intensive technologies and the oligopolistic structure of the domestic market, which are features of the import-substitution model, help to explain the growing concentration of income in Mexico. In a recent cross-section and cross-country study that included Mexico, the distribution of income in a group of countries that have followed the model of import substitution was compared with that of another group composed of countries that have followed the model of export substitution. In the second group the distribution of income was less unequal than in the first group. In countries that followed the model of export substitution, 20 percent of the families in the highest level and 40 percent in the lowest level received 40 percent and 20 percent respectively of the national income, while comparable figures for countries that followed the import-substitution model were 60 percent and 10 percent (Table 4). It seems that the concentration of income is, ceteris paribus, a characteristic inherent in the process of import substitution.

EXTERNAL DEPENDENCE AND IMPORT SUBSTITUTION

During the 1940s, and even during the 1950s, it was thought that the breakdown of the enclave economy (outward-looking growth) and the emergence of an import-substitution model (inward-looking growth)

Table 2 / Index of Relative Capital Cost (Costs of Capital/Costs of Labor), Setting the 1945 Figure at 100

Year	All Manufacturing	Food and Beverages	Tobacco	Textiles	Paper and Paper Products	Rubber and Chemical Products	Non-metallic Mineral Products	Basic Metals
1945	100	100	100	100	100	100	100	100
1946	96	93	95	98	96	93	98	98
1947	94	88	91	98	94	88	98	99
1948	88	78	83	93	87	80	93	94
1949	79	68	74	86	80	70	86	89
1950	69	58	62	76	69	59	76	78
1951	72	63	68	79	77	66	79	73
1952	71	63	69	80	78	68	77	62
1953	68	63	69	78	77	69	73	53
1954	66	63	70	77	78	71	71	45
1955	65	64	74	78	79	72	70	40
1956	63	62	66	76	72	69	67	42
1957	61	60	60	73	64	63	63	44
1958	57	58	52	66	55	54	57	44
1959	52	53	45	61	47	48	51	44
1960	47	48	38	54	40	41	45	44
1961	44	45	35	51	38	39	48	40
1962	42	43	33	48	35	36	41	37
1963	39	41	31	47	33	33	39	34
1964	36	38	28	44	31	29	36	31

Source: Ann Dryden Witte, "Employment in the Manufacturing Sector of Developing Economies: A Study of Mexico, Peru and Venezuela" (Ph.D. dissertation, North Carolina State University, 1971).

Table 3 / *Relation of Labor to Output: The Values of R in Man-Years Per 100,000 Pesos Real Value Added/Year*

Year	All Manufacturing	Food, Beverages, and Tobacco	Textiles	Paper and Paper Products	Chemical and Petroleum Products	Non-metallic Mineral Products	Basic Metals
1945	9.6	10.1	10.7	12.8	5.0	12.5	5.8
1948	7.8	4.6	12.4	6.8	4.4	12.1	3.4
1949	7.7	5.3	12.8	6.7	4.2	10.8	3.1
1950	7.2	4.5	12.2	6.1	4.1	9.3	3.1
1951	6.8	4.3	12.3	5.7	4.1	8.9	2.9
1952	6.4	3.3	12.2	7.1	3.9	9.0	3.1
1953	6.7	4.5	12.4	7.0	3.9	8.9	3.0
1954	6.1	4.4	10.0	7.6	3.9	9.4	3.0
1955	5.7	4.1	9.7	8.1	3.4	8.9	2.8
1956	5.2	4.2	9.0	6.1	3.4	9.3	2.4
1957	4.9	3.8	9.0	5.2	3.2	8.5	2.2
1958	4.6	3.4	9.4	5.2	2.9	8.7	2.1
1959	4.1	3.3	8.2	5.0	2.4	8.5	1.9
1960	3.9	2.9	7.4	5.4	2.3	7.8	1.7
1961	3.6	3.0	7.3	5.4	2.0	8.1	1.7
1965	2.8	2.8	7.3	4.7	2.2	8.6	1.5

Sources: Dirección General de Estadística, *Censo industrial 1950* (Mexico, D.F., 1953); United Nations, *The Growth of World Industry,* 1938–1961 and 1953–1965 (New York, 1963 and 1965); Ann Dryden Witte, "Employment in the Manufacturing Sector," Table 8.

Note: The function R, as estimated by Ann Dryden Witte, is the production function of constant elasticity of substitution:

$$R = \frac{L}{V} = \frac{\left[\delta\left[\frac{r}{w}\left(\frac{1-\delta}{\delta}\right)\right]^{1-\sigma} + (1-\delta)\right]^{\sigma/1-\sigma}}{\gamma}$$

where R = labor/product, L = labor, V = value added, σ = elasticity of substitution, r/w = relative price (capital costs over labor costs), δ = distribution parameter, and γ = efficiency parameter.

Table 4 / Distribution of Income by Pattern of Development

Pattern	Country	Income Shares (Percentages)		Gini Index
		Upper 20%	Lower 40%	
Import Substitution	India	54.0	14.0	.46
	Ecuador	73.5	6.4	.66
	Brazil	66.7	6.5	.61
	Colombia	59.5	9.4	.54
	Chile	56.8	13.0	.49
	Mexico	65.8	10.2	.58
	Uruguay	47.4	14.3	.42
	Argentina	52.0	17.3	.42
Industrial Specialization				
A. Normal Capital Inflow	China (Taiwan)	40.1	20.4	.32
	Yugoslavia	41.5	18.5	.33
B. High Capital Inflow	Pakistan	45.0	17.5	.37
	South Korea	45.0	18.0	.36
	Tunisia	55.0	10.5	.50
	Lebanon	61.0	13.0	.52
	Puerto Rico	50.6	13.7	.44
	Israel	39.4	20.2	.30

Source: Hollis B. Chenery, *Alternative Strategies for Development,* World Bank Staff Working Paper no. 165 (October 1973), Appendix, Table 2.

Note: The Gini Index indicates the degree to which the distribution is skewed toward one extreme.

would lead to a reduction in the economy's vulnerability and its dependence on the external sector. However, in the historical experience of Mexico, even though the nature of external dependence has changed, no tendency toward reduction has been noted. Indeed, external dependence has become more obvious in the structure of imports and exports, in rental payments to foreign capital, and in foreign investment.

1. The vulnerability of the growth process and its dependence on the volume of imports have increased. While in 1929 the imports of intermediate and capital goods represented 55 percent of total imports, by 1970 the proportion had increased to 90 percent. Consequently a reduction in the capacity to import is likely to have a greater impact on production and employment than in 1929.

2. The continuous and growing deficit in the balance of payments in current account from 1940 to 1970 was financed through external indebtedness and foreign investment. However, during the late 1960s rental payments to foreign capital (transfers of rents and interests) reached the high level of 500 million dollars per annum, and this amount more than offset the net income from tourism; the old balance of services surplus was transformed into a growing deficit after 1968.

3. Even though by 1970 the structure of merchandise exports was more diversified than it had been (25 products accounted for three-fourths of the total exports), 75 percent of the exports were primary products, and 75 percent of the total trade was with the United States.

4. The industrialization process has been, in good part, the substitution of an inflow of foreign investment for an inflow of imports. The concentration and control of foreign investment in the manufacturing sector have been increasing, in qualitative and quantitative terms. In 1965 less than 1 percent of the firms in the manufacturing sector were foreign firms, but they controlled one-third of the sector's production. In the sector of nondurable consumer goods 0.2 percent of the firms were foreign and controlled 15 percent of the total production; however, in the most strategic sectors (intermediate and capital goods) foreign firms controlled 50 percent of the total production, despite the fact that they accounted for only 3.5 percent and 0.1 percent respectively of the number of firms. This illustrates not only the degree of concentration of foreign investment in the strategic sectors, but also the imperfection of the market structures in which these firms operate.[6]

The import substitution model was thus characterized not only by a process of growth without development, but also by a continuous and permanent external disequilibrium which itself tended to reinforce dependence on foreign capital. Before we look at the transitions evident in recent years, we should analyze this external disequilibrium in more detail.

External Disequilibrium in the Process of Import Substitution

EXTERNAL DISEQUILIBRIUM AND PARTIAL BALANCES

The growth of the Mexican economy during the last 20 years has been characterized by a continuous and accelerating deficit in the current account balance (B_{cc}). This deficit in the B_{cc} represents a value, in absolute terms, of outstanding importance. During the period 1951–70 the deficit increased from 126 to 1,115 million dollars (m.d.), and grew at an average annual rate of 9.0 percent and 12.8 percent during the 1950s and 1960s respectively. It has also increased in its relative significance: in 1951–52 the deficit in current account represented only one-tenth of the total imports of goods and services; by 1969–70 it accounted for one-fourth of the same total. The factors that have determined the evolution of this external disequilibrium can be detected from a careful examination of the partial balances (Figure 2, Tables 5 and 6).

The continuous and growing deficit of the merchandise balance (B_m) has been a crucial factor in the disequilibrium of the current accounts. The merchandise balance deficit increased from 65 m.d. in 1950 to 955 m.d. in 1970, and grew at an annual rate of 7.5 percent during the 1950s and at a rate of 8.3 percent during the 1960s, which serves to underline the reduction of exports as compared to imports. Thus, while merchandise exports financed 77 percent of imports in 1951–52, by 1959–70 this figure had been reduced to 64 percent. If the dependence on foreign investment and debt as a compensating mechanism is to be reduced, pressure has to be put on the net income from services as a source of funds to finance the deficit. This is of course assuming a constant level of international reserves.

Even though the amount shown in Table 6 as balance of services A (B_sA), or net income in the services account without including rent payments to foreign capital, has traditionally financed a substantial part of the growing deficit in the B_m, its relative importance as a compensating mechanism has decreased in recent years. This is explained by the enhanced importance of the service imports, in particular border trade and tourism. During the period 1951–52 to 1969–70 the imports of services in category A rose from 38 percent of the total exports of services to 61 percent. This was due to increased tourist expenditures abroad, which were equivalent to about one-third of the tourism income in 1951–52, and increased to approximately half the total (48 percent) in 1968–69.

As for balance of services B (B_sB), which includes the rental payments to foreign capital, since 1968 it has failed to be a compensating mechanism for the deficit in the merchandise balance (see Table 6). Even though payments for direct foreign investment have been greater than payments of interest on the foreign debt, both of these items have grown rapidly,

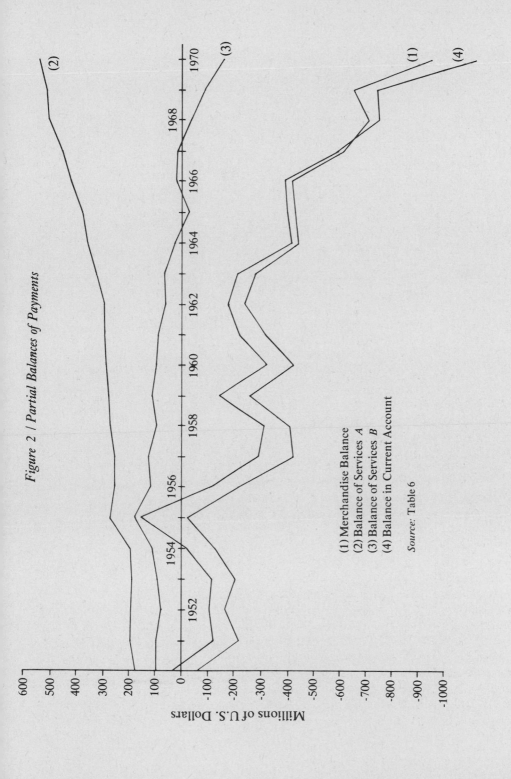

Figure 2 / *Partial Balances of Payments*

(1) Merchandise Balance
(2) Balance of Services *A*
(3) Balance of Services *B*
(4) Balance in Current Account

Source: Table 6

Table 5 / Mexico: Balance of Payments, 1950–70 (Millions of Dollars)

	1950	1951	1952	1953	1954	1955	1956	1957	1958	1959	1960
						Current Account					
1. Exports of Goods and Services	803	980	974	930	1056	1332	1333	1258	1227	1314	1340
(a) Goods	533	667	658	599	668	861	844	740	736	753	764
(b) Services	270	313	316	339	388	471	489	518	491	501	576
2. Imports of Goods and Services	−695	−1006	−955	−966	−903	−1086	−1305	−1421	−1364	−1207	−1482
(a) Goods	−597	−809	−829	−807	−800	−884	−1072	−1160	−1143	−1015	−1192
(b) Services	−98	−117	−126	−159	−193	−202	−233	−261	−221	−282	−290
3. Payments for Rent of Foreign Capital (Net)	−76	−100	−123	−94	−86	−93	−143	−134	−143	−169	−191
(a) Foreign Investments	−65	−91	−113	−83	−75	−79	−128	−117	−123	−128	−142
(b) Interest	−11	−9	−10	−11	−11	−14	−15	−17	−20	−41	−49
4. Private Donations	1	2	2	2	−10	−6	−2	2	1	−3	−7
5. Current Account Balance	33	−124	−102	−120	−33	147	−117	−295	−279	−155	−340
						Capital Account					
6. External Financing (Net)	−33	124	102	120	33	−147	117	295	279	155	340
7. Direct Investment	87	124	63	41	105	107	129	126	100	81	−38
(a) Loans (Long and Medium Term)	−2	−4	16	−4	23	14	41	82	113	62	173
(b) Inflows	29	35	55	32	79	78	107	165	243	224	363
(c) Amortizations	−31	−40	−39	−36	−56	−64	−66	−83	−130	−162	−190
8. Official Donations	14	6	3	3	4	2	—	1	−1	2	2
9. Errors and Omissions	40	−10	−1	38	−125	−68	8	72	−10	66	194
10. Movements in Reserves	−172	8	21	42	26	−202	−61	14	77	−56	9

Table 5 (continued)

	1961	1962	1963	1964	1965	1966	1967	1968	1969	1970
Current Account										
1. Exports of Goods and Services	1436	1547	1683	1824	1965	2136	2165	2448	2719	2875
(a) Goods	826	913	969	1054	1146	1199	1152	1258	1435	1445
(b) Services	610	634	714	770	819	937	1013	1190	1284	1430
2. Imports of Goods and Services	-1460	-1494	-1634	-1912	-2024	-2133	-2324	-2648	-2862	-3290
(a) Goods	-1143	-1155	-1248	-1499	-1577	-1619	-1767	-1968	-2089	-2400
(b) Services	-317	-339	-386	-413	-447	-514	-557	-680	-773	-890
3. Payments for Rent of Foreign Capital (Net)	-204	-237	-266	-324	-339	-394	-473	-551	-602	-700
(a) Foreign Investments	-148	-159	-186	-236	-236	-277	-322	-368	—	—
(b) Interest	-56	-78	-80	-88	-103	-117	-151	-183	—	—
4. Private Donations	-14	-17	-16	-9	-5	-5	5	13	14	15
5. Current Account Balance	-242	-201	-233	-421	-403	-396	-627	-738	-731	-1100
Capital Account										
6. External Financing (Net)	242	201	233	421	403	396	627	738	731	1100
7. Direct Investment	120	127	118	162	214	183	130	227	302	—
(a) Loans (Long and Medium Term)	165	133	195	384	3	160	367	318	451	—
(b) Inflows	352	401	426	755	372	645	839	890	976	—
(c) Amortizations	-187	-258	-231	-371	-389	-485	-472	-572	-525	—
8. Official Donations	1	2	-1	-2	—	4	2	—	—	—
9. Errors and Omissions	-66	-44	31	-91	165	55	168	242	26	—
10. Movements in Reserves	22	-17	-110	-32	21	-6	-40	-47	-48	—

Source: La política industrial en el desarrollo económico de México, p. 92.

making the original B_sB surplus into a deficit that increases the external disequilibrium. Rental payments to foreign capital increased from 76 m.d. in 1950 to 700 m.d. in 1970, having grown at an annual rate of 9.16 percent during the 1950s, and at a rate of 13.9 percent during the 1960s. Direct payments for foreign investment grew at rates of 8.11 percent and 12.6 percent yearly during the 1950s and 1960s respectively, reaching a rate of 16 percent during the last years (1965–68). Interest payments grew at a rate of 16 percent during both periods, reaching an average level of 21 percent during the last four years.

In summary, while rental payments to foreign capital represented 10 percent of total imports during the first years of the 1950s, this item increased its share to 20 percent during the late 1960s (see Table 5). Thus, the B_sB grew at a negative rate of 5.3 percent during these two decades. It declined from a surplus of 96 m.d. in 1950 to a deficit of 160 m.d. in 1970. Indeed, during the last three years of the period (1968–70) the net income in services account B not only did not help to finance part of the B_m deficit, but helped to increase it considerably (6 percent, 15 percent, and 17 percent for 1968, 1969, and 1970, respectively; see Table 6). All of this implied a growing dependence on capital inflows for financing the overall disequilibrium.

During the 1960s external financing (direct and indirect, foreign investment and foreign loans) increased its relative share, thus evening the total balance of payments. However, the role of foreign investment as a compensating mechanism had decreased compared to that of foreign indebtedness. While during the 1950s the total of foreign investment amounted to 963 m.d., the net inflow of foreign loans (medium- and long-term loans less amortizations) amounted to 341 m.d. These shares reversed during the 1960s, when the net inflow of foreign investment amounted to 1,545 m.d. and the net external loans to 2,349 m.d. This reversal was a sign of the growing inability of the economy to finance imports through the sale of goods and services and, furthermore, of the insufficiency of foreign investment to make up for such inability. This was true even though the government offered "open doors" to foreign investment during this period.

It is also important to note that net foreign investment (foreign investment less rental payments) proved a liability to the balance of payments during the later years. The net inflow of foreign investment (55 m.d. in 1951–52) became a new outflow of 334 m.d. in 1967–68. For the entire period of 1950–68 the inflow of foreign investment reached the level of 2,206 m.d., and the rental payments reached a total of 3,076; this implies a net negative balance of 870 m.d. during the period, which by itself was a stimulus for foreign indebtedness to increase in order to play its role as a compensating mechanism.

The alternatives to foreign indebtedness as a way of financing the

Table 6 / Partial Balances of Payments (1950–70)

Year	Merchandise Balance (I)	Service A Balance (II)	Service B Balance (III)	Commercial Balance (IV)	Balance in Current Account (V)
1950	−64	+172	+96	+108	+32
1951	−222	+196	+96	−26	−126
1952	−171	+193	+67	+19	−104
1953	−208	+180	+86	−28	−122
1954	−132	+195	+109	+63	−23
1955	−23	+269	+176	+246	+153
1956	−228	+256	+113	+28	−115
1957	−420	+257	+123	−163	−297
1958	−407	+270	+96	−137	−311
1959	−262	+279	+110	−17	−152
1960	−428	+286	+95	−142	−333
1961	−317	+293	+89	−24	−228
1962	−242	+295	+58	+53	−184
1963	−279	+328	+62	+49	−217
1964	−445	+357	+33	−88	−412
1965	−431	+372	−33	−59	−398
1966	−420	+423	+29	+3	−391
1967	−615	+456	+17	−159	−598
1968	−710	+510	−41	−200	−751
1969	−654	+511	−91	−143	−743
1970	−955	+540	−160	−410	−1115

(I): Exports of goods − Imports of goods
(II): Exports of services − Imports of services, without payments for rent to foreign capital
(III): (II) + payments for rent to foreign capital
(IV): (I) + (II)
(V): (I) + (III)

Source: René Villarreal, "External Disequilibrium," Table 35.

external disequilibrium did not seem to be very encouraging. In the first place, amortizations of medium- and long-term loans represented more than 50 percent of the inflow of funds (indeed, in 1968, out of an inflow of loans for the amount of 976 m.d., 525 m.d. were in amortizations). In the second place, payments of interest on the debt had not only reached high absolute values (almost 200 m.d. in 1968), but the relative share of this item in the total rental payments to foreign capital had increased. While interest payments on the debt represented 8.5 percent of rental payments to foreign capital in 1951–52, their share increased to 33 percent in 1967–68.

In this way the circle seemed to close; while rental payments to foreign capital had become an element that increased the disequilibrium in the current account, they were of necessity exacerbated as the government recurred to direct foreign investment and more indebtedness to compensate for such disequilibrium. Moreover, since net foreign investment (foreign investment less rental payments) was clearly a negative item during the latter years, external debt was left as the only compensating mechanism. This in its turn led to a diminishing ability to negotiate the acquisition of foreign debt; on the one hand, payments for amortization and interests increased substantially, in relative as well as in absolute terms, and on the other, the cost of servicing the debt seems to have increased:

> between the end of 1967 and the end of 1969, the conditions of contracting external public debt had deteriorated, as the proportion of external public debt to which rates of interest up to 5 percent had been attached was reduced from 11.0 percent to 8.1 percent of the total; the proportion to which rates of between 5 percent and 7 percent were attached decreased also, from 78.8 percent to 67.5 percent; the proportion of debt to which rates between 7 percent and 9 percent were attached increased from 10.3 percent to 20.8 percent; finally, the proportion contracted at rates higher than 9 percent increased from zero percent to 3.6 percent.[7]

The continuous and growing deficit in B_m and in B_sB together with the net drawback on the balance of payments represented by foreign investment and by the increasing cost of the debt service (amortization plus interest), is an important trend. Without the use of econometric projections for the balance of payments, it is possible to say that the external disequilibrium is and will be in the near future one of the most severe restrictions on growth in the Mexican economy. If no measures are taken to counteract the tendencies that have been observed, the consequences will be serious.

Before proceeding to study the most plausible economic policies that could serve to correct the external disequilibrium, it is necessary to delve into its origin and causes.

THE BACKGROUND TO EXTERNAL DISEQUILIBRIUM

In order to study the nature of the external disequilibrium in the Mexican economy, we will divide the reference period (1940–70) into two subperiods clearly characterized by the stages of import substitution and the commercial policy used to correct the consequent imbalance.

In the first period (1940–58) substitution of consumer goods was promoted; this had been achieved by 1950, and in 1950–58 the process of import substitution stagnated. Movements in the exchange rate were the principal mechanism used to correct the imbalances. As we mentioned earlier, the Mexican peso was devalued twice: from 4.05 pesos/dollar, which was the exchange rate prevailing in 1945, to 8.65 pesos/dollar in 1948–49 (a time when the peso was floating), and to 12.50 pesos/dollar in 1954, a rate which remained constant until September 1976. Even though quantitative controls were initiated in 1947, it is only during the second sub-period that these controls became relevant to the overall balance.

In the second period from 1959–70, the substitution of intermediate and capital goods was promoted. During this time the exchange rate was *not* utilized as an adjustment mechanism for the external disequilibrium. The policy of fixed exchange rates, and the growth of domestic prices as compared with international prices, gave rise to an overvaluation of the Mexican peso in terms of the U.S. dollar; this fluctuated between 15 percent and 20 percent in 1970.[8] This means that the exchange rate was rather an "unprotective" instrument of the import-substitution sector; it decreased the price of imports by approximately 20 percent. Despite this, the process of import substitution was intensified during 1959–70, by means of changes in the tariffs and, even more important, quantitative controls.

The general tariff for imports underwent significant changes in 1958, and again in 1961 and 1962, remaining unchanged from that year to the present. In 1958, about 57 percent of the items in the tariff, accounting for approximately 75 percent of the imports, increased ad valorem in an average proportion of 5.6 percent. In 1961, more than 600 items of the tariff were revised with the purpose of limiting imports, because of domestic and balance-of-payments maladjustments. This change implied a further decomposition of the tariff into its specific components, thus making the tariff structure even more discriminatory. In 1962, an additional ad valorem tariff was established on a group of import goods, the purpose being to use the fiscal revenues to subsidize some exports.

Quantitative controls had steadily increased in importance as a protectionist device. In 1956 only 25 percent of the imports were controlled, while in 1970 about 75 percent were controlled. About 50 percent of the 14,000 items on the Mexican tariff were subjected to import licenses that year.

In summary, while the exchange rate was an "unprotective" instrument after 1958, the tariffs were a "compensating" instrument, and quantitative controls turned out to be the effective protectionist device and the means to control imports.

GENERAL HYPOTHESES

Two general hypotheses can be derived from what we have said:
    1. A *structuralist* hypothesis would explain the origin of external dis-

equilibrium as intrinsic to the stage of growth in the process of development. In the first stage of import substitution, that of substitution of consumer goods, import demand is characterized by elasticity of income greater than unity $(N_y > 1)$, owing to the intensity of imports in the process of substitution itself. At the same time, given the lack of internal substitutes at this stage, the relative price elasticity of import demand is very low (both in absolute terms and relative to income elasticity) and substantially less than unity. Exports, on the other hand, generally limited to a few primary products, can increase, but not in the desired proportion to avoid external disequilibrium. This is due to the facts that exports of primary goods depend to a great extent on international demand and not only on internal conditions; the internal process of industrialization requires mineral and energy resources, slowing actual and/or potential export of them; and finally the nascent industry, precisely because it is nascent, is not yet efficient enough to compete in the international manufacturing market, except perhaps under unusual conditions of world shortages. All of these factors accelerate growth of imports and slow growth of exports, and thus create the external disequilibrium.

2. A hypothesis of *overvaluation of prices and costs* would explain external disequilibrium as a consequence of the greater rise in prices and costs in the domestic market relative to the international market. This scenario assumes a fixed exchange rate policy, import tariffs along with export subsidies, and an overvalued domestic currency—all inducing accelerated growth of imports and a slowing of exports. The combination of these two factors ultimately leads to a deficit in the current balance of payments account.

The data in the case of Mexico indicate that during the first stage of import substitution (1939–58), when the focus was on consumer goods, the external disequilibrium was of a structural nature; in the advanced stages of import substitution, those involving intermediate and capital goods (1959–70), the process was of a semistructural nature.[9]

During the first stage of import substitution the structural nature of the external disequilibrium can be explained as much by imports as by exports.

1. Once the economy has entered the first stage, substituting domestically produced consumer goods for imports, a derived demand is created for the importation of the intermediate and capital goods necessary for the continuation of the process of industrialization; these the economy cannot provide, precisely because it is in the first stage. This structural dependence on the importation of intermediate and capital goods, arising from the intensity of the substitution process itself, is manifested in a high marginal propensity to import $(P_{mam} = 0.22)$. This becomes greater than the average propensity to import $(P_{mem} = 0.15)$. A consequence is an

income elasticity of import demand greater than unity ($N_y = P_{mam}/P_{mem} = 1.5$), and this also implies a low relative price elasticity (significantly less than unity, approximately -0.08) which can be explained by the lack of domestic substitutes, particularly for intermediate and capital goods. Thus, during the first stage of import substitution the nature of the external disequilibrium, as far as imports are concerned, is structural.

2. Exports, still limited to a few primary products, cannot increase sufficiently fast enough to finance the imports required in the first stage.

(a) Mineral and petroleum products, which represented nearly two-thirds of total merchandise exports in 1939, were reduced to one-third in 1950. This was due to the fact that, as internal production of manufactures increased by 10 percent, exports of mineral and petroleum products declined by 5 percent ($N_{PIMX} = -.48$), since they were required for the substitution process itself.

(b) Livestock exports depended on world demand more than on internal conditions. The data indicate that such exports did not significantly respond to the effective real rate of exchange: as world demand (real GNP of the United States) increased by 10 percent, exports increased by 8.7 percent ($N_{DM} = 0.87$).

(c) Although exports of manufactures reacted to the effective real exchange rate, they did not reach the level of efficiency necessary to compete on the international market. Exceptions occurred in cases of world shortages, as during World War II, when manufacturers accounted for over 33 percent of total exports. (This figure decreased to 10 percent in 1950.)

In short, during the first stage of import substitution the deficit can be characterized as an external structural disequilibrium; consequently, devaluation and/or other commercial and economic policies designed to affect relative prices cannot correct the commercial deficit and simultaneously promote growth. Devaluation ceases to be effective from the moment import demand becomes characterized by a high income elasticity and low relative price elasticity.[10] In other words, in spite of the fact that overvaluation of the exchange rate can occur, the principal determinant of the level of imports would seem to be increases in income rather than increases in domestic prices in comparison with the international price level. And, although some exports might have been encouraged, these did not and could not increase sufficiently to diminish the commercial deficit.

It therefore seems obvious that to promote growth in this stage, it is necessary to finance a continuous and accelerating external disequilibrium or commercial deficit. This, in turn, implies a structural dependence on foreign capital (external loans and/or foreign investment) which constitutes the only mechanism of adjustment for such a disequilibrium. In actual fact, during the period of 1939–58, as we have seen, Mexico twice tried to use devaluation as a mechanism of adjustment. The devaluations of 1948–49 and 1954 meant a rise in the price of the dollar by more than 200 percent, but in spite of this change the disequilibrium continued to be financed by foreign capital. Of the deficit accumulated in 1939–58, foreign investment financed 1,134 million dollars of it and external debt 505 million. According to the theory of parity of purchasing power, the exchange rate was overvalued only during World War II and the immediately succeeding years (1943–48). Thus, it is very difficult to explain the external disequilibrium for the whole of the period 1939–58 by the overvaluation of prices and costs.

However, when the economy moved on to the advanced stages of import substitution, those involving intermediate and capital goods (1959–70), the external disequilibrium was of a *semi*structural nature:

1. During the advanced stages import demand goes through a structural change which differentiates it from the first stage. The substitution of consumer goods has virtually been exhausted and that of intermediate and capital goods is now in operation. More internal substitutes are now available to compete with imports, a fact that ensures that income elasticity must decrease significantly (from 1.50 to 0.81) and relative price elasticity must increase (from a value not significantly different from zero to 1.53). The external disequilibrium (as regards imports of goods) can now be characterized as being semistructural in origin. The hypothesis of overvaluation of prices and costs explains much of the increase of imports ($N_{P_d/P_m} = 1.53$); but income elasticity, although less than unity, is still significant ($N_y = 0.81$), and the imports are basically made up of intermediate and capital goods.

The reduction in income elasticity (from 1.5 to 0.81) can be explained by a greater reduction in P_{mam}, the marginal propensity to import (from 0.22 in 1945–58 to 0.063 in 1959–70), than in P_{mem}, the average propensity (from 0.1509 to 0.077 in the same period). That is, the average propensity to import decreases as the economy advances in import substitution, but the intensity of imports within the process is reduced still further (Figure 3).

2. Although the economy has advanced in the production of manufactures and the capability of exporting them, the overall model of import substitution is characterized by a commercial and protectionist policy which generally slows down the exportation of manufactures.

(a) The export industry receives domestic inputs which are a result of import substitution, but they are more expensive than internationally traded goods because of the existence of overprotected markets; this produces an implicit tax on exports.

(b) A generally overvalued exchange rate (from 15 percent to 20 percent in 1959–70) also establishes an implicit tax on exports and an effective subsidy for imports.

Figure 3 / Evolution of the Average and Marginal Propensities to Import in the Stages of Import Substitution (1940–70)

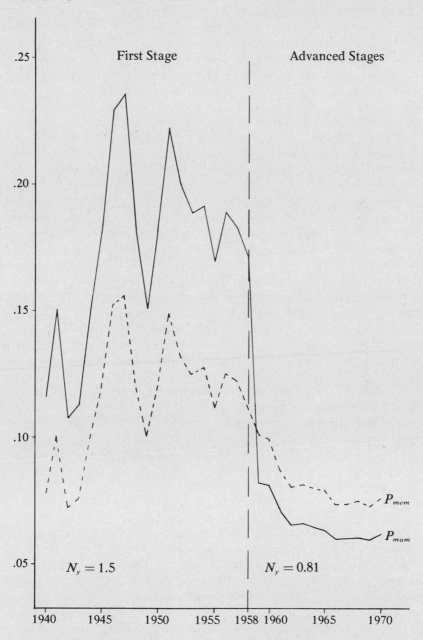

Source: René Villarreal, "External Disequilibrium," Table 41.

(c) The existence of a captive domestic market and the low level of subsidies for exports means that the export of manufactures cannot be either attractive or competitive.

3. Thus the commercial balance must continue in a state of disequilibrium; the current account balance of payments deficit increased from 152 million dollars in 1959 to 1,115 in 1970. Imports of services such as the rent of foreign capital (foreign investment and external loans), which were used during the first stage of import substitution, continue to be used as mechanisms of adjustment for the disequilibrium. When these payments are added to the balance of tourism and border services (which had traditionally financed the deficit in the merchandise balance), we find a deficit in the total balance of services; this, together with the deficit in the merchandise balance, exacerbated the disequilibrium in the current account balance. This was particularly pronounced after 1968.

For these reasons the external disequilibrium in the advanced stages of import substitution is of a semistructural origin. Even if imports of intermediate and capital goods continue to be significant, overvaluation of prices and costs makes the continuation of an external disequilibrium inevitable. The solution would seem to be a better commercial policy (devaluation, tariffs, subsidies) and an adequate strategy for development; these could considerably reduce the commercial deficit and in the long run promote the growth process.

In conclusion, during the first stage of import substitution the structural nature of the external disequilibrium leads to the judgment that, since devaluation does not work, development can only be promoted at the cost of a dependence on foreign capital. During the subsequent advanced stages of import substitution the semistructural origin of the disequilibrium means that its continuation, together with the dependence on foreign capital, is due in good measure to an inadequate strategy of development and an inadequate commercial policy.

The Continuation of Import Substitution and the Transition to Stabilized Growth

To understand the evolution of the Mexican economy in the period 1970–75, and the possible alternatives available for the latter part of the 1970s, it is necessary to link the external disequilibrium or foreign exchange gap with the import substitution model (1939–70) and its component parts: growth with devaluation and inflation (1939–58) and stabilized growth (1959–70).

In the long-run policy model, the primary objective was and is economic growth. The strategy was industrialization via import substitution, and it was assumed that the objectives of employment, income redistribution, and external independence would naturally follow the advance of the industrialization process itself. The protectionist policy (commercial and industrial), together with the State's activity as an investor in areas of infrastructure and strategic sectors, played a central part in the implementation of the model. For the *short*-run success of the policy model it is important to attain both external equilibrium (in the balance of payments) and internal equilibrium (stability of prices and development).[11] Such a scenario requires the union of instruments of commercial, fiscal, and monetary policy.

In the stabilized growth model (1959–70), fiscal and monetary policies were directed toward increasing internal savings in order to reduce the savings-investment gap $(S - I)$; the instruments were tax exemptions on capital income, low tariffs for public services, financing of the public deficit with internal and external debts rather than primary emissions of money, and so on. In this policy mix, the foreign exchange gap $(X - M)$ is taken for granted, as is its financing with foreign capital $(-I_f)$, and commercial policy is characterized by a fixed exchange rate. In the growth model with devaluation and inflation (1939–58), on the other hand, the reduction of the foreign exchange gap is an objective and devaluation is used as a mechanism of adjustment.

As we have shown, during the first stage of import substitution the external disequilibrium is structural, and devaluation as a mechanism of adjustment cannot correct it. During the advanced stages, however, the external disequilibrium is of a semistructural nature and devaluation as a mechanism of adjustment (linked with other policies) could significantly diminish the current account deficit. This also implies that, given the two "bottlenecks" (the savings-investment and the exchange gap) which an economy faces in its growth process, the "optimum" short-run model during the first stage should be directed primarily toward elimination of the savings-investment gap $(S - I)$. This is because the exchange gap $(X - M)$ is structurally determined and cannot be eliminated through devaluation (or any other type of fiscal, commercial, or monetary policy). It is this latter fact that accounts for the structural dependence on foreign capital to finance the disequilibrium $(-I_f)$. In the advanced stages, on the other hand, the short-run model cannot be exclusively focused on eliminating the savings-investment gap; it must also be concerned with the exchange gap. This can be acted upon as much on the side of imports as on that of exports, and an intelligent policy can contribute to diminishing dependence on foreign capital.

Comparing our theory with historical reality, we can now see that the two short-run policy models were applied at stages of import substitution when they were least effective. In many ways, the stabilized growth model was the "optimum" and most logical strategy during the first stage, when the external disequilibrium was of a structural nature in terms of both imports and exports. Such a model presupposes a foreign exchange gap (and its financing through foreign capital) and is directed chiefly toward the elimination of the savings-investment gap, promoting savings through various fiscal and monetary instruments. In contrast, during the advanced stages the semistructural nature of the disequilibrium would have allowed exports to be increased and imports to be diminished through adequate commercial, fiscal, and monetary policies. So the "optimum" short-run model here would have been directed toward the elimination or reduction of the exchange gap and would have been based on a system in which the real exchange rate (not the nominal one) increased or at least remained constant. In other words, this stage required a system in which the nominal rate of exchange had greater flexibility, as it did in the period 1939–58.

It seems that those responsible for economic policy making in Mexico during the 1960s were considerably influenced by the failure of the model of growth with devaluation and inflation (1939–58) and decided to abandon it in favor of a new short-run policy model, that of stabilized growth. They did not notice, however, that import substitution had already entered the advanced stages, when the original short-run model would have had greater ability to act on and reduce the exchange gap.

Economic Policy from 1970 to 1975

Before analyzing the economic policy of the first half of the 1970s, it is worth remembering the effects of the import substitution model and the costs that the stabilized growth model implied. Import substitution generated industrialization and growth during the whole period under study (1939–70), but by the end of the 1960s there were clear signs of unemployment, concentration of income, and dependence on foreign capital. The recent short-run model (1959–70) had allowed growth and price stability with a continuous and growing external disequilibrium that by 1970 had reached the level of 1,100 million dollars deficit in the current account balance; this was financed chiefly by external debts. At the same time private internal saving was encouraged in order to prevent taxation increases and to maintain low prices on public goods and services; this produced a situation in which the public debt represented more than a fifth of the gross domestic product. It was in this context that Mexico started the 1970s.

During President Echeverría's administration, beginning in 1970, the costs of industrialization were recognized openly and explicitly for the first time in 30 years; that is to say, the problems of unemployment, concentration of income, dependence on foreign capital, the public debt, and the low capacity of the public sector to finance itself were all acknowledged. Although inflation and the world recession (1973–74) complicated and limited the implementation of new policies, there were significant changes.

The most important changes were directed at the stabilized growth policies. The first thing to change was the policy of encouraging private saving at the expense of public saving. Taxes were raised (1971, 1973, and 1974 fiscal reforms), and so were prices and the tariffs of public services. The fiscal reforms implied, among other things, taxing income from fixed revenue bonds; these had been virtually tax-exempt in the stabilized growth period.[12] Among the public services, principally the energy sector (oil and electricity), prices and tariffs were raised with the intention of increasing fiscal revenue and financing expansion in these sectors.

In 1975 the import substitution policies were changed with the general aim of rationalizing the protectionist structure, but this was done without any attempt at changing the model itself. In January of that year a modification of customs policy was designed to eliminate the excessive and discriminatory character of the protectionist structure of Mexico. The number of tariff items was reduced from 12,887 in 1970 to 7,275 in 1975; products were to be taxed according to their grade of manufacture, and no rate would be greater than 75 percent except in the case of cars (see Table 7).[13] Duties were increased on 2,517 items, reduced on 2,576, and left unaltered on 2,180; "the effective impositive coefficient, i.e., the percentage that import revenues represent in relation to the value of imports, is

Table 7 / Tariff Structure in Early 1975

Type of Product	Tariff Rates (%)
Agricultural machinery	exempt
Raw materials	5 to 15
Intermediate products of industrial use	15
Machinery and tools	20 and 25
Other manufacturing products	25 to 35
Unnecessary or superfluous goods	50 and 75
Cars assembled abroad	100

Source: Luis Bravo Aguilera, "Las nuevas tarifas de los impuestos generales de importación y exportación de México," *Comercio exterior de México*, vol. 21, no. 3 (March 1975): 290.

expected to increase from 16 percent in 1974 to 17 percent in 1975."[14] The object, then, was not to boost protectionism or to raise fiscal revenues, but to establish a new structure of duties that would eliminate the highly discriminatory and excessive character of the tariffs.

The specific tax which had been in use since 1927 disappeared completely in the new tariff, leaving only an ad valorem tax. At the same time, it was decided that the official price (the price on which import duty was set) should be fixed along the lines of that existing for that particular product on the international market.[15]

In December 1975 Rule XIV was eliminated by the change of tariffs, along with the Law for New and Necessary Industries.[16] This put an end to the fiscal encouragement of industrialization, which, apart from being inefficient, implied a considerable sacrifice of revenues and a slowing of industrial employment because of the freedom to import machinery and equipment tax-free.

But because the import substitution and stabilized growth models remained the principal strategy for industrialization, and the deficiencies of only the fiscal policy (not the commercial policy) were taken into account, the external disequilibrium continued through 1975. A result was that, owing to balance of payments pressures in August 1975, all imports were subjected to an import permit and tariffs on 5,845 items were increased, 75 percent of them receiving a duty of between 5 percent and 25 percent (see Table 8).[17] In addition, a 75 percent subsidy on duties of machinery imports was again considered, providing this was used for the production of export or capital goods.

In other words, in spite of the rationality of the new tariffs, the elimination of Rule XIV and the Law for New and Necessary Industries, and in spite of the fact that the intention was not to increase protection, the high levels of external disequilibrium caused all imports to be subjected to a quantitative control, thereby increasing protection in the worst possible way. The new policy permitted the existence of redundant effective tariffs, and therefore a greater inefficiency in the allocation of resources.[18]

Another important characteristic of Echeverría's period was a larger participation of the State in the process of capital accumulation and industrialization. The proportion of federal public investment in the gross domestic product increased from 6.8 percent in 1970 to 10.9 percent in 1975. In addition, the share of public investment in total investment increased from 40 percent in 1970 to more than 56 percent in 1975. It is also important to point out that public investment in the industrial sector grew at an annual rate of 35 percent, moving from 11,000 million pesos in 1970 to 46,000 million projected for 1976.

Table 8 / Changes in the Tariff in August 1975

Tariff Rate (%)	Number of Items	
	Preceding Tariff	New Tariff
Exempt	142	65
5	219	252
10	673	331
15	2,763	531
20	1,292	2,720
25	652	1,515
35	910	569
50	417	861
75	230	291
100	5	168
Forbidden	7	7
Total	7,310	7,310

Source: Secretaría de Hacienda y Crédito Público, *Revista numérica* (September 1975): 9.

Evolution of the External Disequilibrium from 1970 to 1974

In the period 1970–74, the external disequilibrium continued and, indeed, worsened compared with the preceding period (1959–70). The deficit in the current account balance (B_{cc}) increased at an annual average rate of 28 percent and reached the 3,010 million dollar mark in 1974 (in 1970 it had stood at 1,115 million dollars); in other words, it amounted to one-third of the total imports of goods and services for that year (see Table 9). The merchandise balance continued to be a determining factor in explaining the B_{cc}'s increase; from 955 million dollars in 1970, the merchandise deficit grew to 2,423 million in 1974.

The balance of services *A* (border and tourism transactions), although still in surplus, grew at an annual average rate of only 6.1 percent. Therefore, when interest payments on foreign capital are included, giving us the figure for balance of services *B*, the continuing deficit tendency is clearly evident. The deficit grew at an annual average rate of 38.5 percent from 1970 to 1974, thereby emphasizing the indirect costs of using foreign capital as a source for financing the current account deficit.

Partial accumulated balances for the period 1970–74 (see Table 10) reflect the limits the external disequilibrium sets on economic growth.

Table 9 / Balance of Payments, 1970–74 (Millions of Dollars)

	1970	1971	1972	1973	1974
Merchandise balance	−955	−681	−737	−1,269	−2,423
Service A balance	540	682	666	611	684
Service B balance	−160	−37.9	−62.1	−285	−587
Balance in current account	−1,115	−718.9	−799.1	−1,554	−3,010
Liquidity balance*	−1,651	−1,174.9	−1,303.1	−2,399	−3,633
Foreign direct investment	323	307	301	374	557
Long-run loans	626	765	827	1,855	3,218

*Balance in current account plus amortizations.

Source: International Monetary Fund, International Financial Statistics, September 1975.

Table 10 / Accumulated Balances (Millions of Dollars)

	1939–48	1959–70	1970–74
Merchandise balance	−3,071.2	−5,778	−6,065
Service A balance	2,897.2	4,110	3,183
Service B balance	1,488.8	234	−1,132
Balance in current account	−1,582.4	−5,544	−7,197
Net foreign investments	1,133.9	2,025	1,862
Net foreign loans	504.5	3,460	7,291
Reserves	369	−310	−646
Errors and omissions	−425	−369	1,310
Liquidity balance	−2,283.4	−9,912	−10,161

Source: International Monetary Fund, *International Financial Statistics,* September 1975.

The merchandise balance showed an accumulated deficit of 6,065 million dollars, a gap which could not be bridged by balance of services A. The current account balance reached a deficit of 7,197 million dollars. The principal sources of finance were net external loans (7,291 million dollars) and, to a lesser extent, net foreign investment (1,862 million).

We can now see not only the costs of using net external loans and net foreign investment in such magnitudes, but also the difficulty of making more than 10,000 million dollars available in five years, particularly at a time when dollars are scarce on the international market and therefore their costs are greater (shorter terms and higher interest rates). Without any doubt, world stagflation and internal hopes for devaluation are factors in explaining the high levels of disequilibrium. Nevertheless, the disequilibrium as of 1974 was primarily a result of the continuation of the import substitution and stabilized growth models:

1. The continuation of the models slowed growth of exports and stimulated that of imports.

(a) Captive markets and greater profits for investment in the internal, as opposed to the external, market were still operative factors.

(b) The export sector continued to suffer from implicit taxes (overvaluation of the exchange rate, high costs of national inputs because of protection, and so on). The subsidies an exporter received (in the form of access to special drafts) were not large enough to compensate. At the same time, they did not allow the exporting firm to operate on a margin and were therefore of benefit to existing exporters rather than potential exporters.

(c) Imports continued growing, for in spite of complete control of imports between 1970 and 1975 the system was based more on prior permits than on fixed import quotas.

(d) As regards services, imports continued to be stimulated and exports slowed, for until September 1976 both faced the same nominal rate of exchange set in 1954 (12.50 pesos to the dollar), which meant a real 1975 exchange rate of 10.45.

2. With regard to the stabilized growth model, fiscal policy was modified in order to increase the participation of State savings by raising taxes and tariffs on public services. The emphasis, then, was still on closing the savings-investment gap and the foreign exchange gap continued to be taken for granted. These attitudes increased dependence on foreign capital.

The early 1970s, therefore, are an indication not only of the difficulty of promoting a new economic strategy independent of foreign capital, but also of the limits that a permanent disequilibrium sets on growth itself. In short, a new model is called for, one in which economic strategy will be directed toward reducing and eliminating the foreign exchange gap, while at the same time increasing employment and promoting income redistribution in a context of independence from foreign capital.

A Proposed New Policy: Export Substitution

I now wish to suggest that the project of development requires that the model of import substitution be replaced by a model of export substitution. The economic policy of transition would have the following features: devaluation, expenditure stabilization, and trade liberalization.

In the model of export substitution, manufactured goods would displace primary goods as the dominant exports. Industrialization would still be the engine of growth, but emphasis would be given to specialization in the industrial sector and orientation toward foreign markets. For example, the abundant supply of labor which is underutilized or unemployed in the traditional agricultural sector could be absorbed by an expanding industry, which would simultaneously be developing its ability to export labor-intensive goods.

This project of economic development through export substitution can be justified with the following reasoning:

1. To continue import substitution in the intermediate and capital goods sectors, as a way of promoting industrialization, implies not only increasing costs but also a limit to the possibilities of success. This is due to the size of the domestic market and the complex technology that is required for these stages of the process. Moreover, unemployment and concentration of income would show a tendency to increase because of the

protectionist policy and the characteristics of the process itself. In addition, in order to keep the balance-of-payments deficit from acting as a brake on growth, foreign capital would have to be utilized continuously and increasingly as a financing mechanism. This would, in turn, increase both the dependence on foreign capital and the balance-of-payments deficit—because of the growing amounts that would be sent abroad as rental and interest payments.[19]

2. Substitution of exports would tend to reduce and even to eliminate the balance-of-payments deficit and would consequently provide not only a greater flexibility in the economic structure, but also a means to decrease the dependence on foreign capital. Industrial employment would increase rapidly, as long as:

(a) The traditional agricultural sector is modernized, for increasing productivity in this sector will make it possible to provide the industrial sector with food and labor at a real cost close to the opportunity cost.

(b) The relative prices of capital and labor reflect the true social opportunity costs; this would stimulate the use of new technology and labor-intensive innovations and improve the distribution of income.

In particular, I would like to stress that the transition to a model of industrialization via export substitution would be characterized by *devaluation, stabilization, and trade liberalization.*

Devaluation is an instrument of policy which serves the purpose of *general expenditure-switching.* It directs expenditure or demand toward the acquisition of home-produced goods, and domestic production toward the export-supplying and import-competing sectors. The devaluation of the peso in September 1976 was a step in this direction. This policy would imply that both sectors—export-supplying and import-competing— would receive initially the same degree of stimulus, that is, the relative prices of their goods would increase in the same proportion. However, because of the protectionist effects of devaluation, the characteristics of the present structure of protection (which is excessive, permanent, and discriminatory), and the stage of import substitution in which the country finds itself, it would not be efficient to undertake more import substitution as a primary objective of the development strategy. For this reason I suggest also a policy of *selective expenditure-switching* that in the medium and long run will allow the economy to move from the stage of industrialization via import substitution to the more advanced stage of industrialization via export substitution.

This policy would have as an objective, in the medium and long run, the stimulation of resource allocation to the exporting sector. It would consist of a policy of *gradual liberalization* of imports—the tariffs being equalized and quantitative controls taking their place. This would improve the efficiency of resource allocation in the industrial sector itself, and it would oblige this sector to confront, in the medium and long run, a given top price—the international price plus the tariff. This factor would improve competitiveness, enabling Mexican industry to enter the international export market.

However, given that the supply elasticity of the tradable-goods sector (exports and import substitutes) is not infinite or instantaneous, the increased domestic demand generated by devaluation would not be translated into an equal growth of production. For this reason prices would tend to increase. Therefore a deflationary fiscal and monetary policy would be necessary, to reduce demand temporarily and allow time for resources and factors of production to be reallocated in the tradable-goods sector. This would guarantee that the increased demand for tradable goods would be accompanied by an increase in production, thus avoiding inflation. However, it should be noted that, given the present characteristics of the Mexican economy, devaluation in itself will produce important deflationary effects. We should consequently worry more about a policy of *expenditure stabilization* than about one of expenditure reduction.

A further point is that, even when unemployment and the unused capacity of industry allow domestic demand to react positively to devaluation, the inevitable "bottlenecks" that exist in some sectors, and the recent world inflation, are drawbacks for such a policy in the short run. However, this policy of transition is both possible and necessary in the medium run.

The "optimum" policy mix of devaluation, expenditure stabilization, and trade liberalization thus takes shape as an adjustment mechanism for the external disequilibrium of the Mexican economy. It implies changing the economic strategy of growth and industrialization via import substitution to a strategy of growth and industrialization via export substitution. This policy is necessary not only for economic growth during the present decade, but also as a precondition for improving employment, redistributing income, and decreasing external dependence.

Conclusion

External dependence and disequilibrium, together with the unemployment, concentration of income, and population explosion which now characterize Mexico, endanger both economic and political stability. This analysis has shown that these problems are currently intractable.

At the present time there are three alternative mechanisms of adjustment for the external disequilibrium in the Mexican economy:

1. First, the policy of allowing the disequilibrium to continue and financing it with foreign capital. This would involve accentuating depen-

dence and at the same time limiting the possibilities of this type of financing, because of the additional costs of interest payments on such capital and the volume of resources needed (5,000 to 6,000 million dollars annually). It would prove to be extremely difficult to finance such disequilibrium in an international credit market which is more and more restricted, that is to say, one that is characterized by higher interest rates and shorter-term loans.[20]

2. Second, a policy of reduction in the rate of growth to the level dictated by the foreign exchange gap. This would be done without altering commercial policy and would entail diminishing the present pressure on the balance of payments at the expense of present growth—in a sense, postponing the whole problem until tomorrow. It is important to note that over the past few years it has already been necessary to reduce the rate of growth to the limits set by the external disequilibrium.

3. Finally, a new strategy which would stimulate growth of exports (of both goods and services) and slow that of imports, thus reducing the disequilibrium.

The above alternatives have led us to propose a new economic development project whose first stage would involve an export substitution model. Its implementation would require an economic policy of transition along the following lines: devaluation, stabilization of expenditure, and liberalization of trade. Later, a new short-run model would take effect, one in which a principal objective would be the maintenance of a real effective exchange rate favorable to the export sector.

The viability of the policy of transition would depend on the existence of various factors: flexibility of internal supply (so that no bottlenecks arise in strategic sectors), favorable international market conditions, price and salary controls, discipline in the administration of the stabilization policy, a gradual process of trade liberalization, and an adequate political framework that would allow for efficient control of the policy and process of transition.[21]

Nevertheless, such a policy of transition would still be insufficient to guarantee the fulfillment of all the objectives of economic development. In the first place, in order to attain growth, employment, income redistribution, and independence from foreign capital, within a framework of price stability and equilibrium in the balance of payments, the State would need a large number of efficient and independent instruments of economic policy.[22] These do not exist in contemporary Mexico. Fiscal policy as an instrument of stabilization and/or income redistribution has been generally applied on the side of expenditure and has been used hardly at all on the taxation side. In any case, fiscal policy also determines to a great extent the possibilities of monetary policy; the financing of the budget deficit fixes the level of the reserve requirement and thus directly affects credit.

Commercial policy has relied on quantitative controls and tariffs, and, since it has not used the exchange rate as a policy instrument, has had to depend on foreign capital.

It can be seen, then, that to reach the various objectives of the proposed development project the State will have to make changes that will permit effective utilization of present and potential economic policy instruments. However, one would have to be either very naive or an orthodox neoclassical economist to believe that in a country like Mexico (even under the export substitution model) the indirect action of the State through its various economic policy instruments, and market forces working through monopolistic and oligopolistic structures, could simultaneously and efficiently guarantee employment, redistribution of income, growth, independence of foreign capital, price stability, and an equilibrium in the balance of payments. Without doubt, the role of the State as an economic agent, both in its direct actions (such as specific employment projects and income redistribution programs) and its indirect actions (incorporating new and more efficient instruments of economic policy), would have to be broadened. And, at the same time, the efficiency of the State's actions would depend on large-scale and integral economic programming.

Notes

1. The experiences of Mexico, Argentina, and Brazil, between 1880 and 1930, show the intrinsic limitations of the export promotion model as a means of industrialization. The recent experiences of Malaysia and Thailand offer other examples. See D. Paauw and J. Fei, *The Transition in Open Dualistic Economies* (New Haven: Yale University Press, 1973).

2. We use the Chenery import substitution index:

$$ISI = M_i/[M_i + (VA)_i]$$

where M_i = imports of commodity i at constant prices and $(VA)_i$ = domestic value added of commodity i at constant prices. In other words, the ISI is the ratio of imports to total supply on the basis of value added.

3. Grupo de Estudio del Problema del Empleo, *El problema del empleo. El problema ocupacional de México: magnitud y recomendaciones* (Mexico, D.F., 1973), pp. 14–57.

4. Almost all the Mexican industries (90 percent) showed elastic production function (elasticities significantly different from zero). For the manufacture sector as a whole, the estimations of the elasticity of substitution had a variation range between 1.47 and 0.95. See Ann Dryden Witte, "Employment in the Manufacturing Sector of Developing Economies: A Study of Mexico and Peru," *The Journal of Development Studies*, vol. 10, no. 1 (October 1973).

5. Ann Dryden Witte, "Employment in the Manufacturing Sector."

6. CEPAL-NAFINSA, *La política industrial en el desarrollo económico de México* (Mexico, D.F.: 1971), Appendix, Table 76.

7. Jorge E. Navarrete, "Desequilibrio y dependencia: las relaciones económicas internacionales en los años sesentas," in M. Wionczek (ed.), *Crecimiento o desarrollo económico?* (Mexico, D.F.: Colección SEP/SETENTAS, 1971), p. 176. My translation.

8. Gerardo M. Bueno, "Consideraciones acerca de la sobrevaluación del tipo de cambio en México," *El trimestre económico*, vol. 41, no. 162 (1972).

9. All of the information that follows is based on my Ph.D. dissertation, "External Disequilibrium, Growth Without Development: The Import Substitution Model. The Mexican Experience (1929–1975)," 1975, Chapter 3, Part 3.

10. Obviously, given the high income elasticity, the way to correct the disequilibrium is by slowing growth; this fact is ignored here, since the objective is to analyze the disequilibrium during the process of growth and not under conditions of permanent economic stagnation.

11. The latter is also, of course, a long-run objective.

12. A 16 percent rate is applied when the owner is unidentified; 12 percent when he is identified. In January 1976 the rates were increased to 21 percent and 15 percent.

13. Luis Bravo Aguilera, "Las nuevas tarifas de los impuestos generales de importación y exportación de México," *Comercio exterior de México*, vol. 21, no. 3 (March 1975): 291.

14. *Ibid.*, p. 292. My translation.

15. *Ibid.*, p. 292.

16. *Diario oficial*, December 15, 1975, p. 8.

17. Secretaría de Hacienda y Crédito Público, *Revista numérica* (September 1975).

18. The changes in commercial policy of August 1975 provided for exports a reduction in the base for the concession of Drawing Special Drafts (DSD) to a minimum of 40 percent (as opposed to 50 percent previously), in which case exporters would receive returns of 50 percent of indirect taxes. If national integration stands at between 50 percent and 59 percent, 63.6 percent of such taxes are granted in returns, and if integration is greater than 60 percent, DSDs will amount to the return of all indirect taxes. Among other important measures during President Echeverría's government are the Law for the Promotion of Mexican Investment and the Regulation of Foreign Investment (*Diario oficial*, March 9, 1973), and the Law Concerning Registration of the Transference of Technology and the Use and Exploitation of Patents and Brands (*Diario oficial*, December 30, 1972).

19. In 1973, the deficit in CAB was 1,487 million dollars and the payments for rent on foreign capital represented 83 percent of the deficit (1,232 m.d.). On the other hand, the net inflow of foreign investment and foreign loans amounted to 1,842 m.d. (International Monetary Fund, *Balance of Payments Yearbook*, May 1974).

20. The deficit in the commercial balance was estimated at 3,500 to 4,000 million dollars for 1975; if a conservative value of 1,500 to 2,000 million dollars is set for the payment of amortizations, then the liquidity balance will have shown a deficit of 5,000 to 6,000 million dollars. This is the minimum net revenue from foreign capital (given the constant level of reserves) required to maintain parity of the exchange rate.

21. René Villarreal, "External Disequilibrium," Chapter 2, Part 4.

22. J. Tinbergen, *On the Theory of Economic Policy* (Amsterdam: North Holland Publishing Company, 1970).

The State and Foreign Capital

RICHARD S. WEINERT

Foreign capital has played a central role in Mexico's industrialization, especially since 1955. Mexican planners in the 1950s deliberately encouraged foreign investment and designed policies to attract foreign capital into new or undercapitalized areas of industry.[1] How has the state dealt with the numerous consequences of foreign investment? I shall argue that, as foreign investment grew, the state consistently and successfully resisted threats to its own authority, while it tolerated social and economic consequences which many have deplored but which did not affect state power.

As much literature on multinationals has stressed, foreign capital threatens to undermine state sovereignty and power because it presents a source of significant economic strength not subject to state control.[2] Traditionally, foreign capital dominated key economic activities in Mexico and state control over basic economic policy was thus circumscribed. By 1940, however, most key sectors were in Mexican hands, and in the 1950s Mexican control of traditional activities increased.

A more modern challenge stems from the growth of multinational enterprise, which can treat each foreign subsidiary as a unit in a global enterprise and seek to maximize its own global profits and rate of growth. To the extent that this is true, a Mexican subsidiary may not respond to local market conditions but may orient production patterns to the global needs of its multinational parent. If this occurs, state economic policy making can be frustrated, since firms operating in Mexico may not respond to the economic signals of state policies.

This would clearly conflict with the state's goal of maintaining and increasing its control over the economy and society. Other essays in this volume show how the state has manipulated popular sectors to minimize their challenge to state development policies. The state has also tried to shape foreign capital's role in the economy, in order to retain decision-making power in Mexican hands. The state's relationship with foreign capital has obviously not been static but has evolved as conditions have changed. From Cárdenas through the late 1960s, the state's strategy was twofold: (1) to gain control over key sectors of the economy, and (2) to direct new foreign investment into undeveloped economic activities. By the late 1960s, nationalization had given the state control over oil, electricity, transportation, and communications. Banking, insurance, steel, and fertilizers were also firmly in Mexican hands. We shall examine later how new foreign investment was directed into nontraditional activities.

The particular challenge from multinational enterprise emerged in the mid- to late-1960s as foreign investment grew. The state's response has been to encourage majority Mexican control of companies through legislation, regulations, and incentives. The implicit theory is that decision making in firms which are majority-owned by Mexicans would be likely to respond to state initiatives and Mexican market conditions, so that power is retained in Mexico and ultimately in the state. This Mexicanization strategy has roots in the 1940s but has been especially stimulated since 1970; we shall review it later.

In addition to a political challenge, foreign capital produces some negative social and economic consequences. These may be roughly grouped under three headings: (1) inequality, (2) market distortions, and (3) balance-of-payments pressures.

Inequality is stimulated and aggravated in several interrelated ways.[3] The capital-intensive industries characteristic of the multinational sector create a wealthy managerial class and an elite of highly paid skilled labor. Foreign technology and products distort consumer preferences toward luxury goods consumed by the elites employed by foreign firms. As various analysts have argued, industrialization stimulated by foreign capital both creates and becomes dependent on increasing inequality, thereby creating strong political imperatives for its continuation. While these consequences undermine the social goals of the Mexican Revolution, they do not challenge the political power of the State, which can command support from sectors created by this industrialization. Other essays in this volume demonstrate that the state has tolerated these social consequences of foreign capital and prevented resulting political tensions which might threaten the economic structure.

Foreign investment may distort local markets in several ways.[4] Since foreign investors have greater technological and capital resources than are available locally, they may significantly distort revenue allocation in ways which do not best promote social goals. By drawing on their superior resources and experience, foreign firms may dominate the sectors in which they operate, thus aggravating market concentration. Further, through such market concentration, acquisition policies, and unfair competition, they may weaken local firms, thereby retarding instead of stimulating indigenous industrialization.

Unlike increasing inequality, market concentration, and domination of Mexican industry *can* diminish state control. The state has resisted these effects in two ways. First, by using its own market power and by subtle cajoling, threats, and fiscal incentives, it has tried to direct foreign investment from established areas into new areas of the economy. Second, since 1970, Mexicanization pressures have defended Mexican industrialists against the superior resources of foreign firms. These pressures on local markets which tended to reinforce inequality did not affect State power, and the state did little to counter them.

Finally, balance-of-payments pressures often result from foreign investment. A country may suffer a tightening circle of outflows resulting from a trade deficit and profit remittances which are financed by foreign debt, thus increasing debt service and ultimately worsening balance-of-payments pressures. Villarreal ably analyzes this process elsewhere in this volume,[5] concluding that the problem became acute in the late 1960s. Perhaps in part because the effects of balance-of-payments pressures have not directly challenged state power, the state has paid insufficient attention to them. Villarreal argues that by the mid-1970s they have come to represent a severe strain on future economic growth and new economic policies are required.

Foreign Investment

How successfully has the state circumscribed the role of foreign capital in the economy? We have suggested that, in promoting industrialization, the state was acutely concerned about the political challenge of foreign capital but was relatively unconcerned about effects on inequality, market distortions, or balance of payments. After the 1950s, the state's primary goal was to direct foreign capital into new economic activities, so that it would open up new areas of the economy, thereby promoting industrialization. At the same time, the state did not want foreign capital to increase its overall importance in the economy, further threatening state control over policy making. Success in preventing such an increase may be seen in Table 1, which shows the importance of foreign capital in the Mexican economy since 1961. Foreign investment as a percentage of gross national product declined from 8.5 percent in 1961 to 7.7 percent in 1975. When foreign debt is added to foreign investment, total foreign capital as a percentage of GNP grew only slightly until 1973, and then bulged in 1974

Table 1 / Importance of Foreign Capital in the Mexican Economy, 1961–75 (Dollar Figures in Millions)

Year	Total Direct Foreign Investment	Total Foreign Debt Outstanding	Total Foreign Capital	GNP	Foreign Investment as % of GNP	Foreign Capital as % of GNP	Imports as % of GNP
1961	$1,130	$ 981	$ 2,111	$13,321	8.5	15.8	8.5
1965	1,745	1,771	3,516	20,162	8.7	17.4	10.0
1966	1,938	1,974	3,912	22,407	8.6	17.5	9.5
1967	2,096	2,176	4,272	24,505	8.6	17.4	9.5
1968	2,316	2,483	4,799	27,132	8.5	17.7	9.8
1969	2,576	2,915	5,491	29,992	8.6	18.3	9.6
1970	2,822	3,260	6,082	33,496	8.4	18.2	11.6
1971	3,018	3,711	6,729	36,192	8.3	18.6	10.8
1972	3,208	4,257	7,465	40,984	7.8	18.2	11.1
1973	3,495	5,627	9,122	49,656	7.0	18.4	12.1
1974	3,857	7,627	11,484	52,586	7.3	21.8	16.5
1975	4,219	10,578	14,797	55,084	7.7	26.9	18.1

Sources:

Foreign Direct Investment and Foreign Debt from Table 8.

GNP: 1965–68 from Bernardo Sepúlveda and Antonio Chumacero, *La inversión extranjera en México* (Mexico, D.F.: Fondo de Cultura Económica, 1973). 1961 and 1969–73 from Mexican bond prospectuses. 1974 and 1975 estimates from *Comercio exterior de México*, vol. 22, no. 2 (February 1976).

Imports: 1965–68, from René Villarreal, "El desequilibrio en el crecimiento económico de México: su naturaleza y mecanismo de ajuste óptimo; devaluación, estabilización y liberalización," *El trimestre económico*, vol. 41, no. 164 (October–December 1974). 1961 and 1969 from Mexican bond prospectuses. 1970–75 from *Comercio exterior de México*, vol. 22, no. 4 (April 1976).

and 1975 as foreign debt leapt forward while GNP growth fell as a result of a world recession.

The total contribution of foreign investment to the economy is surprisingly small considering the discussion it generates. As Flavia Derossi wrote in 1971,

> The sheer bulk of foreign investment at the beginning of the century was so overriding as to be an obvious economic determinant from every point of view for the whole country. Today, capital coming from foreign sources is so low that its role might appear of minor importance but for the quality of its contribution.[6]

Foreign investment represented only about 5 percent of total fixed investment for the period 1962–70 and has declined since. If state investment were excluded, so as to consider only private investment, the proportion would rise to only 7.6 percent.[7] Companies with foreign shareholders accounted for about 11 percent of total production during this period.[8] From the point of view of political control, these data overstate foreign capital's importance, since they include companies with as little as 5 percent foreign ownership. For example, the sector in which firms with foreign shareholders accounted for the highest percentage of production was mining (63 percent), although 98 percent of mining production is by firms which are majority-controlled by Mexicans. Taxes paid by firms with foreign participation contribute over 20 percent of total federal government revenues.[9]

By the 1940s, the state had forced foreign capital out of such basic sectors of the economy as utilities, oil, banking, steel, communications, and railroads. This process was extended in the 1950s with the nationalization of the telephone company and a remaining electric utility company. The state's success in shifting investment out of traditional areas and into new areas can be seen in Table 2, which summarizes foreign investment by sector from 1940 to 1970. Total foreign investment grew slowly from 1940 to 1950 but rapidly after 1950, and it changed sectors dramatically. Investment in mining dropped from 24 percent of the total in 1940 to 6 percent in 1970, and investment in electricity and transportation/communication dropped from 31 to 32 percent respectively to practically nothing. Investment in industry, however, grew from a small 7 percent in 1940 to an overwhelming 74 percent in 1970. These data demonstrate the success of state efforts to divert foreign capital from traditional activities into industry.

Investment also shifted within the industrial sector, though less dramatically. These data are summarized in Table 3 for the period 1950–70. Investment stayed constant in textiles and dropped significantly in food

Table 2 / Value of Foreign Investment by Activities, 1940–70

Year	Value (Millions of Dollars)	% Mining	% Industry	% Electric	% Commerce	% Transportation and Communication
1940	$ 449	24	7	31	4	32
1945	569	24	18	24	5	26
1950	566	20	26	24	12	13
1955	953	18	35	20	15	6
1960	1,081	16	56	1	18	3
1965	1,745	7	69	0.7	16	0.5
1970	2,822	6	74	0.1	16	0.3

Source: Adapted from Sepúlveda and Chumacero, *La inversión*, Table 1.

Table 3 / Foreign Investment: Selected Areas of Industry, 1950–70

Field	% of Total for Each Field				
	1950	1955	1960	1965	1970
Food products	12	8	7	7	7
Tobacco	12	10	3	4	3
Textiles	2	2	3	2	2
Rubber	10	7	9	5	4
Chemicals	26	27	35	30	30
Metal products	3	3	4	5	6
Machinery					
(not electrical)	1	4	3	5	5
Electrical equipment	5	9	9	8	10
Transportation	13	10	6	13	10

Source: Adapted from Sepúlveda and Chumacero, *La inversión*, Table 2.

products, tobacco, and rubber, while it rose in chemicals, metal products, and equipment.

Since foreign capital is concentrated in industry, we should examine that sector more closely. Do foreign firms dominate the industrial sector? The answer depends very much on how the question is analyzed. One starting point is to examine the prominence of foreign firms among the giants of the Mexican economy. Data presented in Table 4 show foreign firms to represent 20 percent of the 50 largest nonfinancial firms and 32 percent of the 500 largest. These data, however, define a foreign firm as one with 25 percent or more foreign capital and thus include as foreign certain mining companies in which foreign ownership is now limited to 34 percent, or Westinghouse's large manufacturing affiliate, in which Westinghouse owns only 26.5 percent. In a list of the 50 largest companies in Mexico, one finds that there is no foreign capital represented among the top 20.[10] Only 12 firms among the remaining 30 have some foreign participation, and in several cases majority control is in Mexican hands. In general, it does not appear that foreign capital dominates the giants in the Mexican economy.

More detailed analyses, however, have argued that foreign firms do dominate the industrial sector. Using a broad sample of foreign firms operating in different sectors, Fernando Fajnzylber found that foreign firms account for 35 percent of total industrial production and represent 45 percent of the share capital of the 290 largest industrial firms.[11] The influence of foreign capital is magnified because it is mostly found in sectors dominated by a few firms. Fajnzylber constructed a ratio of con-

Table 4 / Ownership Distribution of Largest 500 Nonfinancial Firms, 1972

| | Total Foreign | | Mexican | | | | | |
| | | | Private | | State | | Total | |
Size Class	Number of Firms	%	Number of Firms	%	Number of Firms	%	Number of Firms	%
Largest 50	10	20	19	38	21	42	40	80
51–100	23	46	18	26	9	18	27	54
101–100	35	35	52	52	13	13	65	65
201–300	34	34	57	57	9	9	66	66
301–400	27	27	48	48	25	25	73	73
401–500	32	32	63	63	5	5	68	68
Total	161	32	257	51	82	16	339	68

Source: Richard S. Newfarmer and Willard F. Mueller, *Multinational Corporations in Brazil and Mexico: Structural Sources of Economic and Noneconomic Power*, Report to the Subcommittee on Multinational Corporations of the Committee on Foreign Relations, U.S. Senate, August 1975; adapted from Table 3-4 on p. 53.

centration which measured the percentage of production represented by the four largest firms in each sector. He found foreign firms dominant in sectors with high ratios of concentration. Where the ratio of concentration was 75 percent or more, 71 percent of total production came from foreign firms; where the ratio of concentration was 25 percent or less, only 13 percent of total production came from foreign firms.[12] This finding is supported by a U.S. Senate subcommittee study of U.S. firms operating in Mexico.[13] This study found that U.S. firms tend to operate in highly concentrated markets in Mexico and that they are frequently the leaders within those markets. Over 86 percent of firms surveyed ranked themselves among the four leading firms of their main product line, and 44 percent ranked themselves first.

Fajnzylber also developed interesting data comparing foreign with national firms. The general conclusions are not surprising. Foreign firms are more capital-intensive than national firms, have higher labor productivity, pay higher wages, and own larger plants. These characteristics led to a further finding that foreign firms are growing more rapidly than national firms; between 1962 and 1970, they grew at an average annual rate of 17.4 percent, while Mexican firms grew at a rate of only 11.0 percent. A parallel finding was that sectors dominated by foreign firms grew more rapidly than sectors dominated by Mexican firms. These conditions threaten to denationalize Mexican industry.

The U.S. Senate subcommittee study of U.S. companies operating in Mexico noted a similar trend toward denationalization resulting from foreign acquisition of Mexican firms. Table 5 traces a steady rise of new manufacturing affiliates established by acquisition of a Mexican firm, from 6 percent in 1946–50 to 75 percent in 1971–72. The study further showed that these were not all failing firms. In the year prior to takeover, 74 percent of the acquired firms were profitable, one-half earning 9 percent or more before taxes.

The conclusion which emerges from these studies is that the dynamic area of Mexican industry is dominated by foreign firms, and that this domination is growing. There is, however, a significant qualification to this conclusion. The data on which it is based define a foreign firm as one with 25 percent or more foreign ownership. I suggested earlier that state policy was oriented toward meeting the political challenge of foreign capital while accepting negative social and economic consequences. The political challenge is substantially met if foreign capital is in a minority position within a firm. Because the analyses summarized above do not distinguish between minority and majority foreign ownership, they reveal little about how successfully this political threat has been met. Indeed, proper analysis would probably establish several categories of foreign ownership, to distinguish, for instance, among 25 percent, 49 percent, 51 percent, and 75 percent ownership. Unfortunately, the various studies of foreign capi-

Table 5 / Percentage of New U.S. Manufacturing Affiliates Established by Acquisition

Time Period	% Established by Acquisition	Number Newly Established
Prior to 1945	9	35
1946–50	6	18
1951–55	11	18
1956–60	39	54
1961–65	43	60
1966–70	64	77
1971–72	75	32
Total, all periods	43	294

Source: Newfarmer and Mueller, *Multinational Corporations,* Table 4-4, p. 68.

tal in Mexico do not rigorously distinguish between majority and minority ownership. Available data are suggestive, however.

Table 6 shows the percentages of production in selected industrial sectors accounted for by firms with majority, minority, and no foreign ownership. Only 17 percent of total industrial production was by firms with majority foreign ownership: the balance was roughly evenly divided between firms with minority or not foreign ownership. Market shares of majority foreign-owned firms ranged from 54 percent in textiles and 46 percent in chemicals to zero in several other areas. Thus, when viewed with this distinction in mind, the role of foreign firms in the industrial sector appears less awesome.

Analysis of data on market concentration of U.S. affiliates suggests that concentration is highest where minority ownership is most prevalent (Table 7). The three sectors with greatest market concentration are rubber (80 percent), primary and fabricated metals (72 percent), and instruments (80 percent). Of U.S. affiliates surveyed, an average of 19 percent were minority owned, but in these three sectors 25 percent, 24 percent, and 29 percent were minority owned. This suggests that market concentration is more common in the industrial sector as a whole than in majority foreign-owned firms, since concentration seems to be even greater where Mexican capital is dominant.

The implication of this is that, despite the importance of foreign capital in industry, its political challenge is not overwhelming. While the presence of foreign capital may distort industrialization and increase inequality, management control is largely in Mexican hands and so accessible to state pressure and economic policy signals. The state thus retains power. However, meeting this political challenge has remained the major theme of Mexican policy on foreign capital, and several signficant measures have been taken since 1970.

Control of Foreign Investment

In July 1970, shortly before Echeverría took office, an important decree was promulgated prohibiting foreign investment in certain well-established and important economic activities.[14] It reserved five sectors to the state and eight others to companies wholly owned by Mexicans. The sectors closed to foreign investment were electricity, banks, insurance companies and related financial services, and all the areas previously reserved for majority Mexican ownership, such as communications, transportation, and fishing. This merely ratified practice which had developed informally, since these areas were all dominated by Mexican firms.

The decree also extended the requirement of majority Mexican own-

Table 6 / Foreign Investment in Industry, 1969

Sector	% of Sales Accounted for by Firms with:			Total Sales (Millions of Pesos)
	Majority Foreign Ownership	Minority Foreign Ownership	No Foreign Ownership	
Textiles	54	39	7	3,134
Vehicles	—	100	—	1,996
Beverages, tobacco	—	8	92	3,250
Construction	—	15	85	558
Paper	30	—	70	1,231
Chemicals	46	16	38	727
Mining	—	79	21	1,763
Others	—	79	21	1,122
Total	17	43	40	13,781

Source: Adapted from Sepúlveda and Chumacero, *La inversión*, table on pp. 30–31.

Table 7 / Majority Ownership and Market Concentration of U.S. Affiliates in Mexico, 1972

	% of U.S. Affiliates Minority Owned	% of U.S. Affiliates with Market Share of 25% in Their Product Line
Food	6	30
Textiles	0	50
Paper	0	8
Chemicals	21	38
Rubber	25	80
Stone, glass, clay	44	44
Primary & fabricated metals	24	72
Nonelectrical machinery	17	63
Electrical machinery	13	57
Transportation	36	50
Instruments	29	80
Other	9	45
Total	19	46

Source: Richard S. Newfarmer and Willard F. Mueller, *Multinational Corporations;* adapted from Tables 4-8 and 4-14 on pp. 73 and 84.

ership to steel, cement, glass, fertilizers, cellulose, aluminum mining, chemicals, and rubber. In some cases, such as steel, this formalized what had already been achieved, but in other cases the decree would strongly affect new investments. Moreover, since these restrictions applied to expansion programs of existing companies, they represented a strong incentive for such companies to seek local partners. This resulted in several large firms selling majority control to Mexican groups in the 1970s.

Two later decrees also formalized previous practice.[15] A decree of February 1971 reserved the basic petrochemical industry to the state and required 60 percent Mexican ownership for companies processing petrochemicals; 66 percent Mexican ownership was required in mining companies. A decree of October 1972 required 60 percent Mexican ownership in companies manufacturing auto parts.

The most far-reaching set of restrictions since the 1930s, however, was contained in the Law to Promote Mexican Investment and Regulate Foreign Investment, passed in February 1973.[16] In addition to incorporating and reaffirming all previous restrictions, it required that all new companies have at least 51 percent Mexican capital irrespective of activity.

The law further established a National Commission on Foreign Investment which was empowered to approve or reject foreign investment in new or established companies. It laid down 17 criteria to be considered in deciding whether a proposed investment would be permitted and what percentage of foreign ownership would be allowed. The criteria reflected considerable sophistication in identifying and examining areas of potential abuse and gave the Commission broad discretion to evaluate proposed investment. Some of the more important considerations in evaluating proposed investment are:

1. It should not displace national enterprises which are operating satisfactorily, nor enter fields adequately covered by such enterprises.

2. It should have beneficial effects on the balance of payments and on increasing exports.

3. It should not occupy a monopolistic position in the national market.

Other factors to consider are:

4. The effects which it may have on employment, both as to the level of employment which will be generated and the remuneration which will be paid, should be taken into account.

5. The use and training of Mexican technicians and administrative personnel should be taken into account.

6. The degree to which operations are financed from foreign resources.

7. The contribution to the development of undeveloped zones and regions.

The long-range effect of the law will depend on the interpretations and regulations of this Commission. There are indications that, by mid-1975, the Commission had begun to examine proposed investments more critically, and it issued various resolutions establishing harsher and more specific criteria than previously.[17]

In addition, the law moved to curb two practices which have been much criticized, the use of *prestanombres* and the acquisition of existing companies. *Prestanombres* (literally, "borrowed names") are Mexicans who hold shares in trust for foreigners, giving them control in violation of Mexicanization regulations. The 1973 law tightened existing law by requiring that all shares owned by foreigners be issued to them and not in bearer form, and that foreigners owning shares in Mexican companies register their ownership. Further, it established criminal penalties for violations. Conversations with Mexican businessmen suggest that the use of *prestanombres* will wither in response to these regulations.

To restrict foreign acquisition of existing companies, the National Commission on Foreign Investment was empowered to review all new foreign investments, including acquisitions. The Commission has stated that it will not approve new investments which simply acquire an existing Mexican company without adding significant new technology or managerial know-how. The policy has apparently been successful, for the study of U.S. acquisitions cited earlier noted that "apparently because of changes in the Mexican law, the acquisition rate has declined since 1972."[18]

Complementing the law regulating foreign investment was a law regulating royalty and licensing agreements, also passed in 1973.[19] Under the law, a Registry of Technology was established to review all such agreements. Such agreements permit a foreign company to charge a Mexican company for technological or marketing know-how. When properly used, they represent a politically innocuous form of foreign capital, since no ownership or management control need pass with the know-how.

As numerous commentators have complained, licensing agreements lend themselves to abuse.[20] Fees are often excessive and the technology outmoded or unsuited to the local market. Restrictions are sometimes imposed which impede the firm from exporting or producing other products and are thus detrimental to the country. Such agreements are sometimes made between a parent and its subsidiary; since royalty payments are a valid business deduction for tax purposes, they can be used to remit untaxed profits.

The law has two purposes: to prevent abuses and to assist Mexican entrepreneurs in negotiating with foreign firms. The first is relatively straightforward. Criteria such as price, term, export restrictions, and purchase requirements are established and each proposed agreement is examined. If an agreement is judged too harsh, it is denied registration. In the Registry's first 15 months of operation, it denied about 35 percent of proposed agreements. Most will be redrawn and resubmitted on terms more favorable to Mexico.

The second purpose, to assist Mexican entrepreneurs in their negotiations, is more interesting and illustrates the informal control of foreign capital. Since the staff of the Registry reviews all proposed licensing agreements, it can compare terms. It can then help each Mexican firm obtain the most favorable terms drawn from all previous agreements. Camp and Mann have cited the case of a licensor in the chemical industry which had renegotiated a proposed $4 million royalty to $2 million. The licensor was advised by the Registry that similar technology was available from another country for $100,000. The Mexican firm subsequently obtained this price from the original licensor.[21]

There are other instances of informal pressures under this law that are designed to increase Mexican control in industry. While the law does not deal specifically with Mexicanization, the Registry applies different criteria depending on the degree of foreign ownership. For instance, the

Registry prohibits trademark royalties to 100 percent foreign-owned companies, permits 0.5 percent royalties with 49 percent ownership, and permits 1.0 percent royalties with no foreign ownership. Similar practices may be expected in other areas.

The restrictions summarized above are essentially directed toward maximizing Mexican management control and thereby maintaining state power. For reasons analyzed by Villarreal elsewhere in this volume, Mexico's need for foreign capital inflows grew during precisely the period when the state was imposing restrictions on direct investment. As a result, foreign indebtedness grew at a more rapid rate. This may be seen in Table 8, which compares foreign direct investment with foreign debt. They were about the same in 1965–67, but by 1975 total foreign debt was two and a half times total foreign direct investment. Although this may worsen balance-of-payments pressures in the future, it challenges state sovereignty less than direct investment, since the use of loans is determined by the borrower, while the use of direct investment is determined by the investor. A Marxist author has drawn a similar conclusion in analyzing U.S. development in the nineteenth century. He writes that "foreign capital did not apparently jeopardise its independence. That is because the users of the capital were not its provider and were not very subject to their control."[22]

Table 8 / Comparison of Foreign Direct Investment and Foreign Debt, 1961–75 (Dollar Figures in Millions)

Year	Total Foreign Direct Investment	Total Foreign Debt Outstanding	Foreign Debt as % of Foreign Investment
1961	$1,130	$ 981	87
1965	1,745	1,771	102
1966	1,938	1,974	102
1967	2,096	2,176	104
1968	2,316	2,483	107
1969	2,576	2,915	113
1970	2,822	3,260	116
1971	3,018	3,711	123
1972	3,208	4,257	133
1973	3,495	5,627	161
1974	3,857	7,627	198
1975	4,219	10,578	251

Sources: 1961–70 debt figures from *Bond Prospectuses*. Total Foreign Investment from Sepúlveda and Chumacero, *La inversión*, through 1970. Thereafter calculated by adding new foreign investment and debt from balance-of-payments statistics taken from *Comercio exterior de México*, vol. 22, no. 4 (April 1976).

Political Consequences

Mexico's strategy with respect to foreign capital has had important internal political consequences. First, since the State took the lead in controlling and directing the activities of foreign capital, the State grew stronger. Only the State had the resources to confront foreign capital and offer an alternative. Hence it was inevitable that, regardless of ideological leaning, the State became more and more active in the economy. The State not only nationalized industries such as oil, electricity, and railroads but was also the only available investor to salvage ailing but economically important firms. Furthermore, only the State commanded sufficient resources to develop basic industries like steel or fertilizers, where foreign capital was not desired. As Derossi observes, "The state has not limited its role to supplying nurturing encouragements [to Mexican entrepreneurs] but has also acted as a counterweight, balancing the power foreign firms might derive from their higher investment capacity and greater technical experience."[23]

The result is a large State sector. Regrettably, there are no detailed studies of State participation in the economy analogous to those made of foreign capital. However, we do know that the State controls all utilities and dominates basic industries and finance. A report issued by the Ministry of National Patrimony in June 1975 covering 50 State-affiliated enterprises estimated their value added to be about 10 percent of GNP. Though no estimate of total production was given, this would normally translate to about 25 percent of GNP.[24] Investments are concentrated in such basic industries as banking, steel, fertilizers, mining, energy, and tourism, but they cover a bewildering array of activities in hundreds of firms.[25] Most are wholly stateowned entities, but many are mixed firms, some with foreign capital and some with the State as a minority partner. Table 9, which shows a representative list of some of these, illustrates the range of activities and the varied pattern of State ownership.

The State has always acted within a capitalist context, however, and has encouraged private national capital where possible. The State has viewed its role as complementing, not replacing, private capital. Mexicanization requirements have therefore benefited Mexican entrepreneurs enormously, since foreign firms have been forced to take Mexicans as partners—often as majority partners. According to Derossi, the pressures went beyond the written law: "even though this may not be formally acknowledged, domestic industries are given preferential treatment by Government."[26] In order to develop a strong private sector capable of interacting with foreign capital as equal partners, the State also established a variety of government agencies and programs designed to aid Mexican firms. The most important is Nacional Financiera, S.A., which variously

Table 9 / State Participation in Some Representative State Enterprises

Enterprise	% State Participation	Total Assets (Millions of Pesos)
Química Fluor, S.A. de C.V.	17	500
Minera de Cananea, S.A.	26	1,242
Teléfonos de México, S.A.	51	12,198
Mexicana de Cobra, S.A.	44	5,000
Tereftalatos Mexicanos, S.A.	35	800
EXIMIN, S.A.	50	5
EXMEX, S.A.	51	3
Minera Lampazos, S.A.	32	30
Cia. Minera Cedros, S.A.	20	16
Exportadora de Sal, S.A.	25	400
Cia. Minera Autlan, S.A.	51	317
Cia. Exploradora de Istmo, S.A.	64	291
Cia. Minera Nacozari, S.A.	15	10
Banco Internacional, S.A.	51	2,700
Consorcio Minero Benito Juárez-Pena Colorada, S.A.	53	616
Siderúrgica Lázaro Cárdenas-Las Truchas, S.A.	*	6,560
Motores Perkins, S.A. de C.V.	67	125
Fábrica Nacional de Máquinas Herramientas, S.A.	50	30
Tabamex, S.A.	52	153
Azufrera Panamericana, S.A.	96	514
Univex, S.A.	10	624
Renault Mexicana, S.A.	40	175

*Pending subscription

Source: *Comercio exterior de México*, vol. 19, no. 12 (December 1973).

acts as lender, guarantor, or investor to assist the growth of Mexican firms.[27]

The result is that the powerful Mexican industrial private sector has been an indispensable ally in what would otherwise have been a one-sided confrontation of Mexican entrepreneurs with foreign capital. The state has promoted the strength of the industrial private sector in several ways. It has kept foreign capital out of certain sectors. It has required foreign firms to take Mexican partners, and in the future will require all foreign firms to have majority Mexican partners. It has restrained the denationalization of Mexican industry by putting strict limits on foreign acquisition of Mexican firms. And it has provided financing on special terms to Mexican firms to help equalize their competitive disadvantages.

The private sector has obviously supported these measures. However, it has apparently not initiated pressure for them. Although there are no studies of decision making, most observers share the impression that the state itself has initiated restrictions on foreign capital. The state seems to be prompted less by a desire to favor the upper classes than by a commitment to nationalism and to the protection of its own authority from the challenge to sovereignty posed by foreign capital. This view is consistent with the Purcells' argument that there is an identifiable state interest different from and independent of that of the private sector,[28] and is consonant with the view of the Mexican state developed by José Luis Reyna in this volume.

If correct, this view also extends Peter Smith's finding, reported in this volume, that Mexican political and business elites spring from different educational, occupational, and social origins. I have suggested that State policies which have benefited the industrial elite have sprung from different concerns and have been undertaken without particular pressure from that elite. This underlines the independence and autonomy of the two elites.

This suggestion helps explain an interesting anomaly of the Mexican system. Although the business elite have obviously benefited enormously from state policies, they share a distaste and disdain for politicians. They have been particularly critical of and alienated from the Echeverría administration, even though Echeverría promoted the most comprehensive protection of Mexican enterprise from foreign capital. An explanation might be that the Mexican business elite have received benefits without having had to ally themselves politically with the State. The benefits were conferred by the State to further its own goal of maximizing control over the economy. The business elite and the State are therefore not as close as the coincidence of class interest and state policies would suggest. This implies that the political restraints on State policies which challenge business interests may not be as strong as some have believed. Whether State policies and business interests diverge will be one of the most significant questions to follow during the López Portillo administration.

Notes

1. The potential role for foreign capital and Mexico's ability to absorb it was studied closely by Mexican economists at the time. For a fascinating volume summarizing how official economists thought Mexico could and should use foreign capital, see R. O. Mena, V. L. Urquirdi, A. Waterston, and J. H. Haraldz, *El*

desarrollo económico de México y su capacidad para absorber capital del exterior (Mexico, D.F.: Nacional Financiera, 1953).

2. This argument is given sophisticated expression by S. Nymer, "The Multinational Corporation and the Law of Uneven Development," in J. N. Bhagwati (ed.), *Economics and the World Order* (New York: Macmillan, 1972), pp. 113–40. Also see R. Vernon, *Sovereignty at Bay* (New York: Basic Books, 1971).

3. The classic and best statement of this argument may be found in O. Sunkel, "Big Business and 'Dependencia': A Latin American View," *Foreign Affairs*, vol. 50 (April 1972): 517–31. Also see Ronald Müller, "Poverty Is the Product," *Foreign Policy*, no. 13 (Winter 1973–74): 71–103.

4. For an excellent statement of this position, see P. Streeten, "Costs and Benefits of Multinational Enterprises in Less-Developed Countries," in J. H. Dunning (ed.), *The Multinational Enterprise* (London: George Allen and Unwin, 1971).

5. See also René Villarreal, "El desequilibrio en el crecimiento económico de México: su naturaleza y mecanismo de ajuste óptimo; devaluación, estabilización y liberalización," *El trimestre económico*, vol. 41, no. 164 (October–December 1974).

6. Flavia Derossi, *The Mexican Entrepreneur* (Paris: Development Center of the Organization for Economic Co-operation and Development, 1971), p. 69.

7. Bernardo Sepúlveda and Antonio Chumacero, *La inversión extranjera en México* (Mexico, D.F.: Fondo de Cultura Económica, 1973), Table 11.

8. *Ibid.*, Table 14.

9. *Ibid.*, p. 79.

10. The list may be found in David Barkin, "Mexico's Albatross: The United States Economy," *Latin American Perspective*, special issue entitled *Mexico: The Limits of State Capitalism*, vol. 2, no. 2 (Summer 1975): 68.

11. Fernando Fajnzylber, "Las empresas transnacionales y el sistema industrial de México," *El trimestre económico*, vol. 42, no. 168 (October–December 1975): 909–10.

12. *Ibid.*, p. 911.

13. See Richard S. Newfarmer and Willard F. Mueller, *Multinational Corporations in Brazil and Mexico: Structural Sources of Economic and Noneconomic Power*, Report to the Subcommittee on Multinational Corporations of the Committee on Foreign Relations, United States Senate, August 1975, p. 82.

14. The decree is discussed in detail in *Comercio exterior de México*, August 1970.

15. These are discussed in Newfarmer and Mueller, *Multinational Corporations*, p. 58.

16. This discussion is based on the summary of the law prepared by the company Price Waterhouse y Cia. of Mexico City, and published as its *Boletín informativo*, no. 7 (1973).

17. See lead article in *Business Trends*, vol. 5, no. 458 (November 17, 1975).

18. Newfarmer and Mueller, *Multinational Corporations*, p. 68.

19. This discussion is based on Hope H. Camp, Jr., and Clarence J. Mann, "The Mexican Law Regulating the Transfer of Technology—Summary to Date," unpublished mimeo by Council on the Americas, October 1974.

20. The leading work in this area has been done by M.S. Wionczek. See, e.g., his "Los problemas de la transferencia de tecnología en un marco de industrialización acelerada: el caso de México," *Comercio exterior de México*, September 1971; and M. S. Wionczek, G. Bueno, and J. E. Navarrete, *La transferencia internacional de tecnología al nivel de empresa: el caso de México*, mimeo prepared for División de Hacienda Pública e Instituciones Financieras, United Nations, 1971.

21. Camp and Mann, "The Mexican Law."

22. Bob Sutcliffe, "Imperialism and Industrialization in the Third World," in Roger Owen and Bob Sutcliffe, (eds.), *Studies in the Theory of Imperialism* (London: Longman Group, 1972), p. 175.

23. Derossi, *The Mexican Entrepreneur*, p. 89.

24. This is reported in *Comercio exterior de México*, September 1975, pp. 344–48.

25. One list shows 249 enterprises in the public sector. There are surely many more now, since that list was prepared prior to the Echeverría administration. See "Esquema del sector público mexicano," provided by Directorio de Organismos Decentralizados y Empresas de Participación Estatal, Secretaría del Patrimonio Nacional, undated mimeo believed to have been prepared around 1970–1971.

26. Derossi, *The Mexican Entrepreneur*, p. 82. Derossi also confirms my impression that limitations on foreign capital in Mexico are stricter than anywhere else in Latin America (see p. 89).

27. The activities of the state and particularly of Nacional Financiera in assisting Mexico's industry are described in rich detail in Robert T. Aubey, *Nacional Financiera and Mexican Industry: A Study of the Financial Relationships between the Government and the Private Sector of Mexico* (Los Angeles: Latin American Center, University of California, 1966). Also see Charles W. Anderson, *Bankers as Revolutionaries: Politics and Development Banking in Mexico* (Madison: University of Wisconsin Press, 1963).

28. See John F. H. Purcell and Susan Kaufman Purcell, "Mexican Business and Public Policy," in James Malloy (ed.), *Authoritarianism and Corporatism in Latin America* (Pittsburgh: University of Pittsburgh Press, 1977).

Does Mexico Have a Power Elite?

PETER H. SMITH

Virtually all the other essays in this book focus on efforts by the Mexican state to encourage, promote, and defend the development of a capitalistic economic system. Within this perspective it is understandably tempting, and thoroughly reasonable, to conclude that Mexico's political decision-makers operate in conscious behalf of the country's capitalists. The circumstantial evidence gives rise to a compelling syllogism: national entrepreneurs have benefited from government policy, politicians have made government policy, *ergo* politicians have been purposely serving the interests of entrepreneurs. Despite its revolutionary origins, the state, in this view, does not represent an autonomous source of decision-making strength; rather, it reflects and perpetuates the prevailing distribution of socio-economic goods throughout the society at large. Political power goes hand in hand with economic power, and Mexico remains under the firm control of a united, purposeful, exclusive ruling class.

A forceful and articulate formulation of this idea has come from Alonso Aguilar, who, along with other contributors to *El milagro mexicano*, identifies the nation's ruling stratum as "the bourgeoisie." Neither homogeneous nor monolithic, this class has various components, mainly defined by control over means of production—landowners, merchants, industrialists, financiers, and, last but not least, politicians:

> if one could speak of a bureaucratic or governmental bourgeoisie, it would contain the numerous current and former public functionaries who have made great fortunes through their offices (*a la sombra de sus puestos*) and who have sizable investments in farms and ranches, in urban real estate, in luxurious homes, in national and foreign banks and in businesses of the most varied kinds, but who are fundamentally considered to be politicians. To this sector

129

would belong well-known ex-presidents of the Republic, prominent cabinet members, directors of national institutions and state-supported companies, high military officials, governors, deputies, senators, many municipal presidents and not a few labor leaders.[1]

Accounting for less than 2 percent of the economically active population, by Aguilar's estimation, the Mexican bourgeoisie constitutes "a well-defined class, which has grown out of a long historical process and which possesses an ever-clearer sense of its common interests." It is led, at the top, by *la verdadera oligarquía*, a close-knit group of uppermost leaders from each of the component sectors. With more conviction than evidence, Aguilar assures us that "The fundamental thing [about this group] is not the tie to any particular activity, either by itself or in conjunction with others, but the close intercommunication, even the fusion of interests that exists among the upper strata of the bourgeoisie."[2]

But is this true? Does Mexico have a power elite? Phrased in this fashion, the question reveals the enduring legacy of C. Wright Mills. But it is important to remember, and Aguilar would appear to agree, that a "power elite" is not just a minority of people who possess predominant shares of power. As Mills defined the concept, referring to the United States of the mid-1950s: "By power elite, we refer to those political, economic, and military circles which *as an intricate set of overlapping cliques* share decisions having at least national consequences. In so far as national events are decided, the power elite are those who decide them" [emphasis added]. It was the linkages between the political, economic, and military hierarchies that provided the basis for unified action, and the consequent existence of a monolithic elite, and these linkages took three fundamental forms. One was common social background: "In so far as the power elite is composed of men of similar origin and education," Mills wrote, "in so far as their careers and their styles of life are similar, there are psychological and social bases for their unity, resting upon the fact that they are of similar social type and leading to the fact of their easy intermingling." A second linkage grew out of institutional connections, as men moved smoothly from one circle to another, articulating common points of interest and creating complex webs of interlocking directorates. Third, particularly in times of crisis, component segments of the power elite engaged in explicit coordination of various sorts.[3]

In this essay I shall explore the linkages, real or imagined, between political and economic decision-making groups in contemporary Mexico. The task is difficult and delicate, not only because of weaknesses in data but also because of conceptual and methodological problems in the Mills approach.[4] Before moving on to the substantive analysis, therefore, it is necessary to establish the boundaries of this inquiry.

The Problem

My intent is to describe and comprehend some central characteristics and interrelationships of the stratum, strata, or groups that, in Mexico, appear to have exerted predominant influence on key decisions relating to the course of the nation's economic development. Unfortunately, there is very little information on decision-making processes in Mexico, given the propensity for secrecy among upper-level circles, so it is not possible to identify the powerful as those who have triumphed in cases of conflict.

Who possesses power? Even a casual reading of superficial evidence, plus a dose of common sense, would suggest the existence of seven main strata, or categorical groups, with identifiably direct interests in economic policy: workers, peasants, landowners, financiers, national industrialists, foreign investors, and the state. From other essays in this volume— particularly those by Eckstein and Montes de Oca— it is abundantly clear that labor and the peasantry exercise virtually no power over key decisions. Despite their numerical importance and their institutional status within the Institutional Revolutionary Party (PRI), as well as other structures, Mexico's masses are the objects of unceasing (and effective) manipulation, coercion, and control.

It is extremely difficult to say how power is distributed among the other groups. Foreign investors possess considerable influence, to put it mildly, if only by virtue of the capital, technology, and other resources at their disposal. As Richard Weinert shows in his essay, the control of foreign capital, moreover, tends to be concentrated—mainly among multinational companies based in the United States—a fact promoting unity of action in political and economic spheres.[5] Likewise, the Mexican private sector reveals a pattern of concentration and coordination among its component parts—landowners, merchants, financiers, industrialists. The most visible expression of this situation is the preeminence of about a dozen or so investment groups, generally known by the names of their leaders or dominant families (Luis G. Legorreta, Raúl Bailleres, Carlos Trouyet, Bruno Pagliai, Luis Aguilar, the Garza Sada clan, etc.). Instead of specializing within limited fields, these groups typically have complex webs of interests in finance, industry, commerce, and real estate. Organizations within a group work closely together, and there have been alliances between different groups as well.[6] The domestic private sector is far from monolithic, of course, but horizontal linkages of this kind obviously tend to blur distinctions between component segments of it.

The position of the public sector is equally hard to determine. Contrary to the frequently drawn picture of an omnipotent state, several observers have recently noted that governmental expenditures in Mexico have amounted to less than 10 percent of the gross national product, well under average rates in the rest of the world.[7] By 1970, as José Luis Reyna points out in his essay, public investment had declined to around one-third of total investment. In an arresting (if impressionistic) essay, Manuel Camacho has also argued that the economic strategies of the 1950s and 1960s strengthened political and economic "fiefdoms," such as the family-run investment groups, with a concomitant loss of national governmental authority.[8] At the same time, it is undeniably true that political authorities wield major power over development decisions, partly through direct public investment. A more important source of governmental influence is, however, indirect: controls over credits, imports, licensing, and public facilities. Applied in a particularistic (rather than universalistic) way, these regulations provide the State with crucial leverage. As Raymond Vernon said some years ago, "The important point is that the private sector operates in a milieu in which the public sector is in a position to make or break any firm."[9] At this stage of my argument, it does not so much matter if the Purcells are correct in arguing that the State is *more* powerful than the business sector, though I happen to agree.[10] What is clear, and what does matter, is that government officials command impressive power resources.

In order to explore the question of whether Mexico has a power elite, in the Millsian sense, I shall here attempt to analyze relationships and interconnections between political and economic elite groups. Consistent with Mills's formulation of the problem, I specifically propose to examine linkages between these sectors by focusing upon their *social background*, their *career patterns*, and their *modes of interaction*. Because of its relatively minor, albeit substantial, role[11] I shall omit explicit consideration of the Mexican military. Despite their undeniably major role, I shall also leave out foreign investors, since my primary concern lies with the structure of power within *Mexican* society.[12] Even then, I shall concentrate exclusively on the national level; and most of my empirical data are drawn from the 1950s and 1960s, so they shed no direct light on changing patterns in the 1970s. The analytical scope of this study is therefore rather narrow, and the factual information is generally weak. In most instances, I shall have to depend on speculation, suggestion, hypotheses, and even innuendo.

Most of the data for my analysis come from two sources. For politicians, particularly in regard to their social background and career patterns, I shall work with portions of collective biographical material compiled for an as yet unfinished research project on political leadership in twentieth-century Mexico.[13] For data on the economic elite, I shall rely largely, almost exclusively, on Flavia Derossi's study of *The Mexican Entrepreneur*.[14] One limitation of the Derossi book is that it deals with leaders of the *industrial* sector and touches only in passing on bankers, merchants, and other economic groups. Nevertheless, among privately dominated areas of the economy, it is the manufacturing sector which has grown most rapidly since the 1940s,[15] and it is this sector which would therefore seem to have gained the most from government policy. If there has been collusion between the state and private capital, it ought to show up first—and most strikingly—as collusion between the politicians and the industrialists.

Social Background

As indicated above, one of the central characteristics of a power elite (as envisioned by Mills) is common social origin. The question seems deceptively simple: Do politicians and industrialists in contemporary Mexico come from the same sort of background? Would they be likely to have, in Mills's phrase, "psychological and social bases for their unity"? Or do they represent divergent social types?

In an effort to cope with this problem, I shall compare characteristics of Derossi's industrialists, whom she interviewed in the late 1960s, with those of people who held national political office at any time between 1946 and 1971 (a period stretching from the ardently pro-industrial administration of Miguel Alemán through the first years of the Echeverría regime, at which point the data-gathering phase of my research came to an end). Because of uncertainty over comparability between the economic and political groups,[16] I shall work with two sets of politicians: first, a so-called "total" elite for the 1946–71 era, which includes ambassadors (in prestigious posts), deputies, senators, governors, members of the National Executive Committee of the PRI, directors of leading state-supported agencies and companies, members of the cabinet, and presidents ($N = $ 2,008); and, second, an "upper-level" elite embracing only presidents, cabinet ministers, heads of the PRI, and directors of major state-supported agencies and companies ($N = 159$).[17]

Thus identified, Mexico's industrialists and politicians differ in basic respects. According to Derossi, about 20 percent of the entrepreneurs were foreign-born. Considering the birthplace of parents and grandparents, too, it appears that 44 percent of the industrialists were of foreign origin, and to this extent they were newcomers (or outsiders) to Mexican society.[18] In sharp contrast, and partly due to legal restrictions on officeholding, government leaders were overwhelmingly native-born, with well under 1 percent of either political elite having been born abroad. I do not have solid data on the birthplaces of their fathers or grandfathers, but my impression is that Mexico's political decision-makers have tended to come from native stock.

The fathers of entrepreneurs and politicians differed also in their occupations. Table 1 displays the Derossi findings plus my own effort to arrange the (very inadequate) data in a comparable way.[19] Derossi's categories might seem questionable, especially insofar as they distinguish between the middle and the upper class, but the value of the table does not hing entirely upon the precision of the groupings.

The implications are profound. For one thing, it is clear that neither industrialists nor political leaders came in substantial measure from the lower class. Though a fair share (24 percent) of the total officeholding elite came from lower-class backgrounds, *none* of the upper-level politicians had fathers in such occupations, and the same is true for the industrialists. For people starting at the bottom of the social ladder, upward mobility was almost as hard to attain through politics as through business.[20]

At the same time, it is equally clear that industrialists and politicians came from separate strata. According to Derossi's scheme, 54 percent of the entrepreneurs were from the upper class, while the political elites were predominantly middle-class in origin (64 percent for the total group, 82 percent for the top-level group). Even more revealing are the specific kinds of fathers' occupations. Nearly half the industrialists (46 percent) had fathers who were industrialists. Another sizable share (24 percent) had merchant origins. Just about half the governmental officeholders, for their part, came from backgrounds in the professions, civil service, politics, or the military—occupations that brought their fathers into, or at least close to, the political arena. To a considerable extent, therefore, both the economic and political elites have tended to pursue the same sorts of occupations as their fathers. This does not necessarily attest to the existence of family dynasties (though there have surely been some). What it does show is that, with respect to occupation, economic and political leaders have emerged from distinctly separate and partly self-perpetuating social backgrounds.

In some other respects, however, the two groups had similar backgrounds. Both came from urban areas. According to Derossi, 69 percent of the industrialists were born in cities.[21] Though my data have been compiled in a different manner, it is clear that national political leaders were overwhelmingly of urban origin: about half the total elite came from relatively major cities,[22] very often the state capitals, while nearly two-thirds of the upper-level group came from sizable cities. In short, Mexico's entrepreneurs and officeholders both shared the manifold advantages of urban life, one of which is access to education.

Presumably in cumulative fashion, the middle-to-upper class backgrounds and urban life styles of the two elites combined to produce similar educational profiles. As shown in Table 2, both the entrepreneurs and the politicians achieved extremely high levels of education, 68 percent of the industrialists having gone to a university, compared with 73 percent of the

Table 1 / Father's Occupation for Entrepreneurs and Politicians

			Politicians			
	Entrepreneurs		Total Elite		Upper-Level Elite	
Occupation[a]	($N=139$)[b]		($N=192$)[c]		($N=33$)[d]	
Upper class						
Industrialist	60		2		1	
Banker	3		1		0	
Rentier	3		1		0	
Landowner	9		17		4	
Other	0		2		1	
Subtotal	75	(54%)	23	(12%)	6	(18%)
Middle class						
Merchant	33		8		4	
Employee	18[e]		5		1	
Civil servant			5		2	
Professional	13		47		10	
Military	0		16		2	
Politician	0		25		3	
Other	0		17		5	
Subtotal	64	(46%)	123	(64%)	27	(82%)
Lower class						
Worker	0		7		0	
Peasant	0		22		0	
Other	0		17		0	
Subtotal	0	(0%)	46	(24%)	0	(0%)
Total	139	(100%)	192	(100%)	33	(100%)

[a]Categorization and class groupings based on Flavia Derossi, *The Mexican Entrepreneur* (Paris: Development Center of the Organization for Economic Co-operation and Development, 1971), p. 160.

[b]Raw figures computed from percentage data in Derossi, *The Mexican Entrepreneur*, p. 160.

[c]Total N for entire group is 2,008.

[d]Total N for entire group is 159.

[e]The number 18 here is a combined figure for employees and civil servants.

total officeholding elite and 87 percent of the upper-level elite. Parenthetically, the data contain some further implications—suggesting, for instance, that a university experience is a more stringent requirement for political success than for economic attainment—but the basic message is unequivocal. In a society where less than 3 percent of the literate adult male population had attended a university (as of 1960), the industrialists and the politicians both tended to come from the uppermost stratum of advantage. To the extent that educational opportunity reflects "class" status, that is, the distribution of "life chances," it must be concluded, as Aguilar maintains, that Mexico's economic and political elites have grown out of a single and highly privileged class.

But this does not necessarily mean that they went to school together, or that they forged lifelong ties of friendship while at university. Impressionistic evidence indicates that many of the industrialists attended technical universities, such as the Instituto Politécnico Nacional in Mexico City or the Instituto Tecnológico de Monterrey. The politicians, by comparison, showed a strong tendency to cluster together at the National University (UNAM). And even if budding entrepreneurs and future officeholders attended the same institution, their paths may still not have crossed. Among the university-educated industrialists in the Derossi sample, 75 percent had "technical" training, 12 percent studied the "humanities," and 13 percent majored in "business."[23] Since the distinction between technical and humanistic subjects is not spelled out, I cannot order available data in strictly comparative fashion, but my information demonstrates that

Table 2 / Educational Background of Entrepreneurs and Politicians

		Politicians	
Level of Education	Entrepreneurs $(N=143)^a$	Total Elite $(N=1,371)^b$	Upper-Level Elite $(N=151)^c$
Primary or less	2%	6%	0%
Secondary	13	3	3
Higher	17	18	11
University	68	73	87
Total	100%	100%	101%^{d}

[a]Flavia Derossi, *The Mexican Entrepreneur* (Paris: Development Center of the Organization for Economic Co-operation and Development, 1971), p. 164n.

[b]Total *N* for entire group is 2,008.

[c]Total *N* for entire group is 159.

[d]Percentages do not add up to 100 because of rounding.

political cadres tended to specialize in selected fields: those whom Vernon called *políticos* had studied law (by far the most common), engineering, medicine, and education; almost by definition, the *técnicos* had gone to schools of economics (which is to be distinguished from business or accounting). The material suggests that the economic and political elites tended to concentrate in different faculties, even when at the same university, and the chances for forming friendships—or what Mills would call the "psychological and social bases for their unity"—would thereby be diminished.

This point finds further reinforcement in the occupational patterns followed by the politicians (aside from the pursuit of governmental office). Despite imperfections in the data,[24] Table 3 yields two suggestive findings: first, that politicians engaged heavily in the professions (such as doctors, teachers, journalists, and especially lawyers), and second, that they did not, as a rule, join the "ownership" stratum of Mexican society. Officeholders, that is, did not become participating members of the upper economic circles.

In summary, the data on social background produce paradoxical results. On the one hand, it appears that Mexico's economic and political elites have emerged from a common class background—with middle- to upper-class fathers, urban life styles, and exceptional educational privilege. On the other hand, they have also differed—in their national origins, in the specific occupations of their fathers, in the subjects they studied, and in the occupations they pursued. Following the Derossi notion of class (reflected in Table 1), one might conclude that industrialists came from upper-class backgrounds and politicians from middle-class backgrounds. Adopting a somewhat broader view of class, perhaps stress-

Table 3 / Occupational Background of Politicians

Occupational Stratum	Total Elite ($N=1,429$)[a]	Upper-Level Elite ($N=153$)[b]
Worker or peasant	6%	less than 1%
Employee	4	less than 1
Professional	84	91
Owner	6	8
Total	100%	101%[c]

[a]Total *N* for entire group is 2,008.

[b]Total *N* for entire group is 159.

[c]Percentages do not add up to 100 because of rounding.

ing educational opportunity, one might alternatively conclude that *entre-preneurs and officeholders emerged from a single class, but from demonstrably different segments of that class.* Either way, the basic inference remains: the starting points for the two groups were not the same.[25]

Career Patterns

The hallmark of the industrialists' careers in Mexico has been consistency. As already noted, especially in Table 1, entrepreneurs tended to follow occupational patterns established by their fathers. Perhaps reflecting the achievements of their parents, who might have provided necessary start-up capital, more than a third of the industrialists in the Derossi sample (34 percent) went directly into business without acquiring any prior job experience. This pattern was more apparent among those of urban origin than among the rural group, whose fathers and grandfathers were often engaged in agriculture, but it still represents a substantial portion of the total sample.[26]

Of the two-thirds that acquired prior experience, most took jobs in private Mexican-owned industry (43 percent of the entire sample). Some worked for foreign-owned firms, either in Mexico or abroad (14 percent combined). Others started out as self-employed professionals (7 percent), and some engaged in commerce. Only a tiny portion (1 percent) gained experience in the semipublic sector—a figure suggesting that, contrary to possible expectation, state-supported companies have not provided an arena for steady interaction between entrepreneurs and politicians.[27]

It thus appears that most aspiring young businessmen set out in determined pursuit of particular skills, either technical or organizational. The apprenticeship could take quite a long time, often more than ten years, but by the end of this period the great majority had performed important leadership functions. Derossi cites some illustrative cases of deviations from the norm—such as the highly trained electronic technician who went into the cosmetics industry for a fortuitous reason (he married the boss's daughter!)—but the general rule still holds: these men began as entrepreneurs, they worked as entrepreneurs, and they achieved as entrepreneurs.[28]

One thing they have *not* done frequently has been to take overt part in politics. Among the Derossi group, only 12 percent actively participated in political organizations of one sort or another (she does not say which ones).[29] Though precise figures are unavailable, there can be little doubt that an even smaller proportion of the country's leading businessmen acquired governmental office. This does not indicate whether or not there has been constant interaction between the entrepreneurial and political spheres, a theme that I will take up further below. But it does indicate that there has been very little positional crossover from business careers to political ones—in contrast with the United States, where lateral entry into politics has been fairly commonplace.

The careers of Mexican politicians have in some ways been similar to those of the entrepreneurs. Like their industrial counterparts, would-be officeholders started pursuing their goals shortly after finishing their education (and some began while still in school). Within the entire 1946–71 political elite, for example, over 50 percent are known to have started taking an active part in politics before the age of thirty, most commonly in their late twenties. Again reflecting the small degree of lateral entry, less than 10 percent of the group entered formal politics beyond the age of fifty, and many of these were labor-union activists whose roles had long been quasi-political. Though aspiring politicians often began in other occupations, or engaged in professional practice (such as law) even while holding office, a basic dictum has nevertheless been apparent: those who get ahead start young.

Political careers in Mexico have been extremely intense. The norm has been for people, once started in government, to hold between four and six positions, usually in rapid-fire succession. These posts have often been unrelated to each other. It is true, as I have demonstrated elsewhere,[30] that three institutional grooves or "tracks" are discernible: an *executive* track, linking the federal bureaucracy to the cabinet; an *administrative* track, contained within the semipublic sector; and an *electoral* track, tying the official party to legislative and other elected positions. Like the budding industrialists, individuals moving along one of these institutional routes would seem to have acquired specific, task-related skills in a cumulative fashion. Nevertheless, the majority of job changes have not taken place within the tracks. From almost any location in the political system, an ambitious officeholder could entertain at least some hope of moving to almost any other location. Diversity and breadth of exposure, rather than concentrated apprenticeship, have set the predominant pattern.

Just as political careers have started early, they have also tended to end speedily. For a variety of reasons, including the principle that no president can be re-elected, turnover in office has been extraordinarily rapid. A person who has reached national office under one president has had about a 1 in 3 chance of holding a comparable position under another president. A large-scale change in personnel has thus taken place with every sexennial change in the presidency, and those who disappear from the national scene rarely return.[31]

Consequently, most Mexican politicians have left their last major national office while still fairly young—on the average, around the age of fifty-seven. To state the point another way, nearly 25 percent of the total

1946–71 elite left their last office before the age of fifty, over 34 percent did so while in their fifties, and the rest (a minority of about 40 percent) did so at a later age. For most officeholders, the likelihood of such a relatively youthful exit has no doubt had profound implications—making it both desirable and reasonable, for instance, to accumulate as much wealth as possible before their tenure is up.[32]

The age of exit raises another critical question: What have the politicians done afterward? Unfortunately, I do not have any solid data on this matter. It would appear that many of them have set up private professional practices, most commonly in law. Some have moved into private industry, but in restricted ways, usually in fields such as construction where they can make use of their political contacts. Others have obtained minor but useful jobs as "advisers" to friends still holding political office. At any rate, it does not appear that ex-politicians have crossed over into industrial positions any more than industrialists have gained lateral entry into politics. Skills for the two careers have not been viewed as interchangeable, and the "intermingling" between the groups, in Mills's sense, would be accordingly reduced. Yet it is still plausible to suppose that ex-politicians have often served as functional *intermediaries* between the private sector and the state. That is a topic for further research.[33]

Among officeholders in the public sector, there is reason to suspect that *técnicos* have had greater opportunities for crossing over to the private sector than have the *políticos*. Government officials have often held multiple jobs, with economic specialists frequently sitting on the boards of state-supported companies and other corporations; in return they have received handsome fees. By relaying tips on policy to private companies, some decision-makers have no doubt used public knowledge for private gain. And, as almost all observers have stressed, bribery—of both *políticos* and *técnicos*—appears to have been widespread. Such ties between public officials and private interests have been, in Vernon's view, "part and parcel of Mexican life. . . . Any major shift in the existing relations between the private and the public sectors could well disturb the characteristically profitable ties which key public officials have managed to develop with the private sector." The situation, he concludes, offers little incentive for a radical reorientation of governmental economic policy.[34] Within this context, the question still remains: What has been the nature of the relationships between officials and businessmen in Mexico?

Modes of Interaction

One of the central postulates in the Mills formulation was that, in times of crisis, segments of the power elite would act in conscious and explicit coordination. Yet it was precisely on this point that his analysis was weakest. As Robert Dahl insisted, Mills never explored the decision-making process during any crisis, so there is no demonstrable evidence of any such coordination.[35] Referring loosely to the "big decisions" of the 1940s and 1950s, Mills mentioned the dropping of the atom bomb on Japan, the reaction to Korea, the ultimately fateful response to Dienbienphu—issues involving foreign policy, it should be noted, usually decided by the U.S. President and his close advisors.[36] To explore actual linkages between public officeholders and private investors in Mexico, therefore, we cannot rest content with information on social background and careers. Even if the leaders of the sectors are distinct in these respects, as the data so far show, they might still have acted in collaboration.

Since the mid-1940s, in fact, Mexican entrepreneurs and politicians seem to have agreed on at least two basic guidelines for governmental economic policy. One has held that the state should permit the entry of desirable foreign capital but at the same time protect national industry from excessive international competition, principally through import controls and regulations on foreign investment.[37] The other guideline, firmly documented by other essays in this book, has assigned to the state the role of controlling and, when necessary, repressing the masses—the workers, the peasants, and the poor. Together, these policy orientations have furnished a reasonably coherent and workable prescription for maintaining the country's capitalist system.

Within this general consensus, however, specific measures have prompted frequent and substantial disagreement. In the first place, the government has taken steps of its own design that have met with widespread opposition from the business community, some of whose members hold profound *laissez-faire* convictions.[38] Second, and probably more important, the entrepreneurial sector has been far from monolithic—what is good for industrialist A has not always been good for industrialist B (tariff protection for A, for instance, could increase production costs for B). In illustration of these points, respondents in the Derossi sample came up with the results in Table 4 when asked for their opinions of governmental policies. Clearly, industrialists have often been at odds with the state (though not so much regarding labor policy); almost as frequently, they have been at odds with each other. Regrettably, Derossi did not explore the relationships between responses, so we cannot tell if individual businessmen tended to support or oppose the government across the board or to hold selective opinions on specific issue-areas; we do not know how they viewed the policies most directly related to their own companies; nor can we judge the intensity of the responses. Despite these shortcomings, the message still seems unambiguous: there has been considerable conflict between the private and the public sectors.

Table 4 / Entrepreneurs' Evaluations of Government Economic Policies (in Percent; N = 143)

Policy	Favorable	Neutral	Unfavorable
Credit	46	23	31
Fiscal	40	24	36
Pricing of finished products	33	36	31
Pricing of raw material	19	27	54
Import	27	33	40
Customs duties	20	30	50
Export	25	45	30
Labor	41	35	24

Source: Derossi, *The Mexican Entrepreneur*, p. 61.

From the entrepreneurs' point of view, cases of disagreement have been exacerbated by the temporary and discretionary quality of governmental decisions. Permits and licenses can always be revoked, a situation that has made private investors dependent on the state. As an example, listen to the complaint of this entrepreneur:

> The price of containers, both metal and cardboard, is excessive in Mexico. In Mexico metal containers for food cost approximately double their price in America. *At one stage I was allowed to import cans in bond but the permit was not renewed* and I had to fall back on the high-priced domestic article. . . . Were the government to allow the import of Japanese sheeting the price of cans would be halved [emphasis added].[39]

Such disputes have often centered on the implementation of existing law, rather than on the formulation of new laws, with the result that industrialists have engaged in various maneuvers, including bribery, to influence the judgment of the bureaucrats and politicians.

The rapid and periodic rotation of political personnel has affected the interaction between entrepreneurs and officeholders in many ways. For one thing, it has increased the element of risk for industrialists. If their investments depend on some sort of permit, they know that the future holder of the relevant office might or might not extend the particular license. In order to forestall any unfavorable change, the logical strategy for entrepreneurs would be to identify, and curry the favor of, the up-and-coming politicians—as well as the incumbents. This kind of activity demands skill, tact, and usually some inside information. It is an area where ex-politicians could play important roles as go-betweens.

Paradoxically, the high rate of turnover in politics would also appear to give the industrialists a significant advantage in some situations. Because the personnel in upper-level private industry is (or seems to be) stable, it has been possible for entrepeneurs to develop relatively coherent demands, to unify their forces, to muster appropriate technical documentation, and to maintain steady pursuit of incremental concessions and gains. Politicians, by contrast, because they change office so frequently, have often found it difficult to accumulate comparable amounts of expertise, though this problem has been less acute for highly trained *técnicos* than for others. Even more important is the fact that each new set of officeholders must strike its own bargain with the entrepreneurs. If the politicians appear to be favorably disposed toward business, private-sector leaders can seize the opportunity to step up their demands and seek ever-greater concessions. But if the predisposition of the politicians appears to be unfavorable, private-sector leaders have the option of refusing to negotiate and waiting out the difficulty; at least within the short run, time is on their side. And yet this kind of advantage, strategic as it may be, probably pertains only to specific issue-areas that (1) have low public visibility and (2) involve cohesive segments of the entrepreneurial sector. On broad questions of governmental policy, as shown in Table 4, the private sector can suffer internal division, thus affording politicians the chance to play businessmen off against each other.

Given the importance of individual discretion in government policy-making, it is revealing, and somewhat surprising, that industrialists have tended to seek redress for grievances largely through institutional means. As shown in Table 5, fully half the respondents in the Derossi sample said they would seek to counteract unfavorable policies through formal industrial associations (CONCAMIN, COPARMEX, CANACINTRA, etc.). A fairly small minority (12 percent), apparently disaffected, felt that no meaningful action would be possible. About one-quarter, 23 percent to be exact, would rely on an informal pressure group. Only 15 percent thought that individual action might be useful.

To an extent, the tendency to rely on associations is entirely rational. Regulated by national law, Mexico's business organizations have considerable resources at their disposal. Membership in one or another of the key associations is obligatory (there are, in addition, voluntary groupings). Partly as a result of this requirement, the important national organizations have solid financial resources with which they can maintain a paid staff. Their leaders maintain informal contacts among themselves and sometimes act in coordination. Moreover, representatives of these associations often sit on government boards, they consult with political leaders, and they have developed varied channels of communication with policy-making officials.[40]

Table 5 / Modes of Action to Counteract
Unfavorable Government Policies, as
Perceived by Entrepreneurs (in Percent;
N = 136)

Mode	Response
None possible	12
Possible on individual basis	15
Possible through informal pressure group	23
Possible through industrial associations	50
Total	100

Source: Derossi, *The Mexican Entrepreneur,* p. 40n.

Even so, the responses to the Derossi survey convey two further messages. One is the assumption, based on the figures in Table 4, that relationships with political decision-makers can often be of an adversary character. Another is the entrepreneurs' sense of social distance from the politicians. A combined total of 62 percent of the respondents thought effective action was either impossible or attainable through a formal institution. Only 38 percent believed that informal approaches would work, mostly through a collective pressure group, and informality, it should be noted, does not always bespeak harmony: bribery is needed primarily to soften discord. Though a great majority of entrepreneurs (88 percent) expressed feelings of efficacy in dealing with the politicians, in short, they would mostly do so on an adversary basis.[41] The evidence does not present a picture of relaxed and intimate chats among old boyhood chums.

In further testimony to the social distance between the two elites, Mexico's entrepreneurs appear to have an extremely low opinion of political officials. One item in the Derossi survey solicited views on the relative prestige of various occupational groups. The respondents displayed considerable esteem for bankers, industrialists (that is, themselves!), and intellectuals and professionals, in that order. Only 9 percent rated politicians and public officials as commanding the highest prestige, and 34 percent ranked government officeholders as the group of lowest prestige (see Table 6 for a full summary of the data). Attitudes of this sort would hardly seem consistent with the easygoing, familiar intermingling of

Table 6 / Ranking of Prestige Groups by Entrepreneurs

Group	Rankings of Highest Prestige (N Responses = 136)	Rankings of Lowest Prestige (N Responses = 129)
Bankers	42%	2%
Industrialists	26	1
Intellectuals and professionals	18	7
Politicians and public officials	9	34
Priests	4	7
Army generals	1	20
Landowners	0	8
Union leaders	0	18
Merchants	0	3
Total	100%	100%

Source: Derossi, *The Mexican Entrepreneur,* pp. 182, 186.

decision-making cliques that Mills detected within the North American power elite.

Unfortunately, I do not know of any solid data on the politicians' perceptions of Mexican entrepreneurs. Quite clearly, government policy-makers have regarded a vital private sector as essential to national economic growth and as a bulwark against excessive inroads by foreign oligopoly interests. And yet the terms of this collaboration with the business community—what Clark Reynolds has called an "alliance for profits"[42]—seem to reflect suspicion. Making exhortations sound like accusations (or vice versa), presidential speeches have often urged Mexican capitalists to act for the national good instead of for private gain (the latter being the presumption). In the early 1960s, Vernon reported a generalized picture of businessmen as "ruthless, money-grubbing opportunists, utterly devoid of social consciousness, without culture or refinement, imitating the worst in North American society, extravagant without limit." Even the *técnicos,* committed to mixed-economy growth and presumably friendly to the private sector, tended to view businessmen as narrow-minded, unskilled, and, above all, untrained.[43]

Despite their agreement on certain issues, their unquestioned need for each other, and their common commitment to a capitalistic pattern of growth, it thus appears that entrepreneurs and politicians interact in an atmosphere of uncertainty, distrust, suspicion, and even disdain. In essence, they are locked in a tacit struggle for supremacy. The industrialists have been seeking to expand their profits, accumulate capital, and keep governmental regulation to a necessary (albeit critical) minimum. The politicians, for their part, have been attempting to gain and assert control over the entrepreneurial sector. Toward this end they have established (and regulated) the business associations, they have set up an impressive array of licensing arrangements, and, symbolically enough, they have kept big business out of the PRI, thus maintaining the ability to apply pressure on the industrial community.[44]

In summary, relations between entrepreneurs and politicians have rested upon three premises: (1) the popular masses, especially labor, should be kept under control; (2) the public and private sectors must often act in explicit coordination; and, given these conditions, (3) entrepreneurs and politicians can still compete for relative superiority. These three assumptions, paradoxically related to each other, find expression in multiple ways, one of the best-known being the profit-sharing decision of 1961–63. In belated fulfillment of a key clause in the 1917 Constitution, this law seemed on its face to constitute a major victory for labor, since workers would henceforth share in the profits of the company owners. The amount of profits to be shared was so small as to be acceptable to employers, however, and the law was never strictly enforced. So labor had a paper triumph and business had successfully defended its own interests. But by proposing the legislation without consulting business leaders, the politicians displayed their willingness and ability to take autonomous action. And, by getting the law on the books, the politicians acquired another weapon with which they could, in the future, threaten or challenge private capital.[45] A subtle game, this.

Conclusion

Much of the contact between economic and political elites in Mexico remains invisible, at least to scholarly eyes, so it is impossible to draw firm conclusions about the existence of interlocking directorates. The subject stands in need of research, and we need solid information on specific types of elite relationships: socialization patterns, informal associations, kinship networks, decision-making processes. Within the limits of available data, however, we can still focus on the question: Does Mexico have a power elite?

The answer appears to be no. This does not mean that Mexico is an egalitarian society. To the contrary, the data on father's occupation in Table 1 indicate that people of lower-class origin have virtually no chance of gaining access to the upper circles of influence and authority. Moreover, as shown in Table 2, university training constitutes a near-requisite for entering either the economic or political elite, with the result that power is restricted to a tiny fraction of the population. Despite the rhetorical legacy of the Revolution, Mexico remains under the effective control of a small and classbound minority.

Yet a defining characteristic of the power elite, as Mills used the term, was the existence of *overlapping cliques* that, by virtue of their common origin and training, intermingled with each other. This does not seem to hold true for entrepreneurs and politicians in Mexico. Although members of the two elites may have come from the same class background, the data on father's occupation and the prevalence of foreign origins among the industrial group suggest that they came from separate segments of this class. They went to different schools, even while reaching comparable levels of educational achievement. They started their respective careers at relatively early ages, and, once started, they tended to concentrate exclusively upon their separate arenas. Entrepreneurs hardly ever moved into politics and, to the best of our knowledge, government officeholders (with the possible exception of some *técnicos*) did not cross over into private industry (Table 3) before retiring from politics—if even then. Throughout their dealings with each other, often marked by conflict (Table 4), the industrialists and politicians seem to have maintained a sense of social distance (Table 5) plus an admixture of mutual disdain (Table 6).

Instead of a unified power elite, Mexico therefore appears to have a fragmented power structure that is dominated, at the uppermost levels, by two distinct and competitive elites. They have specific common interests, most notably in the continuing subordination and manipulation of the masses and in the promotion of capital accumulation. But aside from this implicit consensus, and the collaboration needed to maintain it, these elites are at the same time struggling for control of the country's development process—and for supremacy over each other. While the leaders of the Mexican state thus attempt to stimulate growth and change within a *capitalistic framework*, they are not operating primarily in behalf of the *capitalist class* (or individual entrepreneurs). From the viewpoint of the state, after all, the private sector represents the major source of rival power.

What I mean to suggest, in conclusion, is that the processes of political recruitment in Mexico have tended to foster the articulation of a relatively autonomous "state interest." Officeholders have come from reasonably uniform social origins, and together they have carved out whole careers within the political realm. It would therefore seem natural for them to identify their interests with those of the state, as distinct from any other social sector. As it turns out, what has been good for the state has been good for the country's capitalists. But this concurrence is a result of governmental policy, rather than the guiding motive for it. In principle, this relationship could change at any time, at least in degree if not in kind, and the threat of such a change constitutes one of the public sector's major weapons in dealing with the private sector.[46]

In operation, Mexico's authoritarian regime thus reflects constant interplay between a relatively coherent state interest and a somewhat less coherent set of business interests. One consequence of this situation has been a considerable degree of flexibility for the formulation of state policy and the regime's ability to play off one actor (or businessman) against another has enhanced its stability and strength. In recent decades, the political and economic elites have maintained a tacit, though uneasy, alliance, in part because of a lack of perceived plausible alternatives. It is possible, but unlikely, that the active pursuit of the state interest will increase the level of conflict in the future.

Notes

1. Alonso Aguilar M., "Problemas y perspectivas de un cambio radical," in Fernando Carmona et al., *El milagro mexicano* (Mexico, D.F.: Editorial Nuestro Tiempo, 1970), p. 311.

2. *Ibid.*, pp. 312, 315. For other comments on the existence of a power elite in Mexico see Robert E. Scott, "Mexico: The Established Revolution," in Lucian W. Pye and Sidney Verba (eds.), *Political Culture and Political Development* (Princeton: Princeton University Press, 1965), pp. 377–384 and esp. p. 380.

3. C. Wright Mills, *The Power Elite* (New York: Oxford University Press, 1959), pp. 18–20. Aguilar does not make explicit reference to *The Power Elite*, but his depiction of Mexico's ruling class has a definite Millsian ring (note, for instance, the phraseology on p. 315 of the essay on "Problemas").

4. For ample presentation of these matters, see G. William Domhoff and Hoyt B. Ballard (eds.), *C. Wright Mills and the Power Elite* (Boston: Beacon Press, 1968).

5. See also Bernardo Sepúlveda and Antonio Chumacero, *La inversión extranjera en México* (Mexico, D.F.: Fondo de Cultura Económica, 1973); and, for a highly polemical statement, David Barkin, "Mexico's Albatross: The United States Economy," *Latin American Perspectives*, vol. 2, no. 2 (Summer 1975): 64–80.

6. Robert T. Aubey, *Nacional Financiera and Mexican Industry: A Study of the Financial Relationships between the Government and the Private Sector of Mexico* (Los Angeles: Latin American Center, University of California, 1966), pp. 76–78.

7. Clark W. Reynolds, *The Mexican Economy: Twentieth-Century Structure and Growth* (New Haven: Yale University Press, 1970), pp. 266–69. Recent changes in tax laws appear to have had a minor impact on this situation.

8. Manuel Camacho, "El poder: Estado o 'feudos' políticos," *Foro internacional*, vol. 14, no. 3 (January–March 1974): 331–51. For suggestive statements on the historical evolution of the Mexican state, see Juan Felipe Leal, "The Mexican State 1915–1973: A Historical Interpretation," *Latin American Perspectives*, vol. 2, no. 2 (Summer 1975): 48–63; and Lorenzo Meyer, "El Estado mexicano contemporáneo," *Historia mexicana*, vol. 23, no. 4 (April–June 1974): 722–52.

9. Raymond Vernon, *The Dilemma of Mexico's Development: The Roles of the Private and Public Sectors* (Cambridge, Mass.: Harvard University Press, 1963), p. 26.

10. John F. H. Purcell and Susan Kaufman Purcell, "Mexican Business and Public Policy," in James Malloy (ed.), *Authoritarianism and Corporatism in Latin America* (Pittsburgh: University of Pittsburgh Press, 1977).

11. On the army's current political roles, see David F. Ronfeldt, "The Mexican Army and Political Order since 1940," paper presented at the Fourth International Congress of Mexican Studies (Santa Monica, California, October 17–21, 1973).

12. It is not uncommon, however, for Mexicans to function in behalf of foreign interests (as, for instance, *prestanombres*). To this extent, international forces, both private and governmental, have gained indirect representation within Mexican society, and it is accordingly impossible to exclude foreign influence completely from any rigorous conceptual consideration of the country's social structure.

13. A description of the project appears in my research note on "Elites, Revolution, and Authoritarianism: Political Recruitment in Mexico, 1900–1971," *Latin American Research Review*, vol. 10, no. 1 (Spring 1975): 183–86. The machine-readable dataset contains information on 6,302 individual officeholders, and it can be obtained (with permission) from the Data and Program Library Service at the University of Wisconsin at Madison.

14. Flavia Derossi, *The Mexican Entrepreneur* (Paris: Development Center of the Organization for Economic Co-operation and Development, 1971).

15. Timothy King, *Mexico: Industrialization and Trade Policies since 1940* (London: Oxford University Press, 1970), pp. 16–17.

16. Derossi interviewed a stratified random sample ($N = 143$) of owners or general managers of private Mexican industrial firms with at least 5 million pesos capital as of 1965, in four regions: the Distrito Federal and state of México, Nuevo León, Jalisco, and Puebla. It is not quite clear whether the scope of her total target population was owners and/or general managers of the 662 such firms in all of Mexico, owners and/or general managers of the firms of that size in the four particular regions, or "important industrialists" in general. By contrast, my political elites are not samples: except for missing data, they represent total populations in themselves. Note that the total elite ($N = 2,008$) embraces a group that might be roughly similar in size to Derossi's target population (whatever that might be); and the upper-level elite ($N = 159$) is nearly the same size as the sample she interviewed. One way or another, I hope that the comparisons are satisfactory.

17. For more detail on the offices, see my paper on "La movilidad política en el México contemporáneo," *Foro internacional*, vol. 15, no. 3 (January–March 1975): 379–413, esp. 412–13. For almost all variables, missing data will reduce the actual number of observations for the computations. Note, incidentally, the similarity between my political elite and the officeholders mentioned by Aguilar in *El milagro*, p. 311.

18. Derossi, *The Mexican Entrepreneur*, pp. 143–44. For supplementary evidence see Vernon, *Dilemma*, p. 156.

19. As the table indicates, data are available for only small fractions of the political elites, and I have no way of knowing whether the distribution of existing vs. missing data follows any underlying pattern. Accordingly, I cannot say whether the politicians for whom we have data on father's occupation constitute genuinely random samples of the total (target) populations.

20. On entrepreneurs, see also the data in Vernon, *Dilemma*, p. 157.

21. Derossi, *The Mexican Entrepreneur*, pp. 164–65. Derossi defined urban communities as those with 2,000 or more inhabitants, presumably as of 1960. (See also Vernon, *Dilemma*, p. 157.)

22. That is, cities with at least 10,000 inhabitants as of 1921.

23. Derossi, *The Mexican Entrepreneur*, p. 164n.

24. Occupational data are rough and sometimes contradictory. For Table 3 the strata were ranked from low to high, from "worker or peasant" to "owner," and individuals with separate occupations in different strata were placed in the highest available stratum.

25. For additional observations on this point, see Roger D. Hansen, *The Politics of Mexican Development* (Baltimore: Johns Hopkins University Press, 1971), chap. 5, esp. pp. 97–98.

26. Derossi, *The Mexican Entrepreneur*, p. 165. Note also the prevalence of family control of enterprises (pp. 101–02, and, more generally, part I, chap. 3).

27. *Ibid.*, p. 165.

28. *Ibid.*, pp. 165–66.

29. *Ibid.*, pp. 187–88.

30. Smith, "La movilidad política," 395–401.

31. This high degree of turnover has not been caused mainly by aging or mortality, since politicians have tended to reach the national level while still fairly young. For further discussion, see my paper on "Continuity and Turnover Within the Mexican Political Elite, 1900–1971," paper presented at the Fourth International Congress of Mexican Studies (Santa Monica, California, October 17–21, 1973).

32. Some rules of the political game have been spelled out in my paper on "La movilidad política," pp. 405–09.

33. See also the comments in Hansen, *Politics*, pp. 124–29.

34. Vernon, *Dilemma*, p. 153.

35. Robert A. Dahl, "A Critique of the Ruling Elite Model," republished in Domhoff and Ballard (eds.), *C. Wright Mills*, pp. 25–36.

36. Mills, *Power Elite*, p. 22.

37. King, *Mexico*, pp. 60–65 and 74–83. Whether the limitations on foreign enterprise have been sufficient or successful is, of course, a separate question.

38. See Robert J. Shafer, *Mexican Business Organizations: History and Analysis* (Syracuse, N.Y.: Syracuse University Press, 1973), chap. 4; and Merle Kling, *A Mexican Interest Group in Action* (Englewood Cliffs, N.J.: Prentice-Hall, 1961), chap. 7.

39. Derossi, *The Mexican Entrepreneur*, p. 61.

40. Shafer, *Organizations*, esp. chap. 5. It would seem especially sensible for entrepreneurs located at considerable distance from the Federal District to rely on the interest-group organizations. Unfortunately, Derossi has not partitioned responses on modes of countering policy according to region, so we cannot explore this point here.

41. Shafer, *Organizations*, chap. 5. Note also that while Kling asserts that his conservative-minded businessmen had "ready access to key government officials," his evidence actually reveals that members of the Instituto de Investigaciones Sociales y Económicas attended political and governmental functions in rather formal capacities. Kling, *Interest Group*, pp. 41–43 and 66.

42. Reynolds, *Mexican Economy*, pp. 185–91.

43. Vernon, *Dilemma*, pp. 157, 147.

44. Shafer, *Organizations*, p. 135.

45. See Susan Kaufman Purcell, "Decision-Making in an Authoritarian Regime: Theoretical Implications from a Mexican Case Study," *World Politics*, vol. 26, no. 1 (October 1973): 28–54; and Shafer, *Organizations*, pp. 167–68. A book-length version of the Purcell study has been published as *The Mexican Profit-Sharing Decision: Politics and Economic Change in an Authoritarian Regime* (Berkeley: University of California Press, 1975).

46. In a perceptive essay, Nora Louise Hamilton has argued that the Mexican state has become a leading bulwark of capitalism and the bourgeoisie—in spite of efforts by Cárdenas and others to establish governmental independence from social sectors and classes: Hamilton, "Mexico: The Limits of State Autonomy," *Latin American Perspectives*, vol. 2, no. 2 (Summer 1975): 81–108. I am not entirely sure that the process is as automatic as Hamilton suggests; and, even within the functional limits of state autonomy, there is much room for alteration and redefinition of the relationships between state interests and private enterprise.

3

Synthesis and Projection

Redefining the Authoritarian Regime

JOSÉ LUIS REYNA

A new trend in world politics is emerging which challenges the supposed relationship between development and democracy. As capitalist development proceeds, concentration of capital is mirrored by concentration of political power. Put differently, the monopolistic tendency of capitalism requires a monopolistic political structure. The political structure which secures capital's interests is incompatible with real political participation. Corporatism, as a form of domination, can be the political expression of the need for capital accumulation in dependent expanding economies.

A recent current in political science literature reflects this trend in world politics: the study of political domination based on corporatist theory.[1] In a very interesting article dealing with this subject, Schmitter suggestively starts with a proposition taken from Mainolesco, a Rumanian political scientist of the 1930s: "The twentieth century will be the century of corporatism just as the nineteenth century was the century of liberalism."[2]

Corporatist regimes are based on a complex network of organizations that mediate between the various class sectors and the state. The new theoreticians of the state and the "corporate group" argue that organizations and corporations are indispensable for four closely related aspects of political domination: (1) the regulation of class conflict, (2) the rationalization of political procedures, (3) the implementation of political and economic decisions, and (4) the effective execution of the mechanisms of political control on which the state depends. By maintaining political domination, corporatist regimes satisfy a basic requirement of capital accumulation: the regulation of popular demands.

Obviously there is no single model, or pure type, of corporatism. To avoid ambiguity, corporatism will be defined here as the "nuclearization" of politically significant groups in society through a complex network of political organizations relating those groups to the decision-making process. A corporatist political structure tends to eliminate competition for power and emphasize conciliation among different societal groups through their vertical or subordinated relationship to the state apparatus.

Within this general and tentative framework, the development of Mexican capitalism and its political base will be analyzed in order to clarify how and why capital and state are mutually indispensable. This will lead to a discussion of the Mexican system and its chances of survival. It is my view that Mexico is still in a rapid process of "corporatization"; its aim is to promote and expedite capital accumulation in spite of the very high social cost, particularly for significant sectors of the popular classes.

Capital, the State, and the Popular Classes

In many developing countries, capitalism—or as Cardoso has called it, "associated-dependent development"[3]—shows great dynamism. Mexico is one of those cases. Mexico's economy has been expanding continuously. Since 1940, GNP growth has averaged more than 6 percent yearly. Despite a high rate of population growth, per capita annual increase in production has never fallen below 2.5 percent. There is evidence that the pace of growth in the last decade surpassed even that of the 1950–60 period. Industrial production has also shown a systematic upward trend, reaching an average growth of approximately 7.5 percent in the 1940–1970 period.[4]

Mexican capitalist expansion has had a high social cost, however. The trend of income distribution shows that between 1950 and 1969 the top 5 percent more or less maintained their share of family income, the next 15 percent were the real gainers, while the lowest 40 percent suffered a dramatic decline in their share.[5] In Mexico, economic expansion and the concentration of income are closely related processes. The stimulation of demand by selected class sectors more than compensates for the inability of the lowest strata to participate in the consumption process.

The means by which capital has been accumulated, as well as the political mechanisms to regulate demands, have varied over time. During the 1940s and part of the 1950s, the latter were based mainly on repressive measures. Since 1960, the emphasis has been on granting more and repressing less.

In the 1940s, capital formation came mainly from domestic resources, especially during the Second World War,[6] while since the 1950s, particularly since 1955, the strategy of development has been redefined to include the overt participation of foreign capital in the economic process. Foreign capital, or direct investment, was certainly present before 1950,[7] but its presence became more obvious as it played a larger role in the economic process.

This qualitative change in Mexican capitalism must be understood in order to discuss the relationships among three central factors in Mexican society: private capital (both foreign and national), the state, and the popular classes. The state's main goal has been to promote capital accumulation. Toward this end, it has consistently strived to create a favorable climate for private capital.

Foreign investment tends to be attracted to developing areas in part by the existence of a cheap and frequently well-disciplined labor force. Because the state has promoted these conditions in Mexico, foreign capital, which is usually channeled into the most dynamic branches of the manufacturing sector, has participated actively. In 1940, total foreign investment, mainly that of the United States, amounted to $450 million, while in 1974 the figure was close to four billion dollars. Multinational corporations accounted for 9.8 percent of total production in 1970 and for 27.6 percent of industrial production. Chemicals, electrical equipment, and machinery were the most dynamic sectors.[8]

In fact, as Weinert shows elsewhere in this volume, foreign investment in the manufacturing sector grew from 7 to 74 percent of total investment in the sector between 1940 and 1974. The big jump took place between 1955 and 1960, going from 35 to 56 percent of total investment in the sector. The "golden age" of Mexican capital during the 1940s has passed. Mexican capital has become a subordinate, although by no means unimportant, partner in the process of capital accumulation.

Another recent study, by F. Fajnzylber, has concluded that multinational corporations have played a leading role in Mexican industrial activity.[9] As an illustration, foreign capital accounts for approximately 75 percent of industrial production in the noncompetitive economic sectors in which it is mainly located. Furthermore, in those sectors profits are 400 percent higher than in the competitive sectors of the economy in which Mexican capital tends to predominate.[10] At first glance, such a contrast would appear to open the way for conflict. However, there are "conciliatory" links between the national and foreign bourgeoisie: technology, coparticipation in firms, loans, etc.

While there is no possibility of a national development dominated by the national bourgeoisie, the national bourgeoisie is a very important factor, capable of exerting political and economic pressure upon the state. To deny its existence would be to ignore a very important factor in the Mexican political and economic system. The Mexican bourgeoisie participates in the capitalist dynamic, but cannot assume leadership. Its competitors are the state and the foreign bourgeoisie. The history of nineteenth-century Europe will not be the history of twentieth-century Mexico.

   The economic policies of the 1970s have clearly been oriented toward the reinforcement of the Mexican capitalist model, not toward its reorientation and much less toward its replacement. Nonetheless, the bourgeoisie has reacted strongly against the state. Echeverría tried to implement some rather mild redistributive reforms, and the bourgeoisie felt threatened. In spite of this apparent conflict, in my view developments point less to a confrontation between the bourgeoisie and the state than to a permanent redefinition of their respective roles in the decision-making process, particularly in the field of economic policies. The fate of one depends on the fate of the other. The bourgeoisie is the son of the state. I do not think the son will do to the father what Zeus did to Chronos.

   Of course this is not true only of Mexico. What is specific to Mexico is the role of the state, which has been crucial in maintaining the capitalist dynamic. The Mexican state has created a climate very favorable to private investment, not only through attractive incentives such as industrial protectionism or tax exemptions but, perhaps more important, through a very effective political infrastructure which absorbs and neutralizes demands. The corporatist structure of the PRI is one of the key elements in the success of this neutralization process.

   This does not mean, however, that there is no political pressure from below. On the contrary, political pressure is increasing systematically in the form of frequent land invasions by landless peasants (and their frequent "control" or repression by the armed forces) and fragmented but politically significant labor protests. Along with this increase in pressure, the system of regulating political demands has become more effective and more sophisticated. This is why the Mexican political system has so far remained stable and why it would be a mistake to assert that deep changes are likely to occur within it. I shall discuss this point later. The point to make here is that the growth of private investment is related to the creation by the state of optimal economic and political conditions. This is an important explanation of the remarkable development of private capital and its prominence in Mexican society.

   It is difficult to find a case in Latin America where the state has so favored the bourgeoisie. The very real "profit alliance"[11] is stronger now than ever before. As mentioned before, the bourgeoisie and the state are mutually dependent. What members of the bourgeoisie appear to fear is increased state intervention in the economy. Thus in the 1970s, paradoxically, "lack of confidence" has grown despite very high profits for the private sector.

   A recent study shows, for example, that 80 percent of the inflation in Mexico is associated with profits, that 80 percent being an average for all sectors of the economy.[12] Thus the last years have been much better for the bourgeoisie than any other period in Mexican history. This is one of the reasons why a confrontation between the state and the bourgeoisie is very unlikely. They continuously bargain but they do not fight destructively. As the Echeverría administration drew toward an end, the bourgeoisie had begun to understand that the economic policies of the state, including the policies of redistribution, had been generally oriented toward strengthening the economic and political system, not toward weakening it.

Within this context, the Mexican state appears to be strong and still consolidating. So far, it has not faced a political or economic crisis serious enough to threaten the stability of the system. Analysts who argue that Mexico is already in the midst of crisis are wrong. The evidence to which they point can be explained in large part by events being experienced worldwide by capitalism. Considering present economic and political conditions, those who argue that a crisis is unavoidable definitely write without thinking. They are merely provoking false expectations.

An important factor in the creation of a favorable climate for private investment which also promotes the legitimacy of the system is the idealogical theme—stemming from the 1910 revolutionary movement—which links the State and the popular classes. The form of this alliance changes in content depending on the political situation. The State emphasizes, sometimes more, sometimes less, the importance of the alliance, which is always of a formal character. Nonetheless, the relationship is an important source of legitimation which is related to the accelerated rate of capital accumulation.

It is true that there have been moments of conflict that have come very close to crisis, but in each case the crisis has been averted. The 1958–59 labor movement, headed by the railroad union, and the student movement of 1968, which involved other groups as well, seriously threatened the state. The 1968 student movement had a corrosive effect upon the legitimacy of the state, and the state reacted by using its ultimate weapon against danger: repression. As an outgrowth of these events, one of the main objectives of the Echeverría administration was to regain the legitimacy that was lost in 1968. It accomplished this by paying unusual political attention to the popular sectors and by an apparently aggressive foreign policy.

If Mexico is far from the ultimate crisis, it follows that capital accumulation proceeds within a rather solid political framework. What accounts for the stability of the system? I would suggest that it is the corporatist, nonfascist structure of the state, which has been able to regulate conflict, although sometimes through very authoritarian solutions. Schmitter's hypothesis that state corporatism is strongly associated with dependent capitalism is applicable to authoritarian Mexico. At the risk of using labels indiscriminately, I would say that Mexico has a sort of populist corporatism. A centralized political structure, effectively functioning political organizations, mild income redistribution policies, and strong populist rhetoric combine to produce a democratic image. Mexico is in fact a flexible authoritarian polity with a very clear capitalist plan. Consequently, those who describe the present administration as leftist have not understood the dynamic of the system.

What is undeniable, as I have already suggested, is the high social cost of the capital accumulation, particularly for the popular classes. From 1940 to 1955, expansion was accompanied by a substantial decrease in the real wages of the laboring class. From 1955 to 1973, expansion was associated with a rise in real wages. Between 1973 and 1974, mainly owing to inflation, there was once more a mild decrease in real wages. In other words, the huge profits that, as I noted before, significantly contributed to the inflation were also related to a deterioration in labor wages.[13] This is one more reason why the government resorts frequently to populistic rhetoric. Rhetoric neutralizes dissatisfaction.

Unemployment and underemployment in 1975 were tragic problems. In a labor force of approximately 16.5 million, between 5 and 6.5 million were underemployed and almost 50 percent of the total labor force was either unemployed or underemployed.[14] Land for redistribution purposes was almost exhausted, and the migration to and expansion of the cities had made it very difficult to find jobs. The growth in population (in 1975 approximately 50 percent of the total population of about 63 million was 14 years old or less) was placing tremendous pressure on the educational system. The demand, particularly for elementary schools, was greater than the supply; in the middle run this will be a disturbing factor in the economic market and the occupational structure unless significant structural changes occur.

These potentially explosive problems cannot be neglected by the state. Solutions, or partial solutions, must be implemented to assure the functioning of the system as a whole. The system must be reoriented since the growing number of demands, particularly from the masses, could lead to protests and then to destabilization of the system.

A legitimate and expanding system like the Mexican one has an alternative: reform and mild income redistribution policies. These are a key to the permanence of the system. For this reason, the Echeverría administration tried to implement such reforms not only to improve the situation of segments of the popular classes but to prevent a potential destabilization which would seriously affect capital accumulation. In the next section I shall discuss this problem further.

In addition to the situation of the popular classes, the problems of an increasing external debt and a rising balance-of-payments deficit have plagued the Mexican regime (see the essays in this volume by Villarreal and Weinert). Yet neither these economic difficulties nor the polarization of the social structure negate the rationality and the success of Mexican capitalism in terms of capital accumulation. In terms of social costs and the real distribution of wealth, of course, it is far from rational. But it *is* rational in relation to the driving force of the system—capital accumulation.

A Populist Corporatism

Populist corporatism implies political mobilization in order, ironically, to *de*mobilize the class groups that can formulate demands. Populism activates strategic class groups and incorporates them into the state apparatus, controlling and "de-radicalizing" their demands. Depoliticization in the Mexican political system has allowed a sophisticated use of the bargaining process within the limits prescribed by the state. It is an alternative to the indiscriminate use of repressive measures. If the demands were not deflected, they would have to be suppressed; therefore political organizations in Mexico act as "contention barriers."

In my view, bureaucratization of the political process has been at the root of the Mexican political tradition since the 1930s. The resulting class relations make Mexico an authoritarian *regime*, in contrast to Brazil, which is today an authoritarian *situation*.[15] The difference lies in the degree of institutionalization and corporatization (or bureaucratization) of the polity. Populist ideology within a corporatist political regime has prevented the development in Mexico of real and representative political organizations of the popular classes. Those who struggle against the system are vulnerable, because of the institutionalization of the system.

The process of subordinating class groups began with the formation of the Partido Nacional Revolucionario (PNR) in 1929 and its redefinition in 1938 as the Partido de la Revolución Mexicana (PRM). The main innovation of the PRM, in relation to the PNR, was to divide class groups and incorporate them into the party. From that moment, the state explicitly segmented the dominated class—peasants in one organization, workers in another. In this way, the state obtained popular support through interest-representation, while preventing real political mobilization of these sectors. The existence of apparently democratic institutions like the PNR is very important, because they give to the incorporated masses a sense of political participation.

Of course, incorporation in itself is insufficient. Incorporation was combined with the meeting of some demands and the granting of some concessions.[16] It is necessary to give something in order to receive something. Once some benefits were given, the state received disciplined labor and peasant organizations.

The public bureaucracy is organized through unions which are linked to the Party through the popular sector of the PRI; many benefits are granted to them. In addition, the entrepreneurs and merchants are organized in their respective chambers (CONCANACO and CONCAMIN).[17]

Because such political organizations in Mexico claim continuity with the revolutionary movement of 1910, they are important elements in the legitimation process. The legitimate subordination of the dominated classes facilitates the decision-making process, since there is only one real political center. The state can activate or exclude the masses according to the circumstances. In some cases, the state stimulates political mobilization to build legitimacy in a context which does not threaten any institutions. In other cases, it demobilizes through incorporation into existing organizations or those created *ad hoc*, in order to exclude or "de-radicalize" demands that may affect the strategic center of the system, capital accumulation. This scheme has allowed limited expression by the popular sectors, which formally participate but in reality are excluded from decision-making. The state can maintain authoritarian control in an ideological context of class conciliation.[18]

The combination of authoritarian control and a conciliatory ideology has been effective in neutralizing demands, particularly those of a redistributive character. Some redistribution is necessary in a conciliatory political scheme like Mexico's, but the distinctive characteristic of this redistribution is its selective implementation. Moreover, benefits, redistribution policies, and the like come from above, frequently before demands are formulated. Demands rarely come from below, because that would imply genuine mobilization.

The corporatization process in Mexico is closely related to economic expansion. As I argued earlier, Mexico's economic growth has depended on control of the working classes, and this control has been achieved by populist corporatism. This depends on a subtle balance of control from above and populist mobilization to defuse popular pressures. Thus, paradoxically, as economic difficulties emerge, the greater is the likelihood of populist rhetoric. A brief historical look at some developments since 1940 may help us to understand the workings of the corporate state and its relation to economics.

In the 1940s, the conciliatory political scheme worked well; there were very few conflicts. The ideology was national unity directed by the state. In 1942 and 1945, during a period of rapid economic expansion, two pacts showed the corporatist nature of the Mexican state. The 1942 pact, *el pacto obrero,* united different workers' unions in order to fight for national independence, economic development, and, above all, national unity. In 1945, two very different classes were united through the industrialists-workers plan. Conciliation was a basic means for unity and development. In spite of the fact that these pacts did not become organizations, regulation and minimization of conflict was assured and thus the economic expansion was not disturbed. This situation helped to consolidate the national bourgeoisie and to create a strong link between it and the state.

In the early 1950s, economic growth became uncertain. Growth of the GNP slowed, and though the Korean War stimulated the economy, its effects did not last as long as expected. Mexico underwent a relatively severe economic recession, which forced the government to take certain measures, of which two were particularly relevant. In order to prevent inflation, an austerity program was implemented, but it led to an economic contraction. The Mexican peso was devalued in relation to the dollar from 8.65 to 12.50. The devaluation immediately set off an inflationary spiral that mobilized segments of organized labor. According to some unofficial estimates, there were between 32,000 and 50,000 threats of strikes.[19] Nonetheless, only 160 strikes (in the textile and movie industries) actually took place. This demonstrates that the potential mobilization was controlled. The test undergone by the union structures was passed satisfactorily.[20]

Nevertheless, this potential mobilization of 1954 seems to have led to a change in economic strategy in 1955. President Ruiz Cortines (1952–58) appears to have arranged a kind of pact with the labor leadership (the leaders of the CTM). The state implemented a more liberal wage policy in return for a more disciplined labor movement. The year 1955 seems to be the turning point for the recuperation of real wages by urban labor,[21] although the 1939 level was not regained until 1966. Nonetheless, the upward trend after 1955 is very clear. Thus, the near mobilization of the labor class that was provoked by the devaluation was handled skillfully by the labor authorities and the labor leadership; the Ministry of Labor correctly predicted that there would be labor calm within the organized labor world.[22]

This was also the starting point for the creation of a favorable environment for private investment. Foreign investment started to grow significantly in 1955, as has been noted. United States foreign investment grew only 4.8 percent in 1954, while in 1955 and 1956, respectively, the rates were 15.8 and 15.3 percent. In these years, moreover, U.S. investment in the manufacturing sector increased by 26.2 and 20.9 percent.[23] This pattern of growth was completely different from that of the previous years.

While the immediate result of devaluation was inflation, after 1956 inflation was effectively controlled through price-control measures and frequent state subsidizing of basic articles.[24] It was at this moment, I believe, that what is known as *desarrollo estabilizador* (stabilizing development) began. The most distinctive characteristics of this period, which ended in 1970, were steady economic expansion, low rates of inflation, and selective rather than society-wide redistribution policies. Although some labor groups gained large wage increases, peasants, unskilled workers, and the so-called "marginals"—the majority of the population—were losers during the *desarrollo estabilizador*.

Juan Linz observes that one of the characteristics of an authoritarian regime is the lack of extensive or intensive political mobilization.[25] An authoritarian regime has only one very drastic solution to autonomous mobilization: repression. If mobilization of this type occurs, the whole system tends to be volatile. For this reason, in confronting different social movements in the decade 1958–68, the response has been the same: strong repression. Without repression there was the danger of destabilization. The process of consolidation that I maintain the state is carrying on depends mainly on the effective control, regardless of the means, of independent political movements.

In spite of the rise in wages which began in 1955, the state and the union structure faced a severe political conflict in 1958–59. Railroad workers demanded a significant wage boost, which was justified, given economic conditions at the time. Their demand was echoed by many other unions[26] and led to a political movement which overthrew the "official" committee of the union and exerted strong pressure on the state.

The final outcome of the railroad movement was severe repression on the part of the state. The leaders of the movement were jailed; the movement as a whole, exterminated. Other movements, such as those of medical doctors in 1964 and students in 1968, met the same fate. It is not my intention to analyze these movements or to indicate their causes, but merely to note something important shown by these uprisings: as strong as it is, the Mexican political system has difficulty combating independent or relatively independent political movements. The corporate political structure is designed for political manipulation of demands, but it has no structure to absorb autonomous political mobilization. The Achilles' heel of the system may therefore be that sort of political protest.

If these movements were a reaction against the absence of a well-defined redistribution policy, the most potentially reactive group might be the peasantry. It is well known that the agrarian sector entered a crisis after 1967.[27] The rate of growth in this sector fell drastically. Furthermore, only 9 percent of the total land delivered to peasants was arable. In other words, during the Díaz Ordaz administration, 91 percent of the land the peasants received was useless.[28]

It is for this reason that Luis Echeverría started his candidacy for the presidency in 1969 with the rhetoric of populism, despite predictions that he would follow the hard-line politics of Díaz Ordaz. His goal was to rescue the forgotten expressions of populism and revitalize the state's formal alliance with the people. His political imperative was to regain legitimacy, which had been undermined by the political events of 1968. This led to the so-called *apertura democrática* (literally, "democratic opening"), and to mild redistributive reforms, particularly through the tax system.

During the 1970s, difficulties have arisen from the re-emergence of a politically dangerous factor: inflation. This phenomenon was virtually unknown in Mexico during the 1960s, but has led once again to increased demands for redistribution. As I have pointed out, some popular groups, specifically laborers and peasants, have started to intervene more frequently in the political scene. The growing discontent evidenced by this political expression has made necessary the introduction of reforms—in order to maintain the system, not to alter it. There seems to be a correlation between the *apertura democrática*—free dialogue, self-criticism, freedom of expression, reforms oriented toward certain segments of the people—and social movements both rural and urban. So far, the state is in control, but this does not mean that discontent is absent. Consequently, the state's efforts have been directed toward neutralizing demands, mainly through a strong populist rhetoric and some reforms which favor these groups without creating risks for the bourgeoisie. It is a situation of unstable equilibrium. Reforms are necessary both to legitimate the system and to smooth the way for capital accumulation. The problem lies in the fact that capitalist groups do not easily accept reforms.

For this reason, the state is caught between two kinds of pressure: pressure from below, which it must partly respond to and partly repress, and pressure from above, to which it generally responds. To bargain with the dominant classes, the state must be able to count on popular support. To bargain with the popular sectors, the state must be able to count on resources which are mainly produced in the private sector of the economy.

In this dilemma, it is important to note that the state is activist and initiating, not passive and reactive. It undertakes policies designed to prevent problems from arising, or to deflect pressures before they create problems. It must therefore offer something to all groups in a kind of delicate balancing act.

During the Echeverría years, the dominant strategy has been to re-orient the Mexican capitalist system. However, Echeverría has not broken the alliance with the bourgeoisie. I showed earlier how the dominant classes have benefited despite high inflation and a recessionary environment. Weinert's essay in this volume demonstrates how state policies toward foreign capital have favored the bourgeoisie in numerous ways.

Thus the most important alliance, that between the state and the bourgeoisie, has been strengthened.

But within this context significant benefits have been extended to popular sectors, and the state has again actively promoted conciliation. The mild tax reforms of 1971 and 1974 mainly discomforted the middle sectors. These reforms were not designed to raise taxes significantly for the higher-income groups, because that could be a source of conflict; but they did reduce the taxes of those who have less, in accordance with populist rhetoric. The new tax structure (combined with significant price increases in oil, gas, and electricity) led to some redistribution of income. In addition, an attempt was made to protect labor from the severe inflation by granting major increases in real wages. For instance, the September 1974 increase was higher than had been expected. While the most optimistic predictions had been for a 16 percent raise, the real increase amounted to 22 percent. One of the statements made by the President was, "In the fight against inflation, the government is with the laboring class." Nonetheless, as previously noted, *real* wages went down in 1974 compared with 1973.

In 1975, 60 billion pesos were earmarked for agrarian reform. The purpose of the investment was to control peasant protest, given the rather dramatic conditions of the Mexican countryside. The agrarian policy of the Echeverría administration has been to organize various peasant organizations around the Confederación Nacional Campesina. The Pacto de Ocampo was signed, amalgamating all the most important peasant organizations except one, the Central Campesina Independiente, which controls sectors of the independent peasant movement. This was an important step toward the expected imminent creation of the Central Única Campesina.

The Pacto de Ocampo illustrates the conciliatory policy which the state has adopted. It ties the largest sectors of the peasant population more tightly to the state. It decreases the chances of peasant mobilization and creates a favorable climate for large investments by the state. The state is becoming a more important "entrepreneur," not to compete but to try to diversify the mechanisms of capital accumulation and thereby become stronger politically and economically. This will alter the monopoly of capital accumulation in the countryside and may have important consequences in the cities as well. Increased employment opportunities in the countryside eventually may ameliorate the severe problem of urban unemployment and underemployment.

The conciliatory policy is evident not only in the Pacto de Ocampo but also in organizations like the Comisión Nacional Tripartita, in which officials, workers, and entrepreneurs cooperate to propose policies dealing with investments, productivity, employment, and so on. While this type of organization represents different sectors of society, its most outstanding characteristic is that it makes it easy for the state to impose control on the decisions made there. This is also the case with the Congreso del Trabajo, in which most of the labor organizations are represented. The proliferation of organizations gives the state a base for regulating conflict and strengthening its role as arbiter in both the political and economic arena.

Conclusions

The present crisis in world capitalism directly affects Mexican society, at both the political and the economic level. Recent recession in the United States and worldwide inflation have influenced Mexico because of its overwhelming dependence on the American market.

Two trends emerge clearly in the Mexican situation today: (1) There is growing discontent because of the capitalist system itself. The state is finding it more difficult to satisfy diverse demands from different groups. (2) Private capital is becoming increasingly important. Although the state is intervening more in the economy, a trend which makes the bourgeoisie uncomfortable, it is undeniable that the economic growth is due in large part to private capital.

If, in fact, Mexico is "more" capitalist than ever before and, as a result, there is popular discontent, what are the political prospects for the near future? In order to discuss them, it is necessary to formulate some assumptions.

First, I assume that the Mexican state will do its best to rationalize and revitalize the capitalist system. In other words, in the short and middle run, only political alternatives within the capitalist system can be considered. This is not the historical moment to consider analyses that point to the widespread effect of the world crisis on Mexican society or proclaim that the socialist revolution is not far off. The Mexican state is well established and still retaining a monopoly on power in spite of popular pressures. That monopoly is legitimate, and I do not believe it will be threatened in the near future. The Mexican state will continue to have the capacity to bargain and to impose its rule.

Second, I assume that the army is more an instrument of the state than a political competitor of the executive power. It will not intervene in politics. This hypothesis can be substantiated by an interesting study by Margiotta. After analyzing the rather sparse information dealing with the military organization in Mexico, he concludes that one of the keys to the army's nonintervention has been the involvement of the military in politics.[29] The main condition for this has been the existence of a well-developed, powerful party which has been able to coopt the military elite of the nation. Thus, individual officers run for political office, participate in Party decisions, and help select candidates. In other words, the military elite is integrated into the political apparatus. Because they participate in the political game, it is highly probable that the army as an institution will keep out of politics. The Mexican state will remain mainly civilian, although the military will play a more important role in preserving order than in the past because of the increasing political unrest.

Third, I assume that no serious confrontation will take place between the bourgeoisie and the State. The two are readjusting within a rather "new" capitalist system and are cooperating in a common effort, the pursuit of capital accumulation. It is not a question of state capitalism, because of the importance of private capital. It is a question of "private" capitalism where complementarity rather than contradiction is the condition.

Fourth, I do not foresee a confrontation between segments of popular classes and the State in the near future. The absence of well-structured politically autonomous organizations is the main factor tending to eliminate that possibility. The leftist political groups, although some are active, are not closely associated with strategic sectors of society, and they are not unified.

Under these assumptions, which I consider to be realistic, I think that suggestions that Mexico is on the road to a competitive democracy or heading toward a socialist system are both wrong. I am inclined to think that Mexico is on her way to a more authoritarian, corporatist political regime. Social exclusion and high social costs are inevitable within an economic model like the Mexican one. This is the price that must be paid by the dominated class to enable the dominant classes to preserve their power in frank alliance with the State.

Any attempt to democratize the polity will be demagogic. It is rather difficult to democratize a system which is neither prepared to meet the growing demands of different class sectors nor endowed with the financial resources to do so. Mexico does not possess the political structures that allow for real political participation. Social exclusion is more feasible in the near future than the political and economic participation of popular classes. The important elements in the political solution of Mexican capitalism are more authoritarianism, persuasion, cooptation, and repression.

Repression will be more intense because it is becoming more difficult to meet popular demands. Repression will develop along with corporatization, or the embracing of more and more potentially mobilizable groups. The Mexican regime has an enormous capacity to create *ad hoc* organizations that give different groups a place in the political system. I speculate that Mexican authoritarianism will continue to be associated with a sort of protective tutelage—covert repression within the system rather than overt confrontation between groups and the system. The political cost of repression, however, will be to weaken legitimacy.

Given the nature of Mexican capitalist expansion, the state must support some type of redistribution. Without redistribution, there will be an increased likelihood of conflict and consequent instability. I do not think the Mexican state will run this risk. Obviously there will be no overall redistribution policy that would alter the dynamics of the whole system. I visualize instead what I would call selective redistribution, aimed at meeting the demands of groups holding strategic positions in the production process, such as oil, railroad, and electricity workers. They will be provided with increased fringe benefits, and these will be supplemented by a deferred redistribution policy containing a dose of the so-called hope factor, that is, high expectation and little redistribution.

Some redistribution is more congruent with political reality than reliance mainly on force. A regime based on force is weak. What the Mexican regime is constantly looking for is the best way to legitimatize the system. For this reason, I believe that the main elements of Mexican politics in the near future will be a combination of some redistribution, populist rhetoric, and some repression within a civilian political framework designed to organize the political pressure from below to ensure order.

Notes

1. From my point of view the most important works are: P. Schmitter, "Still the Century of Corporatism?" *The Review of Politics*, vol. 36, no. 1 (January 1974)—there is an excellent bibliography as addendum to the article; H. Wiarda, "Corporatism and Development in the Iberic-Latin World: Persistent Strains and New Variations," *The Review of Politics*, vol. 36, no. 1 (January 1947); G. O'Donnell, "Estado y corporativismo," paper presented at a seminar held at the University of Pittsburgh, 1974 (mimeo); P. Schmitter, "The Portugalization of Brazil?" in A. Stepan (ed.), *Authoritarian Brazil: Origins, Policies, and Future* (New Haven: Yale University Press, 1973); G. O'Donnell, *Reflexiones sobre las tendencias generales de cambio en el Estado burocrático-autoritario* (Buenos Aires: Centro de Estudios de Estado y Sociedad, 1975); J. Malloy, "Authoritarianism, Corporatism and Mobilization in Peru," *The Review of Politics*, vol. 36, no. 1 (January 1947); S. K. Purcell, "Decision-Making in an Authoritarian Regime: Theoretical Implications from a Mexican Case Study," *World Politics*, vol. 26, no. 1 (October 1973).

2. Schmitter, "Corporatism?" p. 85.

3. F. F. Cardoso, "Associated-Dependent Development: Theoretical and Practical Implications," in Stepan (ed.), *Authoritarian Brazil*, p. 143.

4. HAFINSA-CEPAL, *La política industrial en el desarrollo económico de México* (Mexico, D.F., 1971), Tables 1 and 6.

5. See the excellent paper by D. Felix, "Trickling Down in Mexico and the Debate over Long Term Growth-Equity Relationships in the LDCs," Washington

University, 1975 (mimeo). Felix's sophisticated methological procedures make a remarkable contribution to our knowledge on income distribution in Mexico. In addition, his data seem to be more reliable than those of any previous study dealing with this subject.

6. Cf. R. Ortiz Mena, V. Urquidi, et al., *El desarrollo económico de México y su capacidad para absorber capital del exterior* (Mexico, D.F.: Nacional Financiera, 1953), esp. chap. 1.

7. See Richard Weinert's essay, "The State and Foreign Capital," in this volume.

8. Bernardo Sepúlveda and Antonio Chumacero, *La inversión extranjera en México* (Mexico, D.F.: Fondo de Cultura Económica, 1973), Table 1.

9. F. Fajnzylber, "Las empresas transnacionales y el sistema industrial de México," *El trimestre económico*, vol. 42, no. 168 (October–December 1975): 909.

10. F. Fajnzylber and T. Martinez, "Las empresas transnacionales: expansión a nivel mundial y proyección de la industria mexicana" (Mexico, D.F., 1974; mimeo). The data were taken from a summary of this important work made by Lorenzo Meyer.

11. C. Reynolds, *The Structure of Mexican Economy in the Twentieth Century* (New Haven: Yale University Press, 1971).

12. Cf. P. Uribe, "Some RAS Experiments with the Mexican Input-Output Model," *Annals of Economic and Social Measurement*, vol. 4, no. 4 (1975): 551–65; and P. Uribe, "Bienes y factores en el modelo de insuo-producto de México" (1975; mimeo).

13. See T. King, *Mexico: Industrialization and Trade Policies since 1940.* (London: Oxford University Press, 1970), p. 26; M. Everett, "The Evolution of the Mexican Wage Structure" (Mexico, D.F.: El Colegio de México, 1968; mimeo); and J. Bortz and R. Pascoe, "Salarios reales por rama de actividad en el Distrito Federal de 1939 a 1974" (research in process, Instituto Nacional de Estudios del Trabajo).

14. Carlos Pereyra, "Empleo y desempleo: problemas de incapacidad social," *Excelsior*, September 22, 1975, p. 7–A.

15. J. Linz, "The Future of an Authoritarian Situation or the Institutionalization of an Authoritarian Regime: The Case of Brazil," in Stepan (ed.), *Authoritarian Brazil.*

16. O'Donnell, "Estado." Arnaldo Córdova has oriented some of his work to the corporatist framework, although for the last few years he has only made reference to it. See his "Las reformas sociales y la tecnocratización del Estado Mexicano," *Revista mexicana de ciencia política*, vol. 17 (October–December 1972). C. Pereyra has discussed the semi-corporatist nature of the state. Although I would rather disagree with the concept of "semi-corporativism," his arguments are in the same direction as mine. See "México: los límites del reformismo," *Cuadernos políticos*, July–September 1974.

17. R. Santin, "Monografía sobre la organización y estructura patronal en México" (Mexico, D.F.: El Colegio de México, 1975; mimeo).

18. For this reason, during the Cárdenas administration the organized labor movement increased the real wages of laborers and the peasants were given important land grants.

19. *El nacional*, July 24, 1954, p. 1-A, and *Tiempo*, August 2, 1954, p. 6.

20. José Luis Reyna, "De la inmovilidad a la acción: el movimiento obrero 1952–1959" (Mexico, D.F.: El Colegio de México, 1975; mimeo).

21. Everett, "The Evolution of the Mexican Wage Structure."

22. *Tiempo*, August 2, 1954, p. 6.

23. *Impact of Foreign Investment in Mexico* (Washington, D.C.: U.S. Department of Commerce, n. d.), pp. 65–67.

24. T. Skidmore, *The Politics of Economic Stabilization in Latin America* (Madison: University of Wisconsin, Discussion Paper Series, 1975).

25. See his article "An Authoritarian Regime: Spain," in E. Allardt and Y. Littune (eds.), *Cleavages, Ideologies and Party Systems* (Helsinki: Westermarck Society, 1964).

26. See D. Vallejo, *Las luchas ferrocarrileras que conmovieron a México* (Mexico, D.F., 1967) and A. Alonso, *El movimiento ferrocarrilero 1958–1959* (Mexico, D.F.: Editorial Era, 1972).

27. Rosa E. Montes de Oca, "Reforma Agraria," *Siempre!* January 22, 1975, p. 10.

28. J. Martínez Rios, "Las invasiones agrarias en México," *Revista mexicana de sociología*, vol. 24, nos. 3–4 (October–December 1972): 775.

29. F. Margiotta, "Changing Patterns of Political Influence: The Mexican Military and Politics," paper presented at the 1973 Annual Meeting of the American Political Science Association, p. 38.

The Future of the Mexican System

SUSAN KAUFMAN PURCELL

Speculations regarding the direction of future political change are usually conditioned by the way in which the political system is viewed in the present. Because revolution is a relatively rare phenomenon, most predictions tend to assume the continuation of existing political patterns, with minor adjustments made in response to social and economic changes.

Until recently, a consensus was lacking concerning the nature of the Mexican political system. Basically, there were two schools of thought. One classified the Mexican system as imperfectly democratic (or in transition toward a full-fledged democratic system).[1] The other denied that Mexico was an imperfect version of anything and asserted instead that it was an excellent example of an authoritarian-corporate regime.[2]

The proponents of the democratic view tended to stress the aggressive role of interest associations operating under the aegis of the "official" political party, the Partido Revolucionario Institucional (PRI). Concomitantly, they de-emphasized the role of the Mexican President, who was portrayed as a somewhat passive balancer of interests, engaged in the ever-more impossible task of satisfying the demands of interest groups.

Those who considered the system to be authoritarian reversed the power capabilities of the Party and the executive. Power was seen as emanating from the executive, who orchestrated interest-group demands while enjoying substantial leeway in determining the goals the regime would pursue. Interest groups were in a sense captive associations led by coopted leaders who sacrificed the interests of their rank and file to those of the executive in return for handsome personal payoffs. The PRI was regarded in the same light as interest associations. Its main raison d'être was to support and implement decisions taken by the executive.

Not surprisingly, those who considered the Mexican political system

173

as essentially democratic predicted that the future would bring increased democratization. Underlying this view were several assumptions. First, it was assumed that capitalistic economic growth and democracy were positively related. Therefore, as Mexico's capitalist economy continued to develop into a mature industrial economy, its political system would follow suit and evolve into a mature democracy.[3] Second, it was assumed that where one found interest groups one found pluralist democracy. As an underdeveloped country, Mexico's interest groups were still small in number, but it was taken for granted that with development the interest-group universe would expand and the democratic nature of Mexico's political system would become more apparent.[4] Third, democracy was linked to the existence of a sizable middle class. Industrialization enlarged the middle class. Therefore, the future would bring an enlarged middle class and a determined effort on the part of this middle class to divest the Mexican political system of its undemocratic characteristics.[5]

Data were not lacking to substantiate the interpretation that Mexico would evolve into a more perfect democracy. The middle class was growing, and its growth was paralleled by an ever-larger vote for the Partido de Acción Nacional (PAN), the major opposition party.[6] The PAN received almost all its votes from Mexico's major urban areas, which were precisely where the growing middle class was located. In contrast, the PRI depended heavily on the support of the largely poor, illiterate rural inhabitants.[7] Since it was predicted that by 1980 75 percent of all Mexicans would live in urban areas,[8] it seemed clear that the PAN would continue to gain support at the expense of the PRI. The end result would be the transformation of a "single-party democracy" into a competitive two-party democracy.

Supporters of the authoritarian model of the Mexican political system tended to argue that the proponents of the democratic interpretation treated the political system as a dependent variable and the socioeconomic environment as an independent variable. In other words, the democratic interpretation underestimated the ability of the political system to mold and control its environment.[9] Furthermore, those who saw the Mexican system as authoritarian noted that Mexico was not following the Western European model of industrial development. Rather, Mexico (or Latin America in general) was moving along a distinct development path that was characterized by both delayed and dependent development and an Iberic-Latin cultural tradition. As a result, structures or classes found in Mexico, although labeled with names similar to those in Western European systems did not necessarily serve the same function or behave in a similar manner. Interest associations in countries characterized by delayed and dependent development were not autonomous of the state, a sine qua non of democratic polities. Furthermore, the Mexican or Latin American middle class was not the bulwark of democracy because it lacked the industrial base of its Western European counterparts. Rather, it was a bureaucratic middle class, dependent on the state for its sustenance and characterized by authoritarian values. In sum, the automatic association between interest groups or a middle class and democratic development was fallacious.[10]

These arguments, however, do not deal directly with the specific issue of the steadily growing support for the PAN in Mexico. In this regard, it was noted that there was no simple correlation between a growing middle class and a vote for the PAN. Rather, the PAN appeared to be drawing votes from all classes. Furthermore, the PAN was not increasing its support in all urban areas but only in one or two, while the PRI was continuing to increase its support in almost all of the rapidly urbanizing states. An ever-increasing PAN vote resulting from continued development was considered to be far from inevitable. Also relevant to the argument was the notion that the PAN vote was essentially an anti-PRI vote rather than a pro-PAN vote, and would desert the PAN once the PRI decided to put its house in order. Since it was deemed unlikely that the Mexican political leaders would allow power to slip easily and quietly from their hands, it was assumed that the regime would take measures to undermine the PAN and build up support for the PRI when it felt that such action was necessary or expedient.[11]

A rapid perusal of the essays in this volume clearly indicates that the former divergence of opinion regarding the nature of the Mexican political system has disappeared. Apparently, there is now a consensus regarding the essentially authoritarian or corporate nature of the Mexican political system. Despite this consensus, however, there has not yet been an extended discussion of what the future holds in store for the authoritarian regime of Mexico. The few predictions that have been offered to date usually take the form of rather general assertions that the authoritarian system will be able to deal with its environment and make the necessary minor adjustments required in order to maintain its authoritarian essence.[12] Since the overthrow of Allende and the assumption of power by the Chilean military, however, people appear to be more willing and able to conceive of a political breakdown in Mexico.

The purpose of this essay, therefore, is to explore in some depth the future prospects of political authoritarianism in Mexico. What are the main kinds of challenges with which the regime will be faced, and what kinds of options are available for meeting these future challenges?

This exercise in speculation should not be regarded as purely academic. One has only to read the newspapers to realize that the government has been faced with more than its usual share of problems. Guerilla movements are no longer localized in the state of Guerrero. Business leaders, foreign diplomats, policemen, and members of the Mexican political elite have been kidnapped and even assassinated. Peasants in greater numbers are seizing land. Students have been marching for reforms. Unusually high rates of inflation have been met by threats of a general strike on the part of organized labor. Civilian leaders have been relying with greater frequency on overt military support. And in a country where previously no one ventured even a verbal assault upon the chief executive, Echeverría was physically assaulted by masses of angry students. What does all this mean? How threatening is it to the continued viability of the Mexican political system?

One possible interpretation is that nothing has really changed in Mexico. The political system has always been characterized by periods of relative unrest and discontent. During the 1950s, for example, the Confederation of Mexican Workers (CTM) repeatedly threatened to call a general strike because of the declining purchasing power of its members, while the railroad, petroleum, and teachers' unions actually did stage a series of disruptive work stoppages at the end of the decade. The López Mateos years (1958–64) also brought a substantial decrease in confidence on the part of the private sector, an increased alienation of the intellectual left, and a renewed peasant radicalism that took the form of land seizures and support of dissident leaders such as Rubén Jaramillo. Finally, student unrest reached massive proportions under the presidency of Díaz Ordaz (1964–70).

These crises were dealt with by the political elites in a fairly standard fashion. Initially, attempts were made to negotiate with and coopt the alienated leaders and their followers by means of a partial accession to their demands. Where this strategy failed and illegal or violent behavior ensued, repression was utilized. Examples include the use of the army to break the railroad strike and the incarceration of the railroad union leaders, the murder of peasant leader Rubén Jaramillo and his family, apparently by members of the armed forces, and the "Tlatelolco massacre" that resulted in the death of large numbers of students and the jailing of still others.

The use of force by the government has generally been followed, once order has been restored, by decisions benefiting the dissident groups. Thus the labor unrest of the 1950s eventually brought forth a series of constitutional reforms between 1960 and 1962 that favored the interests of the organized workers, and the student unrest of the late 1960s was in great part responsible for the subsequent doubling of the education budget and the construction of new universities throughout the country. Such decisions aim to rebuild support among the alienated groups and to restore the weakened political legitimacy of the elites.

It can be argued that Echeverría's celebrated *apertura democrática* was yet another series of reforms designed to strengthen government support. Increased freedom of the press, for example, was designed to win back some of the middle-class individuals and intellectuals who had become highly critical of undemocratic procedures and the inequitable distribution of resources in Mexico. Worker discontent was met with a raise in minimum wages that kept pace with the relatively high rate of inflation. The government also instituted a system of price controls for basic commodities and provided for annual adjustments of the minimum wage. And the persistent demand for the implementation of the constitutional provisions regarding worker housing (to be subsidized in part by employers) was granted. The problems of rural poverty and underemployment began to be tackled by means of a vastly increased commitment of public funds (generated in part by new taxes falling heavily on the urban sector) to be used to establish rural industries and cooperatives, to mechanize agriculture on the *ejidos*, and to increase the amount of credit available to *ejidatarios*, to cite just a few examples. The policies to decentralize industry and to set up rural cooperatives in particular represent attempts to come to grips with the perceived impossibility of satisfying peasant land hunger by providing alternative sources of livelihood for the rural population. The response of the government to student discontent has already been noted. It might be added that the construction of new universities also had an obvious political rationale, since it will eventually reduce the number of students concentrated in the Universidad Nacional Autónoma de México in Mexico City and distribute them throughout the country, thereby fragmenting and demobilizing the student movement. Finally, the outcries of business elites and other proponents of law and order were met by a massive military campaign against the guerrillas (who have not proved susceptible to negotiation and cooptation) that resulted in the assassination of their main leader, Lucio Cabañas.

Whether or not these efforts will placate the dissatisfied groups in the long run is a moot question. In the short run, at least, the situation appears to have returned to normal, where it probably will remain at least until José López Portillo has had an opportunity to demonstrate what his policy priorities will be. Those who interpret the events of the late 1960s and early 1970s as the disruptive phase of a recurring cycle in which prolonged periods of general calm are occasionally interrupted by brief outbreaks of unrest may therefore be proved correct.

It seems to me, however, that to reach a conclusion regarding the significance of events since 1968 by comparing them with similar events at earlier periods of time unduly narrows one's perspective. Although the recent events and the regime's responses may be familiar, the *context* in which they are occurring is significantly different. In order, therefore, to assess accurately the prospects for the future of the Mexican political system, additional factors must be taken into consideration.

One such factor is the age of the Mexican Revolution. With the passage of time, the number of Mexicans who participated in the 1910 Revolution has been reduced. Most Mexicans are now one or two generations removed from the event. Although hard data to substantiate this impression are lacking, these Mexicans seem to be less affected by the symbols of the Revolution and more cynical regarding the intention of their leaders to implement the social-justice goals of the Revolution.[13] Mexican intellectuals have even begun to question and revise their opinions regarding the contribution of major revolutionary heroes and to counter official assertions that Mexico is a democracy with analyses of the authoritarian, corporatist nature of the political system.[14]

This posited decline in the emotional appeal of revolutionary symbols is important, because until now there has been an inverse relationship between a group's susceptibility to symbol manipulation and the receipt of tangible rewards from the government. Thus workers and peasants, the two groups for whose benefit the Revolution ostensibly was made, have heard their praises sung by all political leaders and have prospered relatively little. In contrast, the business elites, who have been classified repeatedly as "unrevolutionary," have gladly endured their exclusion from the revolutionary rhetoric in return for sizable increases in their economic assets. If the symbols of the Mexican Revolution are indeed losing their ability to generate popular support, groups that until now have been relatively susceptible to symbol manipulation will begin to make more active demands upon the political system.

While the ability of the political elites to substitute symbolic payoffs for tangible ones appears to be declining, the country's economic situation is becoming more problematic. There is little doubt that the spectacular growth of the Mexican economy during the past few decades has contributed substantially to the viability of the political system. It has enabled the political elites to meet an increasing number of demands by augmenting the *ad hoc* distribution of benefits and rewards. Another way of stating this idea is that a continuously growing economy has allowed Mexico to avoid zero-sum politics. Politically difficult redistributive decisions could be postponed because new demands could be satisfied by the distribution of new wealth.

The admirable economic performance, however, was based on a process of import substitution which, as Villarreal points out in his contribution to this volume, has outlived its usefulness. Although in its early years import substitution gave great impetus to Mexico's industrialization process, recently it has contributed to the large increase in the country's balance-of-payments problems and foreign indebtedness, as well as to the persistence of overprotected, inefficient industries. In order to eliminate these economic problems, Mexico will have to increase substantially its export of manufactured goods.

The problem, however, is that the transition to an economy based on the export of manufactured goods will require the adoption of politically unpopular policies. According to Villarreal, these include devaluation, trade liberalization, and monetary stabilization. The net effect of such policies will be to spur inflation further, thereby decreasing the purchasing power of most Mexicans and adding to their frustration and discontent. At the same time, the group that will profit most from the transition to an export-oriented economy will be that segment of the private sector associated with the multinational corporations and national firms that are highly capitalized, modern, and efficient.[15]

The situation in the countryside can be expected to contribute to the inflationary trend. Until approximately 1970, Mexico was the only Latin American country in which the annual growth of the agricultural sector exceeded the rate of increase of the population. In recent years, however, agricultural production has increased 1 to 2 percent annually, while the population has grown an at average of 3.5 percent per year. As a result, Mexico has had to use scarce foreign exchange to import huge quantities of food, principally from the United States.[16] The shortage of basic foodstuffs is in great part responsible for sharp increases in their price, a development that has further eroded the purchasing power of Mexicans on fixed incomes.

Stagnation in the agricultural sector has also had an impact on rural-urban migration. People who cannot live off the land continue to pour into the major cities, especially Mexico City. They require housing, urban services, and—most important—jobs. The chances that their needs will be met appear small. A recent study estimated that existing federal programs for the construction of low-cost housing will leave 66 percent of the urban population without adequate housing by 1980.[17] The employment situation is equally dismal. Since 1970, only 400,000 jobs have been created each year, while 650,000 have been required. It is estimated that "some 2.5 million *extra* new jobs will have to be created in the period 1976–82 if the target of halving the present rate of unemployment is to be achieved."[18]

Finally, the decline in the productive capacity of the countryside has been accompanied by a substantial increase in demands for land on the part of landless peasants. The government has responded by claiming that there is no more productive land left to be distributed. Revelations by the Minister of Agrarian Reform that 15 million hectares of officially distributed land have been distributed "on paper only"[19] highlight the inadequacy of the existing agrarian reform program. The frustration of the peasants has increased the tempo of land invasions. Landowners, in turn, have responded by massacring invading peasants, slowing down production, repudiating the existing "captive" organization that supposedly represented their interests (the Confederación Nacional de Pequeños Propietarios), and forming a more independent pressure group (the Unión Nacional de Agricultores).

These events in the rural areas indicate that increasing hardship and unsatisfied demands can produce higher levels of mobilization. As long as such mobilization remains unorganized and involves a relatively small number of people, the activists can be either repressed or coopted by means of the distribution of land, money, or political positions, to cite just a few possibilities. The fact that the number of poor, deprived, and suffering people is growing and that they are not localized in any one sector or part of the country means, however, that at least the *potential* for mass mobilization now exists in Mexico.

Higher levels of mobilization, if they should occur, would constitute a serious threat to the continued viability of the Mexican political system. All analyses of the system as an authoritarian regime stress the importance of *low* levels of political participation for "system maintenance." By virtue of the passivity or apathy of large sectors of the population, the political elites are subject to a limited number of demands. This has several interrelated and mutually reinforcing implications. First, it is easier to manipulate demands when they are few in number. Second, with limited resources it is easier to respond to a small number of demands. Third, political elites subjected to fewer demands enjoy greater leeway in the decision-making process. From the point of view of those with a significant stake in the current system, therefore, higher levels of mobilization must be avoided.

To say that the *potential* for higher levels of mobilization exists, however, is not to say that higher levels of mobilization must or will materialize. First, it is theoretically possible for the political elites to undertake a series of reforms that would resolve the problems underlying the discontent, thereby removing the raison d'être of any mass mobilization. Second, leadership is needed to transform the potential for mass mobilization into an actuality. Assuming that such leadership arose, it would probably be either destroyed or coopted by the incumbent political elites, who would accurately consider it a threat to their interests. This is, in fact, what has already happened countless times in contemporary Mexico. What is required, therefore, is a division *among* the political elites. This would severely reduce the capabilities of the regime to recognize and deal with both the problems underlying the potential for mass mobilization and the specific individuals who would constitute the counterelite bent on transforming the potential for mobilization into a coherent anti-*status quo* mass movement. Let us examine each of these possibilities separately.

Assuming for the moment that the political elites remain united, what kinds of reforms are required to eliminate the potential for mass mobilization? It seems clear that the *ad hoc* distribution of disaggregated benefits to mobilized groups that has been the standard operating procedure of the Mexican political system until now will not solve the problem. What are required are more basic structural reforms that demonstrate a renewed commitment on the part of the governing elites to the social-justice principles of the Mexican Revolution. One example of such a reform might be the abolition of the right of *amparo* in agrarian matters, a right that has been used mainly by landowners to delay for approximately twenty years the transfer of their lands to peasants to whom the government has granted title.[20] Another would be the nationalization of privately owned lands in federal irrigation districts, since, as Stavenhagen has pointed out, such lands are among the richest in the nation and the vast quantities of money that the government has invested in them have benefited wealthy private agriculturalists almost exclusively.[21] A third example would be a significant restructuring of the tax system so as to eliminate the issuance of stocks made out only to "the bearer" (a system that makes it impossible for the government to control foreign penetration of the economy or to ascertain accurately the amount of wealth owned by stockholding Mexicans), increase taxes on agriculture (which at present is taxed at only nominal rates), and tax income derived from capital at rates equal to those applied to income derived from labor.

If the implementation of reforms such as these would go a long way toward removing the potential for mass mobilization that now exists in Mexico, what is the likelihood that such a course of action will be pursued? The answer to this question depends on one's perception of the nature of the Mexican state and its relationship to the private sector. There appear to be two main schools of thought in this regard. One argues that the private sector has become so powerful that it has "captured" the political elites. Thus, even if the latter wanted to end what has aptly been termed their "alliance for profits" with the private sector,[22] they no longer have the option of doing so. The opposing view agrees that there has been an "alliance for profits" between the political and economic elites but asserts that it is a marriage of convenience based on a temporary congruence of interests. In this marriage, the political elites represent a "state interest" that is separate and distinct from that of any particular class in the society, including the industrial class. Denying that the private sector has captured the state, the proponents of this view affirm that the state is the dominant partner in the relationship. If the interests of the political elites and those of the private sector should diverge, the state interest would be redefined away from previously favored groups and toward heretofore neglected ones.[23]

Adherence to one or the other of these views regarding the balance of power between the government and the private sector produces different predictions concerning the government's ability to reorient its priorities. If one accepts the notion that the state has been captured by the private sector, it seems reasonable to predict that because of strong opposition from the private sector, the government will be unable to make the kinds of reforms necessary to eliminate the potential for mass mobilization and increase its legitimacy. Whether or not the potential for higher levels of mobilization will become a reality would then depend on the degree of unity within the political elite, a matter that will be considered shortly.

If, however, one accepts the notion of a state interest that is separate and distinct from that of any particular class or group in society, as I do, the question regarding the ability of the regime to redefine its relationship with the private sector and pursue a more equitable development strategy requires a different and more complicated answer. With regard to the immediate present, I would argue that the Mexican government appears to have the wherewithal to institute the kinds of basic reforms required to defuse the potential for mass mobilization. Admittedly, in the absence of such reforms the assertion cannot be proved. Nevertheless, there are several reasons for believing that the government is still able to reorient its priorities.

First, during the Echeverría *sexenio*, there was the beginning of a reorientation of public policy away from privileged groups and toward less-favored ones. Examples of specific decisions have already been provided. Perhaps more important, however, were the efforts of Echeverría to lay the groundwork for more profound changes in the near future. The 1971 purge of Martínez Domínguez, Regent of the Federal District and leader of the faction opposed to Echeverría, removed from power a group of people strongly committed to the *status quo* and intimately linked with important economic interests in the country. They were replaced by a large number of young reform-oriented *técnicos* and professional politicians "who are neither capitalists nor *have direct links with the empresarial bourgeoisie.*"[24] Apparently interested more in power than in money, they supported Echeverría's efforts to expand the role of the state via the creation of countless new government agencies, many of which entailed state involvement in industries such as tobacco that prior to this were the exclusive domain of the private sector. They also backed Echeverría's efforts to eliminate local *caciques* who were more tied to regional than to national elites. The concrete results of these efforts include the removal of governors in Guerrero, Sonora, and San Luis Potosí and their replacement by governors more oriented toward reform.

The culmination of Echeverría's strategy was his selection of López Portillo, his close friend, as the PRI's candidate in the 1976 presidential election. By successfully outmaneuvering Moya Palencia and Cervantes del Río, both of whom reputedly had strong ties with the dominant economic interests, Echeverría at least ensured the nonrepudiation of his efforts and, possibly, their continuation and strengthening. As Echeverría himself explained, López Portillo was the pre-candidate who had the fewest ties to vested interests and would therefore be more able to take the hard decisions that will be required to solve Mexico's problems.[25]

It is therefore conceivable that in the near future the Mexican political system will be capable of reorienting its priorities in order to remove the ever-growing potential for mass mobilization. This does not mean, however, that the opportunity to do so will be unlimited. As has been noted, in recent years a major reorientation of the supposed state interest has never occurred.[26] Those who affirm that a distinct state interest exists therefore base their argument on the fact that there have been numerous occasions when the government has implemented decisions that were strenuously opposed by the private sector. Examples of such decisions include the establishment of employer-subsidized housing for workers, the implementation of an obligatory profit-sharing system, the institution of a law requiring reinstatement of unjustly dismissed workers, the imposition of taxes to finance rural development, the creation and recent major expansion of CONASUPO (the government agency that distributes low-cost food staples), the establishment of price and rent controls, and the granting of periodic large wage increases.

These decisions were at best mildly redistributive and generated less opposition from the private sector than would a program of reforms that included such moves as the abolition of the *amparo* in agrarian matters and the nationalization of federal irrigation districts. Nevertheless, in order to make these past decisions the government had to rely heavily on another characteristic of authoritarian regimes—limited political pluralism. This term describes a situation in which interest groups are substantially dependent upon the state. Dependence is achieved through the cooptation of group leaders, who then subordinate the wishes of their rank and file to those of the government. Limited pluralism enables the political elites to manipulate interest groups, to shape their demands, to mobilize their support when it is needed, and to keep them demobilized when passive acceptance of public policies is preferred.

Until now, the government has used its control of two of the component sectors of the system of limited pluralism, the peasants and the workers, mainly to keep down their demands in order to pursue its "alliance for profits" with the private sector. Occasionally, however, it has used its control over the peasants and workers to mobilize them in support of decisions that the private sector has staunchly opposed. Together with the coopted group leaders, the government has embarked on strenuous campaigns to inform the usually docile beneficiaries of its piecemeal anti-business decisions of what is at stake and has encouraged widespread, visible, and enthusiastic pro-government demonstrations.

There are indications, however, that the government's ability to mobilize the support of peasants and workers has been steadily decreasing. Abstention rates in recent elections have been rising rapidly, and an abstention rate of 60 percent was predicted prior to the 1976 election.[27] A partial explanation is the already-noted cynicism and alienation born of the awareness that other groups have been benefiting from the current system far more than have the peasants and workers. It is obviously difficult to mobilize support among the cynical and alienated. More serious in terms of long-range implications, however, is the fact that the organization of peasants and workers has not been keeping pace with the growth of the rural and urban labor forces. The expansion of the *ejido* system and the organization of the *ejidatarios* into the National Confederation of Peasants was intimately linked to an aggressive policy of land redistribution on the part of the government. In recent years, as was noted, the government has repeatedly argued that there is no more productive land available for distribution to the landless. In the absence of an important new land-redistribution program, therefore, the prospects appear dim for continued growth of the organized peasant sector. With regard to the urban labor force, the fastest growth has occurred in the service sector rather than in the manufacturing sector, which, until now, has been the backbone of the organized labor movement. To date, little effort has been made to organize the service sector, perhaps because its lower-class members are too geographically dispersed, while its middle-class members are too sophisticated to be herded into captive unions. Nor has the government expressed much interest in unionizing workers in new industries in the manufacturing sector.[28]

This absence of organizational growth within the rural and urban labor forces means that, as the economically active population continues to expand, the government will be able to mobilize support for policies opposed by the business interests among an ever-smaller percentage of the labor force. Consequently, the impact of the "countervailing power" available to the government will be reduced. The net result of this development would be a situation in which political elites would *no longer* be able to make politically necessary, although economically unpopular, decisions (from the point of view of the private sector). If this occurs, the state will indeed have become the captive of private economic elites and there will no longer be a state interest as such. The potential for mass mobilization discussed earlier could then not be destroyed and once again the crucial question would involve the degree of dissent within the political elite.

It is well known that the Mexican authoritarian coalition has always been characterized by a heterogeneity of views. Until now, this was expressed by the alternation of the presidency between individuals who were considered conservative with those who espoused views that, in the words of López Mateos, were "within the Constitution, of the extreme left." Nevertheless, despite differences of opinion among the elites, there have been few public indications of serious disagreements regarding political and economic fundamentals. One rare example was the conflict over the democratization of the PRI at the beginning of the Díaz Ordaz presidency. The campaign by Carlos Madrazo, the president of the PRI, in favor of democratization was viewed by many as an attempt to weaken the presidency, since by strengthening "grass roots" forces a new power base was created upon which Madrazo could launch his candidacy for the presidency irrespective of the wishes of the incumbent president. The campaign for democratization unleashed such disagreement within the ruling coalition that Madrazo was forced to "resign" in order to bring the system back to normal. A more recent example of dissensus was the attempt to democratize the organized labor movement, principally by removing the perennial leader of the CTM, Fidel Velázquez. It appears that Echeverría initially favored the idea, probably because it would build support among the rank and file, who regard Velázquez as the *líder charro* (corrupted leader) who has repeatedly sacrificed their interests to those of the political elites. Ultimately, however, the relatively high rate of inflation and the impending 1976 presidential election tipped the balance toward those who stressed the need for experienced and dependable leaders who could keep control of organized labor during difficult times.

It could be argued that there has been little disagreement among elites (or that whatever elite conflicts have existed have been worked out and resolved behind the scenes) because of the political socialization and recruitment processes in Mexico. In order to enter the top elites, an individual has had to work his way up slowly through the ranks. During this long and rigorous recruitment process, there has been ample opportunity to weed out individuals who were not properly deferential to authority, who were unwilling to resolve conflicts privately and refrain from expanding the arena of conflict, and who were unable to master the intricacies of the multiple-clientele networks and patron-client relationships. Thus, only those who were both willing and able to play by the political rules reached the top of the power structure, a phenomenon that surely worked to limit the possibilities of serious elite disagreement.

There are indications, however, that recruitment patterns have begun to change. Most obvious is the above-mentioned appointment by Echeverría of very young technocratic types. This, however, represents the accentuation of what was already a growing trend toward the appointment and election of *técnicos* at the expense of the traditional *políticos*. Two recent studies, for example, illustrate this practice with regard to the recruitment of state governors and members of the president's "cabinet."[29] The current president of the PRI, Porfirio Múnoz Ledo, and his immediate predecessor, Jesús Reyes Heroles, also exemplify this pattern. The latter came to the party after a successful stint as head of PEMEX, the government oil monopoly. This represented the first time that the leader of the PRI had been recruited from a nationalized industry requiring high levels of technological expertise. Múnoz Ledo's career also is conspicuously lacking in party militancy, since he was a former Secretary of Labor, head of the Social Security Institute, and advisor to the Mexican President.

Echeverría's choice of José López Portillo as his successor is in keeping with this trend. López Portillo is the nearest thing to a technocrat President that Mexico has ever had. A professor of public administration and former head of the Federal Electricity Commission and the Treasury, López Portillo had never held an elected office prior to his nomination by the PRI and had had virtually no experience in the official political party.[30]

The second change has to do not with the type of person being recruited but with the recruitment process itself. Most of the *técnicos* brought in by Echeverría are in their early thirties. They have not served a long political apprenticeship in the party or the bureaucracy at state and local levels. For some, their rise to the top has been nothing short of meteoric. This is also true of López Portillo, who is the first Mexican President to succeed a President of the same political generation.

These changes in the recruitment route and in the type of person appointed could have important implications for elite consensus in the near future. Increasing recruitment of technocratic types could divide the elites into two camps, the *técnicos* and the *políticos*. There have already been some signs of conflict based on this cleavage. During the PRI convention in the 1960s, for example, there was considerable discussion of the differences between the new progressive *técnicos*, who desired more rapid and substantial change, and the old-line *políticos*, who wanted the continuation of tried and true policies and processes.

There is also the possibility of increasing dissensus *within* the *técnico* group, however. Many of the *técnicos* who have been working in the public sector for some time now received their training in major, and often conservative, universities in the United States. Many of the younger and less experienced *técnicos*, in contrast, have studied in more "third-world oriented" universities in Europe. One already hears rumors to the effect that there is substantial conflict between the more classically trained *técnicos*, centered in the Banco de México, and the more reformist ones, centered in the Ministry of National Patrimony.

Serious elite dissensus, whether between progressive *técnicos* and old-guard *políticos* or between change- and *status-quo*-oriented *técnicos*, could ultimately produce a political stalemate. The strong convictions of each group would make compromise difficult, if not impossible, with the result that few, if any, decisive decisions could be taken. It would be at this point that the existence of a potentially mobilizable mass of discontented people would become of paramount importance. In order to break the deadlock within the elite, the more progressive elites (convinced that their opportunity for putting through basic reforms was limited) might decide to take advantage of the potential for mass mobilization in order to increase their power and put through the reforms they believed to be necessary.[31] Attempts at mass mobilization by the progressive elites would probably spur the more conservative elites to fortify their position by mobilizing their supporters. The result would be the transformation of the Mexican political system into a competitive populist regime characterized by elite dissensus and high levels of mobilization.[32]

I believe, however, that the period of mass mobilization resulting from elite dissensus would provoke a takeover by the Mexican military. Like the Chilean military before 1973, the Mexican military is usually regarded as "apolitical" or "noninterventionist." The military's subservience to civilian elites, however, has depended on the latter's ability to govern. Until now, the armed forces have had a definite stake in the current political system, which has treated them well and has relied heavily on them for information and cooperation in putting down antisystem groups or keeping them under control.[33] But increased political alienation on the part of major groups, elite fragmentation, and high levels of uncontrolled mobilization could persuade the armed forces to replace the "dysfunctional" civilian elites with military men. A military takeover precipitated by high levels of conflict and mass mobilization would be unlikely to produce a populist regime, at least in its initial stages.[34]

The steps between the existence of large numbers of discontented citizens and the overthrow of civilian rulers by the military are several. There is also nothing predetermined or automatic about the progression. Furthermore, united political elites can probably coexist with a potentially mobilizable mass of discontented people for long periods of time. Nevertheless, to ignore the growing need for basic reforms seems a risky way to govern. Although the scenarios developed in the preceding pages are speculative, they are neither impossible nor improbable. Elite dissensus, mass mobilization, and a military takeover all *could* occur; Brazil, which originally emulated the Mexican model, could, ironically, serve as a model for the future of Mexico.[35]

Acknowledgments

I am grateful to my colleagues who participated in the seminar on "The Relationship between the State and the Economy in Contemporary Mexico" for their helpful suggestions. For their extensive comments on earlier drafts of this paper I particularly want to thank Douglas A. Chalmers, David Collier, Robert R. Kaufman, John F. H. Purcell, Isidro Sepúlveda G., Lois Wasserspring, and Richard S. Weinert.

Notes

1. This argument is made most strongly by Robert E. Scott in his *Mexican Government in Transition* (Urbana: University of Illinois Press, 1959). See also Raymond Vernon, *The Dilemma of Mexico's Development* (Cambridge, Mass.: Harvard University Press, 1963), Pablo González Casanova, *La democracia en México* (Mexico, D.F.: Ediciones Era, 1965), and Martin C. Needler, *Politics and Society in Mexico* (Albuquerque: University of New Mexico Press, 1971).

2. See especially Susan Kaufman Purcell, *The Mexican Profit-Sharing Decision: Politics in an Authoritarian Regime* (Berkeley: University of California Press, 1975), and "Decision-Making in an Authoritarian Regime: Theoretical Implications from a Mexican Case Study," *World Politics*, vol. 26 (October 1973): 28–54; Roger D. Hansen, *The Politics of Mexican Development* (Baltimore: Johns Hopkins University Press, 1971); Frank Brandenburg, *The Making of Modern Mexico* (Englewood Cliffs, N.J.: Prentice-Hall, 1964); and Evelyn P. Stevens, *Protest and Response in Mexico* (Cambridge, Mass.: M.I.T. Press, 1974).

3. For this argument, see especially González Casanova, *La democracia*.

4. This is a major assumption of Scott in *Mexican Government in Transition*.

5. The work that most explicitly links the Latin American middle classes and democracy is John J. Johnson's *Political Change in Latin America: The Emergence of the Middle Sectors* (Stanford: Stanford University Press, 1958).

6. In 1952, the first year that the PAN ran its own presidential candidate, the party received 7.8 percent of the total vote. In 1970, the PAN's candidate received an all-time high of 14.1 percent of the total vote. See James W. Wilkie, *The Mexican Revolution: Federal Expenditure and Social Change since 1910* (Berkeley: University of California Press, 1967), p. 182, and Ronald H. McDonald, *Party Systems and Elections in Latin America* (Chicago: Markham, 1971), p. 253.

7. In most rural states, the opposition vote has rarely exceeded 2 percent of the total vote (González Casanova, *La democracia*, pp. 116–117).

8. Wayne A. Cornelius, Jr., "Urbanization as an Agent of Latin American Political Instability: The Case of Mexico," *American Political Science Review*, vol. 63 (September 1969): 837–38.

9. For this argument see especially Purcell, "Decision-Making in an Authoritarian Regime," and Hansen, *The Politics of Mexican Development*.

10. For a recent discussion along these lines of Latin America's path of development, see Philippe C. Schmitter, "Paths to Political Development in Latin America," in Douglas A. Chalmers (ed.), *Changing Latin America: New Interpretations of Its Politics and Society, Proceedings of the Academy of Political Science*, vol. 30 (August 1972): 83–108. For the cultural argument in particular see Howard J. Wiarda, "Toward a Framework for the Study of Political Change in the Iberic-Latin Tradition: The Corporative Model," *World Politics*, vol. 25 (January 1973), 206–35.

11. Antonio Ugalde, *Power and Conflict in a Mexican Community*, (Albuquerque: University of New Mexico Press, 1970), p. 153, and Barry Ames, "Bases of Support for Mexico's Dominant Party," *American Political Science Review*, vol. 64 (March 1970): 153–67.

12. See, for example, Purcell, "Decision-Making in an Authoritarian Regime," Roger D. Hansen, "PRI Politics in the 1970's: Crisis or Continuity?" and David F. Ronfeldt, "The Mexican Army and Political Order since 1940." The Hansen and Ronfeldt essays appear in James W. Wilkie, Michael C. Meyer, and Edna Monzón de Wilkie (eds.), *Contemporary Mexico: Papers of the Fourth International Congress of Mexican History* (Berkeley: University of California Press, 1975).

13. One Mexican journalist, for example, has argued that the cynicism and disenchantment account for the new style of propaganda that the PRI is using in the 1976 presidential campaign. He notes that instead of the usual slogans, the PRI is using surrealistic messages—white walls painted with the candidate's initials in forms that look Greek and pre-Columbian, and scenes of the Mexican countryside overlaid with an emblem of the PRI. See Heberto Castillo, "Renovados y re-valuados voceros: el recurso del método," *Excelsior*, January 22, 1976, p. 6.

14. With regard to the debunking of revolutionary heroes, note, for example, the emphasis on Lázaro Cárdenas's purposeful attempts to prevent horizontal alliances among peasants, workers, and government bureaucrats in order to ensure the government's control over each of these groups in Arnaldo Córdova, "La transformación del PNR en PRM: el triunfo del corporativismo en México," in Wilkie et al. (eds.), *Contemporary Mexico*. The essays by Mexican authors included in the present volume are good examples of the revisionist tendency to categorize the Mexican political system as authoritarian or corporatist.

15. The recent discovery of apparently large but as yet unspecified reserves of petroleum will not solve Mexico's economic problems. Its main effect will be to reduce the imbalance between Mexico's imports and exports by decreasing the former and increasing the latter.

16. Note the recent statement by Macedonio Barrera, Director of Planning and Studies of the Mexican Institute of Foreign Trade, to the effect that in 1976 Mexico will have to import 5 million pesos worth of agricultural products, including corn, sorghum, oils, and milk, to satisfy its needs (*Excelsior*, January 22, 1976, p. 4).

17. The study was done by the Instituto de Investigaciones Sociales de la Universidad Nacional Autónoma de México and is reported in *Excelsior*, October 13, 1975, p. 1.

18. *The Impact of Foreign Private Investment on the Mexican Economy*, prepared by Harry J. Robinson and Timothy G. Smith for the American Chamber of Commerce of Mexico, Stanford Research Institute (SRI Project 4110), Menlo Park, Calif., January 1976, pp. 30–31.

19. *Excelsior*, January 23, 1976, p. 1. It is not clear whether the 15 million hectares distributed on paper only refer to the Díaz Ordaz administration, the Echeverría administration, or both. See, for example, the assertion by the former head of the Agrarian Department under Díaz Ordaz that 5 of the 15 million hectares distributed on paper only are the responsibility of the Echeverría administration (*Excelsior*, January 24, 1976, p. 4).

20. The need to suppress the right of *amparo* in agrarian matters is argued forcefully by Heberto Castillo in his article, "Violencia inminente en el campo: supresión del amparo agrario," *Excelsior*, December 4, 1975, p. 7. The idea was first aired publicly by several peasant organizations, members of the Pacto de Ocampo. It was immediately attacked by the President of the Supreme Court and no further action was taken on the issue. (See Heberto Castillo, "La lucha contra el amparo agrario: maniobra?" *Excelsior*, December 11, 1975, p. 7.)

21. Rodolfo Stavenhagen made these remarks in an article in *Excelsior*.

22. Clark W. Reynolds, *The Mexican Economy: Twentieth-Century Structure and Growth* (New Haven: Yale University Press, 1970), p. 186.

23. For this argument, see John F. H. Purcell and Susan Kaufman Purcell, "Mexican Business and Public Policy," in James Malloy (ed.), *Authoritarianism and Corporatism in Latin America* (Pittsburgh: University of Pittsburgh Press, 1977). See also S. K. Purcell, *The Mexican Profit-Sharing Decision*.

24. Julio Labastida M. del Campo, "Nacionalismo reformista en México," *Cuadernos Políticos*, vol. 3 (January–March 1975): 48.

25. *Excelsior*, November 14, 1975, p. 4.

26. It can be argued that during the presidency of Lazaro Cárdenas (1934–40) a major reorientation of the state interest did occur. However, this was before the development of a strong and important industrial sector.

27. By the newspaper *Excelsior*.

28. Richard Ulric Miller, "The Role of Labor Organizations in a Developing Country: The Case of Mexico," Ph.D. dissertation, Cornell University, 1966, and Michael David Everett, "The Róle of the Mexican Trade Unions, 1950–1963," Ph.D. dissertation, Washington University, Missouri, 1967.

29. Roderic A. Camp, "The Cabinet and the Técnico in Mexico and the United States," *Journal of Comparative Administration*, vol. 3 (August 1971): 188–214, and Roger Charles Anderson, "The Functional Role of the Governors: Their States in the Political Development of Mexico, 1940–1964," Ph.D. dissertation, University of Wisconsin, 1971.

30. The extent to which the nomination of José López Portillo represented a change in recruitment patterns is captured by a joke which made the rounds shortly after he was *destapado*, or unveiled: Question—What do the letters JLP stand for? Answer—*Jamás lo pensamos!* (Who would have thought it!)

31. If the scenario appears unrealistic, note the statement of Fernando Benítez, an intellectual who is a member of the Executive Council of the Instituto de Estudios Políticos, Económicos y Sociales of the PRI, to the effect that the Mexican President should not be the President of all Mexicans but, rather, should actively further the interests of the peasants over those of other groups, even to the extent of arming them, if necessary (*Excelsior*, January 20, 1976, pp. 1, 11).

32. For a discussion of populist politics in Latin America, see Torcuato de Tella, "Populism and Reform in Latin America," in Claudio Veliz (ed.), *Obstacles to Change in Latin America* (New York: Oxford University Press, 1969), pp. 47–74.

33. Ronfeldt, in Wilkie et al. (eds.), *Contemporary Mexico*.

34. Margiotta's findings that populist sentiments are not entirely absent from

the Army indicate that a populist military regime would not be an inconceivable possibility in the longer run, however (see Franklin D. Margiotta, "Changing Patterns of Political Influence: The Mexican Military," paper presented at the 1973 Annual Meeting of the American Political Science Association in New Orleans).

35. For a detailed discussion of the Brazilian model, see Guillermo A. O'Donnell, *Modernization and Bureaucratic-Authoritarianism: Studies in South American Politics* (Berkeley: Institute of International Studies, University of California, 1973) and Alfred A. Stepan (ed.), *Authoritarian Brazil: Origins, Policies, and Future* (New Haven: Yale University Press, 1973).

Mexico and
Latin American Authoritarianism

ROBERT R. KAUFMAN

For "South Americanists" who seek to understand patterns of political and economic change in such countries as Argentina, Brazil, Chile, and Uruguay, many of the essays appearing in this volume on Mexico will contain a striking, if depressing, ring of familiarity. Virtually every contributor, for example, either assumes or argues explicitly that Mexico is fundamentally authoritarian—that an ongoing, systematic suppression of open electoral competition underlies its democratic and constitutional façade.[1] This feature of Mexican politics offers an obvious parallel with the experience of Brazil since 1964, with Onganía's more abortive effort to take Argentina along a similar path, and with the violent overthrow of constitutionalism in contemporary Chile and Uruguay. The same is true of the essays describing the way "captive" associations in Mexico are used to demobilize and manipulate industrial labor, peasants, and the urban poor.[2] The new regimes of the south have also employed such "exclusionary corporatist" techniques. It is this technique, in fact, that is widely regarded as one of their distinctive traits, setting them apart from more traditional, personalistic forms of authoritarian rule and from the "inclusionary populist" regimes founded between the 1920s and 1950s by such leaders as Perón, Vargas, and Ibáñez.[3] In Mexico as well as the South American countries, finally, such authoritarian corporate controls provide the underpinning of a particular configuration of "technocratic," "orthodox," and "liberal" economic policies: the promotion of growth at the expense of social welfare, increasing reliance on foreign loans and investment, and attempts to "rationalize" and "deepen" an already developed manufacturing sector through the encouragement of large-scale, technologically intensive industries.

193

This apparent convergence between Mexico and the more industrialized southern countries seems quite remarkable when we consider the wide variation in political institutions and style that had previously existed among them. Just a little more than a decade ago, "revolutionary" Mexico appeared to share little in common with "polarized" Argentina, with the "tolerant, compromising" Brazilians, or with "democratic" Chile and Uruguay. How is it that countries with such different traits appeared in the 1960s and 1970s to be arriving at quite similar political-economic "end points"? What accounts for the seeming irrelevance of earlier distinctions which for so long had been embedded in the conventional wisdom about Latin America? As earlier political differences have diminished, scholars outside as well as within the Marxist tradition have attached increasing significance to economic factors at work throughout the area. Common experiences of dependency and delayed industrialization seem to have generated quite comparable shifts in the relationships between capital, labor, and the State, and it appears increasingly useful to analyze the process of political change in Mexico and the South American countries in terms of such concepts and variables.[4]

Along with these political and economic parallels, however, there are also some important differences between Mexico and the south. In the South American cases, the inauguration of what O'Donnell calls bureaucratic-authoritarian (B-A) regimes (the label I will apply to the structural, class, and policy configurations detailed above) occurred in the context of relatively advanced industrial economics and supplanted very different types of class coalitions and political structures.[5] In Mexico, many of the authoritarian and corporatist features of such regimes were already in place at the very onset of the industrialization experience, the outgrowth of the civil war and of the Cárdenas reforms. Whereas B-A policies seem for the time being to have worked in Mexico and Brazil, Argentina's first go-around with such arrangements aborted, and the outcomes of similar efforts in Chile and Uruguay are still very much in doubt. We should also not overlook the fact that, despite episodes of brutal repression, Mexico's version of B-A rule seems blander, less openly coercive, less obviously cruel than those of both the "successful" and "unsuccessful" cases to the south. It is not out of the question, finally, that, whatever the points of convergence reached during the 1960s and 1970s, Mexico will follow a rather different political-economic course from her southern neighbors in the remainder of this decade and beyond.

In this essay I will attempt to place the Mexican experience in a comparative perspective by further elaborating the implications of some of these similarities and differences. At the theoretical level, the study will draw heavily on O'Donnell's work on B-A regimes, with the general assumption that this label applies broadly to contemporary Mexico as well as to the governments of the southern countries. Particular attention will be given, within the Mexican context, to O'Donnell's general thesis that such regimes are linked to a particular phase (or crisis) of capital accumulation encountered in the maturation of dependent, industrializing economies—the phase in which "easy" import-substitution possibilities have been exhausted and further expansion seems to depend upon major new investments in capital-intensive, technologically advanced producers-goods industries.[6] Although I will refer occasionally to Chile and Uruguay, the principal empirical points of comparison will be Argentina and Brazil, the concrete cases from which most of O'Donnell's generalizations are drawn, and the two countries which most resemble Mexico in terms of size and industrial development. My working proposition is that comparisons among these three countries, when informed by the theoretical guidelines suggested by O'Donnell, will lend support to at least three conclusions of interest to students of Mexico and of Latin America in general:

1. All three countries did, in fact, industrialize along similar lines, and during the 1950s and 1960s all three faced similar capital-accumulation problems related to the maturation and deepening of their industrial economies. This is important for establishing a ground of comparison among the three cases.

2. Bureaucratic-authoritarian regimes were functionally related to the medium-run resolution of these difficulties. In Mexico, where such a regime had been established during the early phases of industrialization, the new phase of expansion could be entered relatively smoothly, without major political or economic disruption. In Argentina and Brazil, the problems encountered during this phase led directly to attempts to find new, B-A "solutions." And, in all three cases, the viability and success of the B-A regimes themselves have depended on their capacity to deal with the two central imperatives of the maturation of their industrial economies: the encouragement of large-scale investment and the control of the labor movement.

3. Finally, the formation of Mexican B-A structure *prior* to the new phase of industrialization should alert us to the theoretical mistake of assuming that there is a simple mechanical relationship between economic causes and political effects. In all three cases, and especially in Mexico, the interaction between political structure and policy, class relations, and the economic mode of production is obviously much more subtle and complex. In the Mexican case, the early consolidation of authoritarian-corporatist controls does much to explain why the government of that country could be less repressive in its treatment of labor, and why the new challenges of capital accumulation were more successfully and smoothly resolved. As we shall see, the sequences and timing of political change

relative to industrial transformation may also have important implications for an issue which has concerned most of the contributors to this volume: the future of the Mexican system.

The Theoretical Framework: Industrialization, Populism, and the Emergence of Southern B-A Regimes

Let us look more closely at the economic and political processes which, according to O'Donnell, eventually led to B-A regimes in the South American cases. In his discussion of these processes, O'Donnell reaches rather far back into the past, basing much of his analysis on the well-known works of political sociologists such as Cardoso, of political economists such as Hirschman, and of political scientists such as Schmitter and Stepan.[7] Consequently, most readers will be familiar with at least some segments of the general conceptual framework he elaborates. Given the scope and complexity of the conceptual framework as a whole, however, a fairly extensive synthesis and review seems warranted. Table 1 presents some of the main elements of O'Donnell's argument in schematic form. The remainder of this section will devote particular attention to three important components of the model: the economic aspects of import-substituting industrialization (ISI); the populist politics associated with this process; and, finally, some dynamic aspects and dilemmas of the transition to new, B-A forms of rule.

THE ECONOMICS OF IMPORT-SUBSTITUTION INDUSTRIALIZATION

In Latin America, import substitution has generally been understood in terms of the reaction of dependent, neocolonial economies to the exigencies of twentieth-century war and depression. While the larger Latin American economies contained at least some domestic industry prior to the 1930s and 1940s, they were nonetheless integrated into the world economy primarily as suppliers of raw materials and importers of manufactured consumer products and capital goods. With the great crises, the basis of this expert-led growth pattern collapsed, and the bigger, relatively modernized countries were provided with the incentive and opportunity to significantly expand their industrial sectors by replacing unavailable imports with domestic products. By this time, however, the Latin American countries were already economically far behind and vulnerable in a world order dominated by advanced industrial powers; the constraints of this international context (both real and perceived) served to shape and limit the industrialization process.

Albert Hirschman suggests that one of the distinctive characteristics

Table 1 / O'Donnell's B-A Schema

	A	B	C	D
Economy	"Open" economy	"Closed," import-substituting industrialization (ISI): (a) Transfer of resources from export to manufacturing sector (b) Growth led by expansion of manufacture for domestic market	Economic crisis: (a) Exhaustion of "easy phase" of ISI (b) Inflation (c) External imbalances (d) Slowdown in expansion of economy and manufacturing sector	Bureaucratic-authoritarianism: (a) Where successful, a renewed industrial expansion based on growth of producer-goods and consumer-durables sectors for both export and domestic market (b) Reduction of inflation (c) Expansion of GDP (d) Deterioration in position of urban working class
Class Relations	Dominance of agro-export oligarchy	"Populist" alliance between industrialists and urban working class	Increased class antagonism within industrial sector	Alliance between state technocrats and multinational corporations
State Structure and Policy	Weak state: (a) Little penetration, low extractive capabilities (b) Laissez-faire policies	Expansion of state functions and activities: (a) Promotion of ISI (b) Heavy central-bank borrowing (c) New welfare functions	Increased direct action; weakening of state extractive and distributive capabilities	Expansion or enforcement of corporate controls over urban workers; increased extractive capabilities of state; austerity measures

of this crisis-induced industrialization was its tendency to move forward in distinct, relatively well-defined phases.[8] As Latin American governments and entrepreneurs faced the challenges and opportunities presented by a succession of balance-of-payments difficulties, attention focused naturally on these imported products which were easiest to replace domestically. Thus, in the initial phases, industrial expansion tended to be spearheaded by the formation of relatively small-scale plants applying the last touches to consumer products. Larger, more complex producer-goods industries usually came later on in the process, after the first, easy import-substitution industrialization (ISI) opportunities had been exhausted and as the cost of imported inputs placed new, heavier burdens on foreign-exchange earnings. In contrast to earlier European patterns of industrialization, where large-scale investment in armaments and producer goods frequently led the initial drive toward industrialization, there was in Latin America little public effort or private incentive to move toward the formation of a vertically integrated industrial economy—a feature of ISI which, as we shall see, is highly relevant to an understanding of the capital-accumulation problems of the 1950s and 1960s.[9]

A related feature, which also serves to differentiate Latin American from European industrialization, is that in Latin America industrial production was oriented primarily toward supplying domestic demand. Latin American manufacturers did not, like earlier industrializers, move rapidly and aggressively into international markets. An important exception to this generalization occurred during World War II, when Mexican and Brazilian textile producers enjoyed a temporary export boom, taking up the slack left by the war economies of the more industrialized nations. On the whole, however, domestic markets seemed to be the most natural and urgent area of expansion, for both local entrepreneurs and Latin American policy makers. Hirschman argues that this perception may well have been a self-fulfilling and self-defeating prophecy, based on an exaggerated pessimism about the competitive weaknesses of "technologically inferior" industries and perpetuated by the protectionist policies of postwar Latin American governments.[10] Whatever the reasons, the inward-looking character of Latin American industrialization remained another of its distinctive traits until the 1960s, which meant that the import-substitution process could not materially contribute to the restructuring of the export sector or to the capacity of Latin American economies to generate new foreign-exchange earnings.

The continuing dependence on the fluctuating demand for traditional exports had several other important implications for import-substituting Latin American countries. The recurrent problem, of course, was too little exchange earnings relative to capital needs. This type of squeeze occurred repeatedly—during the 1930s, again in the post-Korean slump of the mid-1950s to early 1960s, and still again in the mid-1970s. During the 1940s, on the other hand, too much foreign exchange chased too few available imports, creating strong inflationary pressures and, eventually, a rapid surge of postwar imports which quickly depleted reserves. These external imbalances were exacerbated by the import-intensive characteristics of many of the new domestic industries, which depended directly on foreign supplies and generated indirect pressures for additional imports through the creation of new domestic income. Although import substitution may have reduced the ratio of imports to domestic production, therefore, it did not reduce the economy's vulnerability to external bottlenecks. As the process wore on, in fact, import requirements tended to become more rigid, with increasing proportions of scarce foreign exchange required simply to fuel the existing industrial structure and decreasing proportions available to finance new expansion or offset balance-of-payments deficits.[11]

One more aspect of import substitution should be noted: its association with varying degrees of intersectoral antagonism. Much of this antagonism, to be sure, was less profound than it seemed to be on the surface, blurred over as it often was by the familial and economic ties that grew up between the older agro-export elites and the newer industrial classes. Yet the economic disruptions generated by international depression and war produced a widespread disenchantment among middle-class politicians and intellectuals with the earlier patterns of export-led growth. And at least some conflict of interest tended to be built into the relationship between protected high-cost industrialists and "free-trading" mineral and agricultural exporters, especially when the former were new, small-scale, and of immigrant stock and the latter were large, aristocratic, or foreign. The general perception throughout much of the industrialization process, therefore, was that the agro-export oligarchy was hostile to the reorientation of Latin American economies. The uncertainty of export earnings and the increasingly growth-related import needs added to this natural rivalry by magnifying the struggle over scarce foreign exchange. And many Latin American governments, anxious to foster the growth of the industrial sector, often attempted to do so at the expense of the exporters, engineering large intersectoral resource transfers through taxation policies and manipulation of the exchange rates of their currencies.

THE POLITICS OF ISI: POPULISM

In the southern countries, the logical political corollary of such economic processes was populism—a coalition of new entrepreneurs and urban workers, cemented by the protectionist and welfare appeals of power-seeking nationalist *políticos*. The entrepreneurial segments of this coalition could not achieve hegemony alone; for, as previously implied, they lacked the prestige and élan that accrued to the European and American "pioneers" of heavy industry and "conquerors" of new foreign markets. Where the protectionist requirements of the Latin American bourgeoisie faced opposition from the exporting oligarchies, their interests coincided quite closely with those of middle-class *políticos*, who were anxious to expand their political power at the expense of such oligarchies. In this context, a "popular" mass appeal was the principal vehicle through which both entrepreneurs and *políticos* could achieve their respective aims. Thus, a vague commitment to social welfare was a central element in the platforms of populist coalitions, translating in more concrete terms into the encouragement and supervision of union organization, toleration of generous wage settlements, and expansion of government services, education, and social security benefits to large segments of the urban working class.

One of the central themes of this essay, which I will take up more directly in the discussion of Mexico, is that the actual political and economic gains of the working-class members of the populist coalition varied directly with the degree of sectoral conflict associated with industrialization. In Brazil, the conflict was more muted than elsewhere. During the 1930s, the government's effort to defend export prices by stockpiling coffee produced a sizable fiscal deficit which had the side-effect of maintaining domestic demand and offering new investment opportunities for local manufacturers.[12] Entrepreneurial and coffee interests thus coincided in this instance and rendered a sustained working-class appeal far less necessary politically. As a result, the workers' organizations found it more difficult to extract political independence and economic benefits from the Vargas administration. On the other hand, in Argentina, where no such pump priming occurred, the overall economic contraction was far more severe and contributed to a persisting zero-sum perception that industry's gain would be agriculture's expense. This situation of extreme sectoral conflict, which reached its peak during the Perón era, produced considerable leverage for the Argentine working class. Not surprisingly, the Peronist regime was far more lavish than Vargas in its wage and welfare policies, and the Argentine workers were eventually much more successful than their Brazilian counterparts in resisting the government's efforts to control them from above.

In virtually all the industrialized South American countries, however, populist coalitions did seem to accompany the import-substitution process to one degree or another. A simple recitation of the names associated with such coalitions—Perón and Vargas in Argentina and Brazil, Ibáñez, Alessandri, and Aguirro Corda in Chile, Battlle in Uruguay—should suffice to make this point. These leaders, and the movements they headed, were major political forces in their respective countries during the entire second quarter of the twentieth century. Later, in the quite different economic context of the late 1950s and 1960s, such leaders as Frondizi, Kubitschek, Goulart, and Frei—along with a host of much lesser-known *políticos*—were the heirs of such movements, attempting to draw on quite similar bases of support. These attempts, to be sure, varied in character from one country and time period to another. They occurred in both democratic and authoritarian frameworks, were launched by both governing and opposition elements, and varied in terms of policy emphasis and degree of political success. Yet, in one way or another, the combined themes of industrialization, social welfare, and nationalism pervaded virtually the entire political history of southern Latin America until the middle of the 1960s.

INDUSTRIAL MATURATION AND B-A REGIMES

This brings us, finally, to a discussion of the contemporary experiences with bureaucratic authoritarianism. The socioeconomic difficulties which provoked such experiments were rooted in two sources. One, already implied, was the exhaustion of the easy phase of ISI, which in the southern countries occurred during the 1950s. It was widely recognized that the new phase would require managerial, planning, and technological skills that were frequently unrelated to those of earlier industries, and a level of capital investment that was not easily financed out of the profits of smaller-scale firms. Second, this need for new types of capital investment tended to coincide with an end to the war-related export booms of the 1940s and early 1950s and a decade-long deterioration in the terms of trade for traditional experts. In the grip of those underlying pressures, all the countries of the south eventually proved unable to escape prolonged bouts with soaring inflation, severe depression, and mounting labor unrest, a syndrome of high political salience that had reached crisis proportions by the early 1960s.

For many of the politicians and "technocrats" who confronted such difficulties, some combination of increased foreign and government investment seemed to offer the most logical way out of this cul-de-sac. Foreign sources, especially the expanding multinationals, possessed the necessary new technology and offered at least short-term relief for balance-of-payments problems. And domestic governments seemed more able than the domestic private sector to generate large-scale risk capital. However, the effective mobilization of foreign and public investment required the implementation of a number of new, highly controversial policies. For the government, the primary requirement was to recoup the extractive powers and investment capabilities which had been steadily eroded by populist pressures and inflation. This implied a drastic expansion of the tax base, the elimination of public sinecures, and restrictions on welfare expenditures. New *private* capital (both foreign and domestic) required, above all, greater stability and predictability. And this, in turn, implied an end to populist demagoguery, fiscal austerity and currency devaluation, long-term agreements about profit remissions, and liberalized policies toward foreign investment and trade.[13]

Not surprisingly, efforts to graft such policies onto older populist social and institutional bases generally ended in economic and political failure. Perhaps the most striking example of such difficulties was Frondizi's unsuccessful attempt in Argentina to find a balance between his initial nationalist and Peronist base of support and a development strategy which relied heavily on accepting the International Monetary Fund's orthodox advice and attracting foreign capital. Frondizi's decision to "capitulate" to the IMF (along with his concessions to the international petroleum companies) helped for a time to generate a substantial inflow of foreign investment, but the cost in terms of domestic political support proved exorbitant. As new elections approached, Frondizi was unable to maintain the austerity programs which had been part of the price of international respectability. By 1962, he was out of office, the investment flow had dried up, and a new round of inflation and depression gripped the Argentine economy. Kubitschek's less orthodox policy mix (combining heavy foreign borrowing with large fiscal deficits and price controls) was somewhat more successful in postponing these problems in Brazil. By the late 1960s, however, his elected successors were confronting a socioeconomic crisis quite similar to that of Argentina.[14]

The lessons drawn from these apparently unsuccessful experiments undoubtedly contributed directly to the B-A regimes which grew out of the armed coups of the past decade. For, as the decade wore on, many of the military leaders and civilian technocrats who engineered these coups were convinced that the policy "imperatives" of the new industrial era could not be sustained without a thorough restructuring of state-societal relations. Partly from design and partly from trial and error, therefore, the now familiar B-A features of the new regimes began to emerge. Authoritarian rulers proclaimed a long-term "transcendence" of open electoral politics. Old-style protectionist nationalism was abandoned in the attempt to build a close working relationship between the state and foreign capital. And efforts were made to demobilize the working-class base of the old populist coalition through exclusionary corporate controls.

The Brazilian case (and, in some ways, the Mexican case as well) indicates that such efforts, if successfully carried through, can convert some of the vicious circles of the previous political economy into what is—from a technocratic perspective—a more virtuous, mutually reinforcing relationship between authoritarian stability, new investment, and economic expansion. As a basis for our subsequent discussion of Mexico, however, this general summary is best concluded on a somewhat different note: that southern rulers who attempted to restructure their political economies along B-A lines have faced serious transitional problems which rendered failure at least as likely as success.[15]

The most immediate task faced by the new southern regimes—the use of military force to tame labor and close down elections—was perhaps the easiest. Middle-class *políticos* and domestic entrepreneurs alike were inclined to welcome the respite from political unrest and conflict, leaving organized labor at least temporarily isolated from its former allies. The harsh austerity measures which followed the coups, however, were far less likely to be greeted with general enthusiasm. Such measures required a number of years before they would pay off in renewed growth rates, more jobs, and greater monetary stability. And, in the meantime, it was the middle sector that was most likely, after the working class, to face the highest costs in terms of losses in salaries, credit, and profits. Finally, as it became clearer that the new regimes intended to remain in power indefinitely and that efforts at economic recovery would involve opening the door to foreign competition, middle-class *políticos* and national entrepreneurs found their interests seriously threatened.

O'Donnell argues that the task of neutralizing this initial threat of domestic entrepreneurial opposition—and of eventually drawing support from this sector—is one of the most difficult aspects of the transition process.[16] In Brazil, this hurdle was surmounted largely because middle-class fear of "another Goulart" helped to forestall open opposition long enough for inflation to be contained and for the alliance with foreign capital to be secured. Once economic recovery had taken hold, the regime could draw segments of the old entrepreneurial elite back into the governing coalition through subsidies and mixed enterprises. The dismantlement of the old populist coalition could then be completed. In Argentina, however, this process was short-circuited. The excluded Peronists were at once far less threatening and far better organized than their Brazilian counterparts, and there was less to inhibit the disaffected *políticos* and bourgeoisie from turning back toward an alliance with the working class. As a result, the repression of labor became ever more costly politically, and by the late 1960s the old familiar spirals had reappeared. The Cordobazo, the prolonged massive rioting in Córdoba, raised serious questions about the capacity of the regime to provide a safe investment climate. The flow of foreign funds diminished, further threatening economic recovery, and the regime collapsed, the victim of the same vicious circles that had destroyed its predecessors.[17]

By this stage of the analysis, many will anticipate some of the contrasts that can be drawn between these southern patterns and the Mexican experience. I will argue more extensively below that the early emergence of authoritarian and corporatist institutions in Mexico allowed her to escape many of the transitional difficulties associated with the new phases of industrialization. Before turning to these issues, however, another set of questions must logically be dealt with first: to what extent does the pattern of Mexican *economic* change resemble the dependent ISI which allegedly occurred in the south? Are the phases and problems associated with this type of industrialization comparable among the different countries? A comparative discussion of political institutions and processes is meaningful only if such questions can be answered.

Industrialization Processes Compared: Mexico, Argentina, Brazil

Is it useful to speak of Mexico, Argentina, and Brazil as sharing a common type of industrial change? Comparisons of this sort are, of course, always rendered difficult and debatable by the uniqueness of the national settings within which industrialization occurs. Argentina, for example, was already a relatively wealthy country when the great depression triggered industrialization, but its overall economy has grown very slowly since—at an annual per capita rate of 0.8 percent.[18] This is the reverse of Brazil and Mexico, which began the century as much poorer countries but have grown at far higher rates. Brazil's population, to mention another difference, is almost twice Mexico's and about four times that of Argentina. There are also significant variations in resource endowment (Argentina's relatively low iron and mineral reserves, for example), and in geography (Mexico's proximity to the United States). These and other factors inevitably intrude on efforts to find a common economic ground of comparison between the three cases.

Notwithstanding such differences, important similarities do exist. In the 1960s, the manufacturing sector contributed between one-fifth and one-third of each country's gross product, a figure matched only by Chile and Uruguay among the other Latin American countries; 60 percent of the manufacturing sector, in turn, was comprised of dynamic rather than traditional industries (see Table 2). In quantitative and qualitative terms, therefore, Mexico, Argentina, and Brazil shared the status of being the most industrialized countries in Latin America. Still more important for our purposes is the fact that, when the historical *process* of industrialization is examined more closely in each country, many of the preceding generalizations about ISI seem to stand up rather well—a fact which, as I have already suggested, is probably attributable to the weight of exogenous influences emanating from a shared international environment.

Table 2 / Levels of Industrialization in Latin America

	Industrial Production as % of GDP (1960)[a]	Traditional Industry as % of Total Industrial Production (1968)[b]
Argentina	32.2	39.8
Brazil	21.4	41.9
Mexico	23.3	41.2
Chile	23.7	47.5
Uruguay	21.2	61.3
Colombia	17.0	63.2
Peru	16.7	57.3
Venezuela	10.6	48.0
Ecuador	15.6	65.5
Bolivia	10.2	71.4
Paraguay	17.3	—
Costa Rica	11.1	—
El Salvador	13.6	—
Guatemala	10.5	91.9
Panama	12.8	73.7
Nicaragua	11.1	—
Honduras	12.1	—
Dominican Republic	14.0	85.9

[a]*Source:* Economic Commission for Latin America, "Industrial Development in Latin America," *Economic Bulletin for Latin America*, vol. 14, no. 2 (1969), p. 4.

[b]*Source:* Economic Commission for Latin America, *Economic Survey of Latin America* (New York: United Nations, 1970), p. 49.

Until very recently, for example, industrial production in all three countries was oriented primarily toward the domestic market, with the single exception of wartime textile exports. In 1969, after almost four decades of industrial expansion, manufactured products accounted for only 21 percent of the value of all Mexican exports and only 14 percent and 10 percent, respectively, of those of Argentina and Brazil.[19] Since the end of the 1960s, all three countries have significantly expanded nontraditional exports, especially to each other and to the rest of Latin America. But this move toward export substitution, described in the Mexican case by Villarreal in this volume, is still at a relatively early stage.

The proposition that ISI is preceded by well-defined phases is slightly less clear. Mallon's data on the composition of Argentine imports from 1925 to 1949 indicate that the inflow of consumer, intermediate, and capital goods all tended to decline at about the same rate, a pattern which he suggests is somewhat at variance with the image of a horizontal spread of "final touch" industries as the first phase of ISI.[20] A fairly clear pattern does emerge, however, when the manufacturing sector is disaggregated into *product groups* requiring successively greater capital and technological inputs. From 1930 to about 1950, textile production led the Argentine manufacturing sector, in terms of both size and rate of growth. Next came the production of consumer durables (washing machines, stoves, bicycles, and automobiles), which had their most rapid rates of growth between 1957 and 1961. During the 1960s, finally, Mallon's data show that the fast growers were the sectors producing relatively complex products: industrial chemicals, synthetic fibers and resins, internal combustion engines, and measuring instruments.[21]

In Mexico and Brazil, there was also some deviation from the general ISI pattern. Each country expanded its steel industry fairly early, in the 1930s and 1940s, and there was considerable attention in both cases to the development of an industrial infrastructure. Each country therefore sustained a somewhat more integrated pattern of industrial development than Argentina, which may have contributed to their considerably more dynamic overall economic performance in the postwar era.

Nevertheless, in most other respects industrialization in Mexico and Brazil appears to have proceeded from easy to successively more difficult forms of investment and production. In both of these countries, as well as in Argentina, light industrial products—most notably, textiles—led the early expansion. In the Mexican case, cotton-textile production expanded by 65 percent from 1939 to 1946, outstripping the 40 percent growth rate of the manufacturing sector as a whole. Comparable industries, though small in total output, expanded at even faster rates during this period: canning and preserving, by 250 percent; beer bottling, by 177 percent.[22] Mosk's description of the "new Mexican industrialist" who emerged in the 1940s also parallels rather closely the type of capitalist generally linked to the early ISI phase: a strong protectionist who generates funds from personal savings and profits to operate small-scale plants.[23]

During the 1950s and 1960s, moreover, the transformation of the Mexican and Brazilian industrial structure also paralleled Argentina's. In Brazil during the 1950s, textiles' share of total manufacturing output dropped from 20 percent to 12 percent, while that of chemicals, electrical machinery, and transport equipment rose from 9.1 percent to 20.1 percent.[24] In Mexico, automotives led industrial expansion during the 1950s, and industrial chemicals from 1960 to 65.[25] By this time, Mosk's "new industrialist" had evolved into (or was superseded by) the managers of massive industrial enterprises, closely linked to commercial banking interests, and with substantial access to foreign creditors and to the Nacional Financiera.

The largest and most important economic difference among the three countries is in the performance of their respective export sectors, with Mexico's considerably more dynamic and diversified than the other two. During the 1940s, Mexico was the only country in which agricultural expansion accompanied the early drive toward industrialization, and the only one in which export sales kept pace with manufacturing output. (In contrast, Argentina was the only country in which export sales *declined* in absolute terms between 1945 and 1961.)[26] Moreover, Mexico has derived substantial advantages from the tourist and border trade, which contributed between a quarter and a half of her foreign-exchange earnings during the post-war era.

Despite these advantages, it can still be argued that Mexico shared many of the external vulnerabilities of the other countries. Her merchandise exports, lower in absolute value than those of Argentina and Brazil (Figure 1a), declined in annual growth rate from 8.0 percent in the 1940s to only 1.8 percent in the 1950s and were virtually stagnant during the critical transitional years from 1956 to 1960.[27] Although the tourist trade continued to grow, an increasing proportion of this growth (about one-half by the late 1960s) was offset by the expense of border imports and by Mexican tourism in the United States.[28] The earning capacity of Mexico's export sector during the 1960s was not appreciably greater than Brazil's when the reverse effect of this border trade is taken into account (see Table 3). And Mexico's lead over the Argentine export sector, while considerable, was substantially less than a comparison of gross export receipts would suggest. As Figure 1b shows, finally, all three countries tended to incur very large current-account deficits during the 1950s and 1960s as they approached their respective drives toward more integrated industrial economies.

If the parallels drawn so far are valid, it follows that the three countries should have exhibited similar types of socioeconomic strains as they approached more difficult phases of industrial transformation. This seems, in many respects, to be the case. Villarreal's data on Mexican import substitution suggest that the easy phase of consumer-goods replacement came to an end in Mexico during the mid-1950s, just a few years after it did in Argentina (circa 1948) and Brazil (circa 1950). From this time until the early 1960s, Mexico encountered the familiar syndrome of problems—although these did not reach the crisis proportions characteristic of the southern countries. Inflationary pressures, so ubiquitous and pernicious in the south, were also present in Mexico from 1955 to 1957, when a major round of domestic price increases was touched off by external disequilibrium and devaluation. Economic growth rates slowed substantially during the late 1950s and early 1960s, leading many contemporary observers to feel that Mexico's long experience with economic expan-

Table 3 / Merchandise Exports plus Net Services for Mexico, Brazil, and Argentina (in Millions of U.S. Dollars)

Year	Mexico	Brazil	Argentina
1960	1,008	966	958
1961	1,084	—	—
1962	1,205	—	—
1963	1,302	—	—
1964	1,396	1,171	—
1965	1,470	1,408	1,320
1966	1,622	1,475	1,389
1967	1,608	1,384	1,272
1968	1,768	1,609	1,143
1969	1,946	1,990	1,311
1970	1,985	2,235	1,476
Total goods and net services (1965–70):	10,399	10,101	7,911
Total goods and services (1965–70):	14,211	13,052	10,561

Source: *Economic Survey of Latin America,* various years.

sion was about to come to a halt.[29] This same period, finally, marked a considerable upswing in the militancy of Mexico's organized labor movement, parallel to that occurring at about the same time in Argentina and Brazil. The number of strikes in Mexico rose from an annual average of only 143 during 1951–57 to 516 for 1958–63, peaking at over 700 in 1958 and 1962, and leveling off sharply to only 96 during the remainder of the 1960s.[30]

It should not be surprising, in view of these difficulties, that writers such as Vernon, looking at Mexico in the early 1960s, took a rather pessimistic view of its future prospects.[31] It was far from unreasonable to conclude that subsequent decades would see an end to Mexico's "economic miracle" and a political time of troubles similar to that of her southern neighbors. Why was it that Mexico, despite similar developmental patterns and tensions, did not collapse into the full-scale crisis characteristic of the south? Has the preceding comparison obscured factors in the Mexican economy that may have permitted her to make a smoother industrial transition?

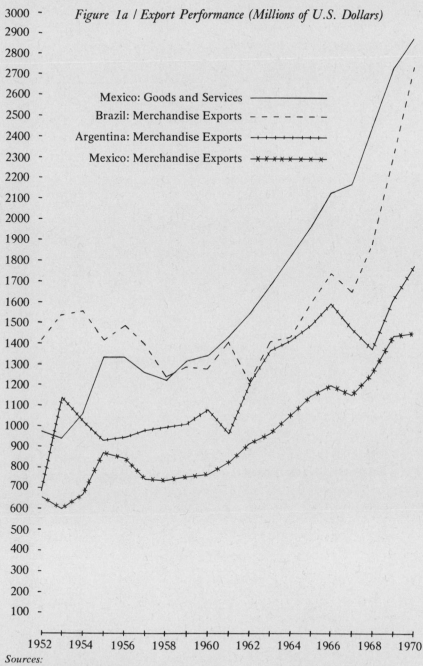

Figure 1a / Export Performance (Millions of U.S. Dollars)

Mexico: Goods and Services ——————
Brazil: Merchandise Exports – – – – – – –
Argentina: Merchandise Exports ++++++++++
Mexico: Merchandise Exports ××××××××××

Sources:

Mexico: René Villarreal's essay in this volume.

Argentina: R. D. Mallon, in collaboration with Juan D. Sourrouillo, *Economic Policymaking in a Conflict Society: The Argentine Case* (Cambridge, Mass.: Harvard University Press, 1975), p. 18.

Brazil: Werner Baer, *Industrialization and Economic Development in Brazil* (Homewood, Ill.: Richard D. Irwin, 1965), p. 273; *Economic Survey of Latin America,* various years.

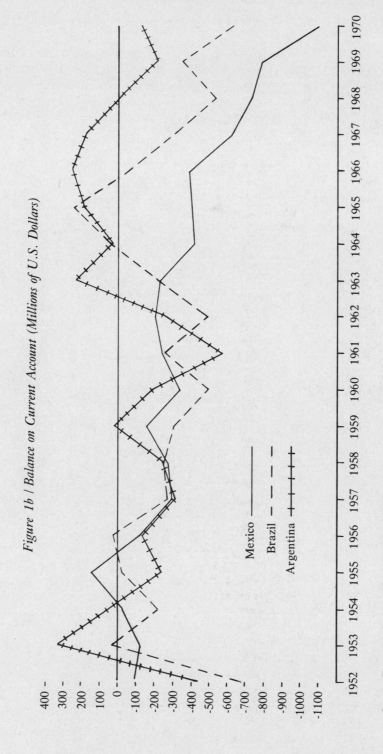

Figure 1b / Balance on Current Account (Millions of U.S. Dollars)

Source: Economic Survey of Latin America, 1972.

Some such factors, most already mentioned above, do of course come to mind: Mexico's large population, compared with Argentina; her relatively more integrated pattern of industrial growth; her geographic proximity to the technology, capital, and domestic markets of the United States. Although the contributions of these and other advantages should not be ignored in assessing Mexico's economic performance, their importance should not be overrated either. Brazil, after all, possessed an even larger domestic market and similar advantages of industrial integration. Yet that country did not escape major economic and political difficulties in the early 1960s. And Argentina, which did not have these advantages, had others of her own—a much higher per capita income at the start of the industrialization process, a more literate population, and a more equitable distribution of income. Similarly, Mexico's unique geographic advantages, while of obvious importance, can by no means explain all of her economic success. The tourist trade, as we have seen, did not prevent the emergence of gigantic current-account deficits. And Reynolds estimates tentatively that the additional merchandise and capital flows made possible by Mexico's shared border with the United States may account for as little as 4 percent of Mexico's total GNP and about one-half to 1 percent of its annual growth rate—a significant, but by no means overwhelming contribution to Mexico's economy.[32]

It should be clear enough by now that Mexico's relative success in containing the tensions associated with the new phases of industrialization is due as much to political as to economic differences among the three countries. The pessimists of the early 1960s proved wrong over the next 15 years not because they had underestimated the seriousness of the transitional problems they had identified, but because they had underestimated the strengths of Mexico's authoritarian sociopolitical order as this interacted with the process of industrialization. Many of these strengths can be highlighted and clarified through further comparison with the political-economic experiences of Argentina and Brazil.

Mexican Authoritarianism and Industrialization

Although students of Mexican development might well acknowledge the economic importance of the industrial transition of the 1950s and 1960s, they would almost universally identify other points in time as being of substantially greater *political* significance. The civil war period, the Cárdenas era of the 1930s, and the policy shifts of the Ávila Camacho and Aleman regimes all would emerge as far more noteworthy historical landmarks than, say, the cautious Ruiz Cortines regime, the vacillating administration of López Mateos, or even the repressive era of Díaz Ordaz.

This historical periodization would be correct as far as it goes. What should be added is that the choices and turning points of these earlier periods are precisely what allowed the 1950s and 1960s to be so comparatively quiet. It was because Mexico had a Cárdenas in the 1930s and an Alemán in the 1940s that it did not have to undergo the traumatic shift to an Onganía or a Castelo Branco later on.

THE FIRST PHASES OF ISI
AND THE EARLY DEMISE OF MEXICAN POPULISM

Like virtually every other analysis of contemporary Mexico, further elaboration of this argument must begin with the Revolution: the cruel armed struggles of the 1910s, the consolidations of the Calles era, and especially the institutional and redistributive reforms of the Cárdenas administration. As every beginning student knows, the first gave Mexico her great political heroes, villains, and myths; the second, social peace; and the third, her corporatist structure and legitimacy-building economic payoffs to the peasantry. By the end of the Cárdenas administration, Mexico's leaders could ground their power in an aura of revolutionary legitimacy which was felt by the very groups that were later to become the *olvidados* of government policy—the peasantry, labor, and the urban poor. As Almond and Verba noted over ten years ago, the support (or, better put, the passive acceptance) which such groups provided for the regime eroded only very slowly, in spite of decades of neglect and abuse.[33]

When viewed from the perspective of the South American countries, the events of Mexico's early revolutionary decades had a second important implication which is less well understood by political scientists. These events, particularly the Cárdenas reforms, eliminated the previously dominant agro-export elites, who, in the south, continued to be perceived as threats to industrialization and to the regimes which promoted it. In Mexico, the absence of this threat left a power-seeking state and a profit-seeking private sector free to promote industrialization. After 1940, there was no sustained need for either to attempt systematically to purchase the active support of labor with social welfare, generous wage settlements, or public employment. Although concern for the welfare of the poor continued to be a part of the rhetoric and policies of post-Cárdenas governments, it is fair to say that populism, as that term was generally understood in the south, died a premature death in Mexico. The only imperative with respect to import-substitution politics was that the workers be "kept in line"—a task that could be relatively easily accomplished by drawing on the political capital built up by earlier reforms, by occasional new concessions, and by the substantial threat of coercion.

The argument that the demise of Mexican populism is related to the elimination of conflict between the industrial and exporting sectors can be given additional force by relating it more explicitly to the comparisons made above between Argentina and Brazil. If we now take all three cases together (as of the 1940s), they fall rather clearly along a continuum in which the treatment of labor is directly associated with the degree of sectoral antagonism.

Perón's Argentina is at one extreme. During the late 1940s, public monoposony powers were deliberately used to depress the incomes of the agricultural elites, to pump resources out of the export sector, and to divert those resources toward industrial and labor supporters. The gains of the organized Argentine workers during this period were probably the most dramatic of the three cases. The real wages of an expanding urban work force doubled between 1942 and 1949 (see Figure 2).

Brazil is an intermediate case with respect to both sectoral and labor relations. The trade and exchange-rate policies of the Vargas government imposed serious burdens on the noncoffee export sector, and its economic policies in general tended to favor industry over agriculture.[34] But the convergence of coffee and manufacturing interests throughout much of this period substantially reduced the degree of sectoral antagonism. And although hard data are not available to substantiate the point, most observers agree that Brazilian workers were more successfully controlled politically and gained less economically than their Argentine counterparts.[35]

Mexico, finally, was at the opposite end of the spectrum from Argentina. During the Ávila Camacho and Alemán administrations, net public funds actually flowed *into* the rural sector (the only case where this was so), providing dams, roads, and credit to the revolutionary *generales* and new landowners who dominated the commercial agriculture of the north. The resulting productivity gains of this sector were in turn funneled through the private banking system into industrial capital, as well as into the consumption of industrial products.[36] Sectoral collaboration, rather than conflict, thus seemed to be the general pattern in post-Cárdenas Mexico, with apparently short-term negative consequences for many members of the Mexican working class. Just how badly the poorer strata fared is, to be sure, a matter of some debate. Overall living standards may have improved slightly as more Mexicans moved into higher-paying occupations and the benefits of economic expansion "trickled down." The general policy of the 1940s regime, however, was to allow profits to rise far more rapidly than wages and welfare. This meant that most of the poorer strata lost in relative terms as income disparities increased, and that the economic and political position of many organized workers deteriorated in absolute terms as well. Whereas Argentine wage rates doubled during the 1940s, Mexican wage rates actually fell—by 50 percent if we accept the data provided by Timothy King (see Figure 2).[37] And, regard-

Figure 2 / Wage Rate Movements

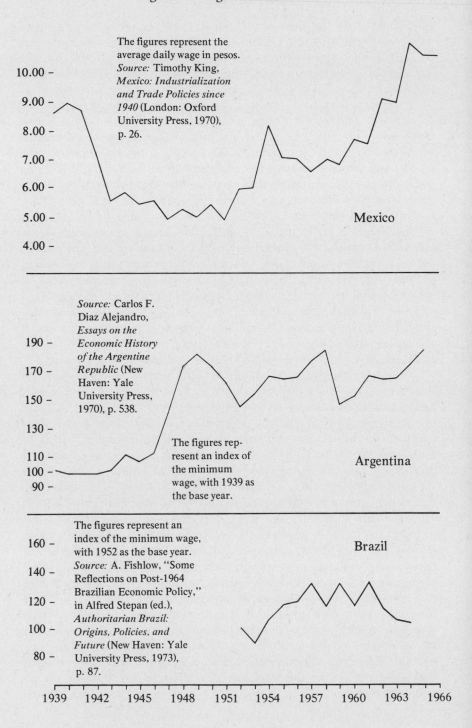

The figures represent the
average daily wage in pesos.
Source: Timothy King,
*Mexico: Industrialization
and Trade Policies since
1940* (London: Oxford
University Press, 1970),
p. 26.

10.00 –
9.00 –
8.00 –
7.00 –
6.00 –
5.00 –
4.00 –

Mexico

Source: Carlos F.
Diaz Alejandro,
*Essays on the
Economic History
of the Argentine
Republic* (New
Haven: Yale
University Press,
1970), p. 538.

190 –
170 –
150 –
130 –
110 –
100 –
90 –

The figures rep-
resent an index of
the minimum
wage, with 1939 as
the base year.

Argentina

The figures represent an
index of the minimum wage,
with 1952 as the base year.
Source: A. Fishlow, "Some
Reflections on Post-1964
Brazilian Economic Policy,"
in Alfred Stepan (ed.),
*Authoritarian Brazil:
Origins, Policies, and
Future* (New Haven: Yale
University Press, 1973),
p. 87.

160 –
140 –
120 –
100 –
80 –

Brazil

1939   1942   1945   1948   1951   1954   1957   1960   1963   1966

less of how much credence one wishes to attach to available quantitative evidence, it seems clear enough in qualitative terms that the emphasis of the corporatist structures established by Cárdenas had changed from the mobilization and politicization of the labor movement to deactivation and control.[38]

Thus, although the Alemán, Vargas, and Perón regimes had certain structural similarities—all were, in some sense, authoritarian and corporatist—they differed substantially in their class base, policies, and use of political and economic resources. These contrasts should help us to understand the even more substantial institutional and social differences which had evolved by the time each country confronted the economic challenges of more recent decades.

By the onset of the industrial transition period of the 1950s, authoritarianism in both Argentina and Brazil had broken down, the casualty of the pressures that powerful domestic enemies placed on the loosely integrated governing coalitions and of the postwar wave of democratic international opinion. Corporatist labor legislation remained on the books in both countries, and the relatively strong enforcement of this legislation remained a feature of democratic Brazil until the late 1950s.[39] In Argentina, however, the political mobilization of the Perón years provided a basis for strong union militancy and class conflict, with the national bourgeoisie divided between the anti-Peronist military and oligarchy and their previous labor allies. In both Brazil and Argentina, finally, the very existence of open politics, with its electoral pressures and partisan competition, offered a continuing incentive for revivals of the old populist coalition in new democratic guises. Such coalitions were employed not only to defeat incumbent regimes but to elect new ones—Vargas himself reappeared on the scene in the 1950s, along with such familiar figures as Kubitschek, Frondizi, and Goulart. The economic result in both countries was the vicious circle described in the preceding pages—less severe and eventually more surmountable in Brazil, but quite different in both instances.

The early demise of populism in Mexico, in contrast, left that country in quite a different situation, with many of the features of a B-A regime already firmly established by the 1950s. For over a decade, the State and the private sector had developed a close, mutually beneficial relationship that Reynolds has aptly termed an "alliance for profits."[40] The exclusionary features of Mexican corporatism, as we have seen, had also taken shape, with organized labor tamed and encapsulated by the institutions of the PRI. With traditional elites eliminated, new industrial capital coopted, and labor contained, there was no real pressure to open the system electorally. Clothed in the symbols of the Revolution, the regime's authoritarian structures were institutionalized and secure.

Mexico was thus constitutionally ready to confront the transition to the new phase of industrialization. It was not necessary in that country to restructure state-societal relations or to endure the politically dangerous and debilitating process of polarization which this restructuring entailed in the south.

In the remaining portions of this section, I will further explore the implications of Mexico's situation by reviewing the way its B-A regime handled three interconnected problems generally associated with the industrial transition: the containment of inflation, the integration of foreign capital into the political economy, and the treatment of organized labor.

STABILIZATION POLICY

Mexico's success in containing inflation during the 1950s and 1960s—in sharp contrast to the performance of the southern countries during these decades—was an important corollary of the early entrenchment of a B-A regime. It should be recalled that Mexico, like the other countries, encountered rather strong inflationary pressures during the war years and again in the mid-1950s—the result, among other things, of the familiar interaction between external bottlenecks, central-bank borrowing, and wage-price spirals. In fact, Mexico's last serious bout with inflation (that is, until the mid-1970s) bears a striking resemblance to the self-perpetuating sequences that proved so difficult to arrest in the Argentine case. In 1954, growing balance-of-payments deficits prompted a sudden devaluation of the Mexican peso, which in turn touched off a wave of compensating wage demands and price increases. In the next 20 months, domestic prices rose by 30 percent, partially neutralizing the effects of the devaluation decision and threatening Mexico with a new round of external imbalances and inflationary adjustments.[41] Unlike the populist regimes of the south, however, the Mexican government was able to engineer the policies necessary to arrest this cycle, in the process displaying a considerable capacity to manipulate its private-sector allies and to assert control over organized labor.

A large number of economists appear to agree that the most important policy change during that period was the decision to move away from central-bank borrowing as a technique for financing government deficits.[42] Although the government budget remained unbalanced, the necessary revenues were generated primarily through placing public securities in the private banking system and increasing reserve requirements —in some cases, to 100 percent. Such measures, together with an increasingly sophisticated system of selective credit controls and an already low general level of public spending, allowed the government to tap private-sector savings without at the same time substantially increasing the tax burden or choking off credit flows into desirable economic activities. Thus, while low taxes helped to compensate the private sector for tighter banking and credit controls, the government was able to keep the expansion of the money supply at quite reasonable levels. During 1961–66, this supply expanded at an annual rate of 12 percent in Mexico, as contrasted with respective figures of 27 percent and 60 percent for Argentina and Brazil, which continued to rely heavily on central-bank borrowing.[43]

Mexico's control of its money supply depended, of course, on its ability not only to compensate and control private-sector credit needs but to resist wage demands and popular pressures that might have advanced the inflationary spiral. But this, as we have seen, was already an important aspect of the Mexican system. Wages did turn sharply upward in 1953, the year preceding the devaluation; but despite the increased strike activity which followed that event, the real wage rate dropped sharply again in the next three years and did not begin a sustained upward climb until the 1960s.[44]

Finally, a similar and even broader capacity of the Mexican regime to resist potentially inflationary popular pressures is amply reflected in the comparatively low level of public social expenditures during that period. During the 1950s, Mexico's investment in education comprised only 1.4 percent of her GNP, as contrasted with 2.5 percent in Argentina and 2.6 percent in Brazil. Only 18.9 percent of the Mexican work force was covered by social security benefits, as contrasted with 66.3 percent for Argentina. In keeping with our earlier characterization of the intermediate position of Brazilian populism, it is significant that the relevant figure there was 20.4 percent, considerably lower than Argentina but still higher than Mexico.[45]

The bottom line of this comparison of the three countries is, of course, their respective rates of inflation. From 1961 to 1966, prices increased at an average rate of 27 percent in Argentina and 60 percent in Brazil. By this time inflation in both countries had assumed a life of its own which seriously distorted savings and investment activities and presented a major obstacle to further economic expansion. Of the "big three" countries, only Mexico was able to contain such pressures and to achieve relative price stability, with price increases averaging only 2 percent throughout the 1960s.[46] The social costs of the political arrangements which made this possible were enormous. Nonetheless, the conditions of stability and predictability which they provided facilitated the investment necessary to the new phases of industrial expansion and economic growth.

THE STATE, FOREIGN CAPITAL, AND THE DOMESTIC BOURGEOISIE

It follows from the preceding discussion that foreign investors and lending institutions would be strongly attracted to the favorable climate provided by Mexican political institutions and economic policies. Mexican officials, in turn, tended to adopt a rather pragmatic orientation toward the prospects of such investment. As the first phases of ISI came to a close in the mid-1950s, therefore, neither the nationalist legacy of Cárdenas nor the protectionism of later years deterred the growing interdependence between the Mexican state and foreign capital. Like its B-A counterparts to the south, the Mexican government relied increasingly on foreign funds to maintain foreign-exchange accounts and to spearhead industrial expansion in new, relatively difficult areas. And as Figure 3 indicates, foreign funds have flowed into the Mexican industrial sector at a generally accelerating rate. While this evolving relationship has not been without its rough spots (suspicions do exist on both sides), in general the distinctive feature of the Mexican experience during the past two decades is the relative political smoothness with which foreign capital has been integrated into the political economy. In the context of our comparison with the southern countries, three aspects of this relationship warrant particular comment.

The first and most general aspect is the overall ease with which Mexican officials could pull on the control reins when general unrest seemed to be shaking investor confidence. This was the case, for example, with the López administration in the early 1960s, when such factors as the Cuban Revolution, internal labor militancy, and the apparent leftward tilt of the López administration itself threatened both the flow of foreign funds and domestic capital formation. By 1962, the President had taken up the slack previously left to the unions and to nationalist elements within his administration and embarked on a series of speeches designed to reassure investors of the government's good will—measures which evidently elicited the desired response from private capital.[47] This ability to pull back was precisely what the more open populist regimes in the south lacked. In Brazil, a renewed flow of foreign funds required a total regime change rather than simply a change of government policy; and, in Argentina, even the new B-A regime itself could not maintain the necessary conditions of order.

Related to this general point is a second, more specific one: the ability of the Mexican regime to neutralize potential entrepreneurial opposition to the growing importance of foreign capital within the Mexican economy. The political threat of an alienated domestic bourgeoisie was, after all, one of the central problems confronted by the B-A regimes of the south. The stabilization of these regimes, O'Donnell argues, depended eventually on their ability to reincorporate segments of this bourgeoisie into the governing coalition—to convert the dual alliance between the state and foreign capital into a ruling trio.[48] O'Donnell suggests that the failure to accomplish this task contributed substantially to the undoing of the Onganıa regime, whereas the more successful stabilization of the Brazilian regime

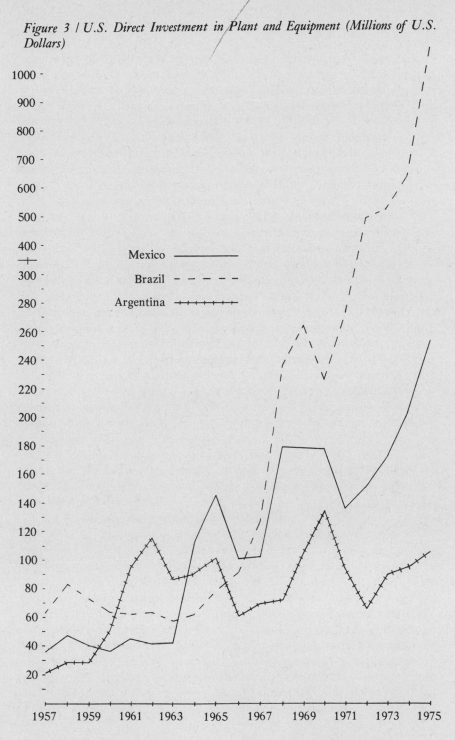

Figure 3 / U.S. Direct Investment in Plant and Equipment (Millions of U.S. Dollars)

Mexico ————

Brazil — — — —

Argentina ++++++

Source: U.S. Department of Commerce, *Survey of Current Business,* various years.

in the late 1960s occurred only after a dangerous period in which the state depended on foreign capital alone. In Mexico, however, a comparable ruling trio was created by *adding* foreign capital, rather than by *re*incorporating national entrepreneurs, for the latter never really left the governing coalition.

As the door to foreign investors opened wider in the 1950s, there was, to be sure, some protest from Mexico's private sector, particularly from the newer industrialists represented by the Cámara Nacional de Industrias de Transformación (CNIT). But such opposition had considerably less political leverage than in the south. For one thing, open confrontation with the regime would have jeopardized the long-established working relationship between the state and the private sector. More important still, the exclusionary basis of this long-standing alliance created an almost insurmountable obstacle to the formation of a nationalist coalition between entrepreneurs and labor, especially since labor was formally a part of the governing party, whereas the entrepreneurs were officially excluded. To the extent that Mexico's restricted electoral process allowed for a protectionist opposition, the principal options were therefore on the right, through the Partido de Acción Nacional (PAN), rather than on the populist left. Given these unpromising possibilities, it was clear that the best choice for the domestic bourgeoisie lay in accomodation and negotiation rather than in serious protest and opposition. In any case, it became evident to many local businessmen in a very short time that the threat of foreign competition was not so great after all—that, in fact, they might profit considerably from Mexicanization policies, from joint enterprises with the State, and from continued government protection in some areas of the economy. In a sense, therefore, Mexico started out its process of industrial transition in a manner quite similar to the Brazilian model which evolved during the late 1960s—with a relatively stable equilibrium between the state, the domestic private sector, and foreign investors.

Finally, in still a third feature of the foreign-investment process, the regime's willingness to impose relatively strict rules of the game on international capital helped the government to maintain its domestic bases of support. In turn, its local allies considerably strengthened the hand of the regime as it looked abroad. Unlike its Brazilian counterpart of the mid-1960s, the Mexican government could afford to maintain an arms-length relationship with foreign capital. This is certainly one plausible interpretation of the data presented in Figure 3. While industrial capital entered Mexico at a rate far surpassing that in unstable Argentina, the inflow was much more modest than the veritable explosion of new investment which has occurred in Brazil since 1964. This was probably not because the Mexican government was less successful in attracting foreign capital, but because it was in a position to be more selective in regulating and directing the flow in ways that were consistent with its own political and economic interest. Weinert's more extensive discussion in this volume of the relationship between the Mexican state and foreign capital seems consistent with this interpretation.

LABOR AND THE MEXICAN STATE

As Mexico moved into the new phases of industrialization during the 1960s and 1970s, exclusionary corporatist arrangements continued to predominate in state-labor relationships. Nevertheless, the recent decades have in many respects been an era of relaxation and concession rather than heightened repression and control. There was, to be sure, the proverbial iron fist concealed in the government's velvet glove. And virtually all "concessions" to the working class (e.g., López Mateos' profit-sharing scheme) turned out on closer examination to be marginal reforms at the very most.[49] Yet the fact remains that, compared with earlier periods of Mexican history, the State treated labor with a relatively light touch; at the very time that the new phase of industrialization induced the Argentine and Brazilian regimes to clamp down, Mexico's B-A rulers were easing up. Further reflection about some of the preceding comparisons should suggest more clearly why this was so, as well as what it implies about the Mexican system.

The B-A regimes in Argentina and Brazil emerged in the midst of a profound political and economic crisis in which an increasingly militant labor movement appeared to be an important propelling force in a soaring inflationary spiral. Just how much of the blame for this inflation should actually be laid at the unions' door is a matter of some debate. At least one distinguished student of the Brazilian economy, Albert Fishlow, has argued that labor's role was in fact minor and that the restrictions imposed by the Castelo Branco regime represented a kind of economic overkill which placed an unnecessarily harsh burden on Brazilian workers.[50] Such a view is at least partially consistent with my earlier observations about the relatively successful containment of Brazilian populist pressures throughout much of the post-Vargas era. Be that as it may, the combination of labor militancy and inflation in both Brazil and Argentina led naturally to perceptions which linked the two; as authoritarian rulers came to power in the mid-1960s, they were impelled to combine the task of political demobilization with the imposition of harsh economic austerity measures.

No such measures were necessary in Mexico. The unions, after all, had been captured by the state decades before, and inflationary pressures, as we have already seen, were nipped in the bud during the mid-1950s.

Within this framework, open coercion was largely superfluous. And, in the absence of serious economic pressures to the contrary, there were many good political reasons for offering increased wage and welfare benefits to Mexican workers.

This apparent trade-off between early repression and later concession is graphically illustrated by the wage-rate movements in Figure 2. While Argentine wages were rising dramatically in the 1940s, Mexico's plunged. Beginning in 1959–60, however, the curve in Mexico began to move steadily upward, finally reaching prewar levels in 1962 and exceeding those levels by the middle of the decade. During the same period, we see "spikey" wage curves for Argentina and Brazil, as the workers in each country struggled (rather unsuccessfully) to prevent inflation from eroding their earning capacity. Finally, although the data for Figure 2 do not extend into the B-A phase, there is considerable evidence from other sources to suggest that the fortunes of the organized working class deteriorated in the South American countries, most markedly in Brazil.[51] The Argentines and Brazilians thus seem to have paid their dues later in the industrialization process, probably with considerable interest.

Whether payment came late or early, none of the three working classes seems to have gained very much in return. Broadly speaking, the class basis of the Mexican political economy appeared roughly similar to that of the southern B-A regimes, especially to the more established and stable Brazilian system. Private capital (domestic and foreign) and the state itself were the gainers in this system, while organized labor and the poor were the political targets and the economic losers, in relative if not in absolute terms. Notwithstanding the leniency with which the Mexican state has dealt with labor recently, it is this framework of state and class relationships that seems to define the parameters of political action.

But Mexico's relatively lenient treatment of its workers, like its arms-length relationship with foreign capital, does suggest that the Mexican regime is in a better position to maneuver within these parameters. Because of the timing of its evolution, the Mexican state is less closely tied than the Brazilian to the short-term interests of its private-sector allies. It is more capable of buttressing relations with groups that are essentially excluded from the ruling coalition. Efforts to make such adjustments may at times give the government the appearance of muddling and indecision; there is certainly little doubt that, on a day-to-day basis, individual decision makers may feel (or actually be) paralyzed by contending interests. From the perspective of the broad historical analysis undertaken here, however, there is a logic to the behavior of Mexican administrations which indicates that the vacillation of recent decades may have been more a sign of strength and flexibility than of fundamental weaknesses in the structure of the authoritarian regime.

Concluding Perspectives: Sequence and Timing in the Industrialization Process

A brief foray into the tangled debates surrounding the literature on political development will bring into sharper focus the concluding aspects of this discussion of Mexico. When this literature evolved several decades ago, primarily from the pens of U.S. scholars, the dominant hypothesis seemed to be that "stable democracy" was the product of economic development and industrialization. Almost immediately, however, this formulation came under attack. A politically *developed* polity, it was argued, was by no means identical with a Western, democratic one. And, in any case, newer third-world countries were modernizing in an historical context which made political development of any kind problematic, and democratic development highly unlikely. Some of the best Latin American scholars, Cardoso and O'Donnell among them, have taken the criticism a step farther by suggesting that, in conditions of economic dependency, industrialization was likely to produce a tendency toward a new, more modernized, more malevolent form of authoritarian rule. While carefully avoiding a simple-minded form of economic determinism, they have come close to turning on its head the conventional optimistic equation between industrialization and democracy.[52]

Meanwhile, however, the intellectual world of the conventional development theorists had not stood still. By the late 1960s, many such theorists had themselves reconsidered earlier formulations relating economic and political change, emphasizing the importance of sequences and rates of change in the interaction of the two.[53] With regard to the question of stable democracies, they also turned earlier formulations around: the dominant hypothesis was now that such systems were most likely to emerge in countries which had achieved a "liberal" constitutional order *prior* to the process of industrialization and modernization.

This study of Mexico suggests an analogous hypothesis about the evolution and consolidation of Latin American B-A regimes.[54] It accepts the O'Donnell-Cardoso thesis that there is a natural affinity between B-A regimes and the more difficult phases of dependent, import-substitution industrialization—that the problems of capital accumulation which occur during this phase encourage unpopular, "technocratic" economic policies, authoritarian controls, and institutionalized restrictions on lower-class political participation. I have argued, however, that it makes a great deal of difference whether such issues are confronted late or early in the industrialization process. Much of the preceding discussion can, in fact, be formally summarized rather simply, in terms of two principal "sequence" variables: (1) whether political authoritarianism had been consolidated by the onset of the difficult industrialization phase; and (2) whether the working class had already been demobilized through exclusionary corporatist institutions. As Table 4 suggests, these two variables seem to account directly or indirectly for a considerable amount of the variance between Mexico, Brazil, and Argentina.

The consolidation of B-A rule is least likely to be successful in countries such as Argentina which have settled neither the authoritarian nor the labor issues by the end of the easy ISI phase. Failure to resolve these two questions is in turn associated with full-scale socioeconomic crises—inflation, stagnation, and labor militancy—as such countries move into the new ISI phase. The B-A regimes which emerge in the course of such crises are thus confronted with the extremely difficult task of engineering fundamental changes on three fronts simultaneously: they must fashion new trade, investment, and wage policies threatening to domestic owners as well as workers; they must forge new controls over the unions; and they must dismantle the apparatus of competitive politics. The antagonisms generated by such measures, *ceteris paribus*, threaten to produce a broad opposition coalition which isolates the regime from much of domestic society and places its survival very much in doubt.

The Brazilian pattern presents a greater likelihood of B-A consolidation. As a result of the relatively mild sectoral antagonisms of the early ISI phase, Brazilian authorities moved more quickly and successfully to deal with the labor question along exclusionary corporatist lines. These arrangements were, to be sure, intermixed all along with populist pressures and policies, which seemed to burst out of control temporarily under the Goulart administration. But, compared with those in Argentina, the Brazilian authorities retained a considerable capacity to manipulate labor throughout most of the post-war period. This may help to explain why the stagnation-inflation crisis was postponed for a longer time in Brazil and why it was surmounted more successfully. It almost certainly made life easier for the new B-A authorities who came to power in 1964. Notwithstanding labor's new militancy, the legal and institutional machinery necessary for the demobilization of the workers was already in place. Without much debate among themselves, the new ruling elites could simply take up the slack left by the previous regime and—as Schmitter puts it—"purge the system" of its "populist imperfections."[55]

On the other hand, Brazil's early failure to consolidate authoritarian government presented serious problems for the post-1964 regime. As long as the electoral arena remained relatively open, competing *políticos* were free to appeal to labor in ways that jeopardized the government's control over the unions. Such competition also inhibited the kinds of stern governmental policies which might have eliminated, rather than simply postponed, the typical crisis of inflation and stagnation. Like its Argentine counterpart, therefore, the Brazilian B-A regime was confronted with the

Table 4 / *The Evolution of B-A Regimes (from Left to Right)*

Country	Easy Phase of ISI (1930/35–1950/55)	Difficult Phase of ISI (1950/55–1970/75)	B-A Regime Changes
Argentina (Chile, Uruguay) — Strong sectoral antagonism	Competitive regime	Very severe inflation; stagnation	Fundamental change in policy
Strong populism	Weak or relaxed corporatist controls	Labor unrest	Restructured state-labor relations; new authoritarianism
Brazil — Weak sectoral antagonism	Competitive regime	Severe inflation; stagnation	Fundamental change in policy
Weak populism	Relatively strong exclusionary corporatist controls	Labor unrest	Tightening of state-labor relations; new authoritarianism
Mexico — No sectoral antagonism	Consolidated authoritarianism	Stagnation, inflation "nipped in the bud"	Incremental policy changes
No populism	Very strong exclusionary corporatist controls		Continued authoritarianism; continued corporatist controls

simultaneous tasks of instituting new economic policies and dismantling a going system of free elections. Opposition to the prospects of long-term authoritarian rule threatened to reinforce the antagonisms generated by the new policy directions. Middle-class fear of "another Goulart," together with the relative weakness of Brazilian labor, helped the regime to fend off this threat and survive. But the political cost of its route to power was a weak base of legitimacy. Coercion remained the principal instrument for dealing with large segments of the middle and working classes; and material rewards, a primary basis of cohesion within the governing coalition itself.

In the Mexican pattern, finally, both authoritarian and labor issues had been settled prior to the onset of the new phase of industrialization. As a consequence, this system's adaptation to the requirements of this phase involved the fewest political and economic difficulties. With authoritarian and corporate structures beyond serious challenge, the regime could move fairly quickly to control inflation. And with full-scale economic crisis nipped in the bud, the regime was free to proceed with an incremental and disaggregated policy style that isolated and neutralized potential opponents. Measures to encourage new heavy investment, often from foreign sources, could be instituted without crippling controversy. Labor could be kept off balance and at least partially tied to the regime by a heavy emphasis on the carrot as well as the stick. For these reasons, the Mexican version of B-A rule was most firmly and easily consolidated.

Successful B-A consolidations tend to generate problems of their own, however. Whereas Argentina continues in the 1970s to wrestle with many of the same issues that gave birth to such regimes, both Mexico and Brazil are confronting a whole series of new challenges, many of which flow in dialectical fashion from the "victories" of the regime itself. Both countries, for example, must now deal with the potentially explosive combination of mass poverty and growing upper-middle-class prosperity, the product in large part of income and investment policies which made a trade-off between growth and welfare. In both countries, also, the alliance between the state and foreign capital has produced a mounting burden of external debt that seriously threatens the viability of earlier growth models. This problem is exacerbated by the soaring import costs which drastically erode both foreign-exchange reserves and the confidence of international lenders and jeopardize the access of both regimes to world capital markets.[56] "Liberalization" and "decompression," finally, have reemerged as issues in both countries. Demands for wider and more meaningful forms of political participation are pressed not only (or even primarily) by the neglected urban and rural poor, but by the middle-class beneficiaries of previous economic expansion.

To speculate extensively on the impact of or response to such challenges would take us well beyond the scope of this paper. In any event,

Purcell's contribution to this volume spotlights in considerable detail many of the variables at work in the Mexican case. Our emphasis on the importance of relative sequences in political and economic change does, however, warrant comment on one relevant issue about the Mexican future: if the early settlement of constitutional issues allowed Mexico to adapt smoothly to the problems of the 1950s and 1960s, will the character of this adaptation in turn facilitate the handling of subsequent challenges? It is by no means clear that the answer to this question is yes—or even whether the challenges of the 1970s and 1980s can be dealt with through B-A framework of any sort. The logic of the preceding analysis does, however, point to some important sources of leverage possessed by the Mexican regime, leverage which has been denied the Brazilian regime as the result of its different, more recent route to power.

Mexico's principal advantages flow from the fact that she entered the 1970s far less polarized along class and political lines than Brazil. This is true in spite of the fact that much of the political capital provided by the Revolution had been eroded by earlier policies and by neglect of social-welfare questions; "revolutionary" Mexico, after all, had far more of this capital to expend than did "counter-revolutionary" Brazil. The Brazilian regime is unlikely to live down the quite recent memory of the repressive demobilization which accompanied its birth or to escape its anti-popular reputation, whereas these elements of Mexican rule are more muffled, distant, and concealed by the incremental changes of recent decades.

The Mexican system is thus much more likely than the Brazilian to withstand the tensions associated with the concept of liberalization. A full-scale democratization which removed all restrictions on peaceful political participation and offered a real possibility of replacing incumbent elites could probably not be tolerated in either system. But in Brazil even more modest forms of liberalization have proved quite difficult. Relaxation of restrictions on the press, on assembly, and on association threaten in that country to open a Pandora's box filled with repressed resentments and antagonisms. Mexicans, on the other hand, have lived with this form of liberalization (in varying degrees, to be sure) for several decades. And although further relaxation of controls (say, wider latitude for trade-union activities) would certainly increase the level of conflict within the Mexican system, it is far less likely to escalate to the point that it gets out of hand.

Having been less repressive than the Brazilians to begin with, moreover, Mexican authorities have less to fear from such liberalization—at least in the short run. Even after the Tlatelolco massacre, there was no Mexican equivalent of the Brazilian security police. The latter, after a decade of the use of torture, are understandably nervous about relaxing political controls and have been instrumental in undermining the liberalization attempts of the past few years. The different routes to B-A consolidation have also cast Brazilian and Mexican technocrats in quite different positions with respect to liberalization. In Brazil (as in Argentina), technocratic elements have tended to rely on hard-line military factions to impose their austerity policies. Thus compromised, their political status and power, as well as the apparent economic gains of their policies, would be threatened by a relaxation of authoritarian controls. In Mexico, where recent decades of growth and stability have been engineered in a less polarized context, the new technocrats have been able to adopt a much more progressive line, operating within the Mexican elite as a force for renovation and social reform.

Can policy innovations go "far enough, fast enough" to prevent the decay of the Mexican regime? The answer, as Purcell argues, will turn in considerable extent on the relationship between the State and the bourgeoisie, domestic and foreign. As a first step in understanding that relationship, it is undoubtedly useful to conceive of the State as having its own distinct objectives and interests—a point emphasized by Purcell, Smith, and Weinert in this volume. However, in my judgment it would be a serious mistake to argue on the basis of that conception that the State can totally transcend class relations or govern independently of society. Historically, the Mexican (like the Brazilian) regime has pursued its interest in close alliance with its private-sector partners, and if the "necessary" reforms involve a fundamental restructuring of that alliance—say, the elimination of foreign or domestic private capital from the governing coalition—they are not likely to be carried through.

It is by no means clear, however, and in fact is highly debatable, that such measures are really necessary for the survival of the system. Social scientists and seasoned revolutionaries alike can attest to how little it really takes for most capitalist (or, for that matter, socialist) systems to manipulate the workers and the poor, to the modesty of lower-class "demands," and to the obstacles that their social position places in the way of generating sustained popular pressures for fundamental change. There is not much to suggest that things are very different in Mexico, and a good deal to suggest the contrary.[57] Moreover, some useful policy innovations (for example, the movement toward export substitution) offer prospects of substantial gain to many parts of the private sector, and can probably be pursued by both the Mexican and Brazilian regimes without serious entrepreneurial opposition. Other factors which vitally affect the survival of the system—the state of the world economy, for instance—are not likely to be affected one way or the other by the outcomes of class conflict or government policy.

Turning back to the adjustments which *do* involve class antagonisms, finally, we should bear in mind the comparative flexibility with which the Mexican regime can operate *within* the prevailing alliance structure. Consider again the contrast with Brazil. Because of the conditions of its birth, the Brazilian governing coalition is bound together primarily by a mixture of pragmatic interest in economic expansion and fear of the sectors which have been excluded from the coalition. The pragmatic basis of cohesion has already, in the mid-1970s, been seriously threatened by a purely exogenous factor—the downturn in world economic conditions. With a few more years of externally induced inflation and recession, the Brazilian regime could be in serious crisis regardless of what it does or does not do domestically. But the second element—fear—weakens its hand even further. In the polarized Brazilian context, even tentative efforts by the government to broaden its base of support risk a loss of investor confidence and a further unraveling of the socioeconomic basis of the "Brazilian miracle."

The Mexican dilemma, while similar, is less severe. However attenuated, the symbols of the revolution continue to provide a cushion against exogenous shocks and economic downturns. And the line between the governing coalition and the rest of society is fuzzier and less defined by recent history than in Brazil. These factors provide the government a more secure basis for maintaining stability and predictability. With this ability more secure, the trade-offs between investor confidence and social reform are likely to be less crippling and less extreme than in Brazil. Where policy initiatives (say, a progressive restructuring of the tax system) bite into the pocketbook as well as the confidence of investors, the government may have more difficulty retaining the support of its private-sector partners. But our argument about the evolution of the Mexican system suggests that the state *can* survive short-term opposition in such instances. In the longer run, as in so many other cases around the world, the bourgeoisie may well discover that the "sacrifices" it found so threatening actually helped to preserve the capitalist system. This, after all, is now the conventional wisdom about the eventual effects of the Roosevelt and Cárdenas reforms. The same conclusion may one day be reached about some reformist Mexican administration of the 1970s or 1980s.

Acknowledgments

This essay is part of an ongoing research project funded by the Center for International Affairs, Harvard University, and by a grant from the Social Science Research Council.

Notes

1. See, especially, the contributions of Susan Kaufman Purcell and José Luis Reyna.
2. See the contributions of Susan Eckstein and Rosa Elena Montes de Oca.
3. For a discussion of "exclusionary" and "inclusionary" corporatism, see Gui-

llermo A. O'Donnell, *Modernization and Bureaucratic-Authoritarianism: Studies in South American Politics* (Berkeley: Institute of International Studies, University of California, 1973); David Collier and Ruth Berins Collier, "Comparing Corporatism: Who Does What to Whom and How?" and James J. Malloy, "Authoritarianism and Corporatism in Latin America: The Modal Pattern," both in James J. Malloy (ed.), *Authoritarianism and Corporatism in Latin America* (Pittsburgh: University of Pittsburgh Press, 1977); Alfred Stepan, *State and Society: Peru in Comparative Perspective* (New Haven: Yale University Press, forthcoming).

4. For a discussion of the Mexican case, see Reyna's essay in this volume.

5. See O'Donnell's *Modernization and Bureaucratic-Authoritarianism;* "Estado y Corporativismo," in James Malloy (ed.), *Authoritarianism and Corporatism in Latin America;* and his *Reflexiones sobre las tendencias generales de cambio en el Estado burocrático-autoritario* (Buenos Aires: Centro de Estudios de Estado y Sociedad, 1975).

6. Especially O'Donnell, *Reflexiones*, pp. 11–21; Fernando Enrique Cardoso, "Associated-Dependent Development: Theoretical and Practical Implications," in Alfred Stepan (ed.), *Authoritarian Brazil: Origins, Policies, and Future* (New Haven: Yale University Press, 1973), pp. 142–79.

7. Fernando Enrique Cardoso and Enzo Faletto, *Dependencia y desarrollo en América Latina* (Mexico, D.F.: Siglo Veintiuno Editores, 1970); Albert O. Hirschman, "The Political Economy of Import-Substituting Industrialization in Latin America," in Albert O. Hirschman, *Bias for Hope* (New Haven: Yale University Press, 1971), pp. 85–123; Philippe C. Schmitter, *Interest Conflict and Political Change in Brazil* (Stanford: Stanford University Press, 1971); and Schmitter, "Paths to Political Development in Latin America," in Douglas A. Chalmers (ed.), *Changing Latin America* (New York: Academy of Political Science, 1972), pp. 83–108; Stepan, *State and Society.*

8. Hirschman, "The Political Economy," p. 91ff.

9. See Alexander Gerschenkron, *Economic Backwardness in Historical Perspective* (Cambridge, Mass.: Harvard University Press, 1962).

10. Hirschman, "The Political Economy," pp. 115–22.

11. Osvaldo Sunkel, "Big Business and Dependencia: A Latin American View," *Foreign Affairs*, vol. 50 (April 1972), 517–31.

12. Celso Furtado, *The Economic Growth of Brazil* (Berkeley: University of California Press, 1968), pp. 193–224.

13. See O'Donnell, *Reflexiones*, pp. 11–21.

14. For a good general review of these issues, see Richard D. Mallon, in collaboration with Juan V. Sourrouillo, *Economic Policymaking in a Conflict Society: The Argentine Case* (Cambridge, Mass.: Harvard University Press, 1975); Thomas E. Skidmore, *Politics in Brazil, 1930–1964: An Experiment in Democracy* (New York: Oxford University Press, 1967).

15. See O'Donnell, *Reflexiones*, pp. 22–41, for an analysis of this process.

16. *Ibid.*

17. *Ibid.*, p. 7; Robert R. Kaufman, "Transitions to Stable Authoritarian-Corporate Regimes: The Chilean Case?" Sage Professional Papers, forthcoming; Stepan, *State and Society.*

18. Carlos F. Diaz Alejandro, *Essays on the Economic History of the Argentine Republic* (New Haven: Yale University Press, 1970), p. 68.

19. Calculated on the basis of data in "Trade in Manufacturing and Semi-Manufacturing," *Economic Bulletin for Latin America*, vol. 17, no. 1 (1972): 45.

20. Mallon, *Economic Policymaking in a Conflict Society*, p. 69.

21. *Ibid.*, pp. 69–72.

22. Sanford A. Mosk, *Industrial Revolution in Mexico* (Berkeley: University of California Press, 1950), p. 317.

23. *Ibid.*, p. 21ff.

24. Werner Baer, *Industrialization and Economic Development in Brazil* (Homewood, Ill.: Richard D. Irwin, 1965), p. 76.

25. Clark W. Reynolds, *The Mexican Economy: Twentieth-Century Structure and Growth* (New Haven: Yale University Press, 1970), pp. 407–10.

26. Economic Commission for Latin America, *The Economic Development of Latin America in the Post-War Period* (New York, 1964), pp. 87–115.

27. *Ibid.*, p. 115.

28. See Villarreal in this volume.

29. Raymond Vernon, *The Dilemma of Mexico's Development: The Roles of the Private and Public Sectors* (Cambridge, Mass.: Harvard University Press, 1963), pp. 116–23 and 176–95.

30. International Labour Organisation, *Year Book of Labour Statistics* (Geneva: International Labour Office, various years). The number of workers involved followed a similar pattern, going from a low of 7,000 in 1956 to over 80,000 in 1958 and then dropping dramatically in the 1960s.

31. Vernon, *The Dilemma of Mexico's Development.*

32. Reynolds, *The Mexican Economy,* pp. 245–51.

33. Gabriel Almond and Sidney Verba, *The Civic Culture* (Boston: Little, Brown, 1965).

34. Nathaniel H. Leff, "Export Stagnation and Autarkic Development in Brazil," in Charles T. Nisbet (ed.), *Latin America: Problems in Economic Development* (New York and London: Free Press and Collier-Macmillan, 1969), pp. 219–37.

35. Schmitter, *Interest Conflict and Political Change in Brazil.*

36. Reynolds, *The Mexican Economy,* esp. pp. 175–80.

37. Timothy King, *Mexico: Industrialization and Trade Policies since 1940* (New York: Oxford University Press, 1970), p. 26.

38. See, e.g., the essay by Reyna in this volume and Susan Kaufman Purcell, *The Mexican Profit-Sharing Decision: Politics in an Authoritarian Regime* (Berkeley: University of California Press, 1975); and Frank Brandenburg, *The Making of Modern Mexico* (Englewood Cliffs, N.J.: Prentice-Hall, 1964).

39. See Schmitter, *Interest Conflict and Political Change in Brazil.*

40. Reynolds, *The Mexican Economy,* p. 185.

41. Vernon, *The Dilemma of Mexico's Development,* p. 110.

42. King, *Mexico,* pp. 36–37; Raymond F. Mikesell, "Inflation in Latin America," in Charles T. Nisbet (ed.), *Latin America: Problems in Economic Development,* pp. 147–48; Roger D. Hansen, *The Politics of Mexican Development* (Baltimore: Johns Hopkins University Press, 1971), pp. 50–55; Reynolds, *The Mexican Economy,* pp. 286–88.

43. Mikesell, "Inflation in Latin America," p. 146.

44. King, *Mexico,* p. 26.

45. Hansen, *The Politics of Mexican Development,* p. 86.

46. Mikesell, "Inflation in Latin America," p. 146.

47. King, *Mexico,* pp. 39–43; Vernon, *Dilemma of Mexican Development,* pp. 116–22.

48. O'Donnell, *Reflexiones,* pp. 22–41.

49. Purcell, *The Mexican Profit-Sharing Decision.*

50. Albert Fishlow, "Some Reflections on Post-1964 Brazilian Economic Policy," in Stepan (ed.), *Authoritarian Brazil,* pp. 69–119.

51. See Philippe C. Schmitter, "The 'Portugalization' of Brazil?" in Stepan (ed.), *Authoritarian Brazil*, pp. 179–233; Economic Commission on Latin America, *Economic Survey of Latin America* (New York: United Nations, 1969), p. 109.

52. See especially, O'Donnell's *Modernization and Bureaucratic-Authoritarianism* and Cardoso's "Associated-Dependent Development."

53. E.g., Samuel P. Huntington, *Political Order in Changing Societies* (New Haven: Yale University Press, 1968); Robert A. Dahl, *Polyarchy: Participation and Opposition* (New Haven: Yale University Press, 1971); Richard A. Pride, "Origins of Democracy: A Cross-National Study of Mobilization, Party Systems, and Democratic Stability," *Sage Professional Papers in Comparative Politics* (Beverly Hills: Sage Publications, 1970).

54. This discussion represents a partial elaboration of my "Notes on the Definition, Genesis, and Consolidation of Bureaucratic-Authoritarian Regimes" (New Brunswick, 1975; mimeo).

55. Schmitter, "The 'Portugalization' of Brazil?" p. 182.

56. Brazil, which imports most of its oil, has been hit considerably harder than Mexico in this respect. But the Mexican import bill has also risen substantially as the cost of capital goods and industrial inputs has increased.

57. See, e.g., Wayne A. Cornelius, "The Impact of Governmental Performance on Political Attitudes and Behavior: The Case of the Urban Poor in Mexico City," in Francine E. Rabinovitz and Felicity M. Trueblood (eds.), *Latin American Urban Research* (Beverly Hills: Sage Publications, 1973); and "Urbanization as an Agent of Political Instability: The Case of Mexico," *American Political Science Review*, vol. 63 (September 1969): 833–57.

List of Acronyms

CAM	Congreso Agrario Mexicano
CANACINTRA	Cámara Nacional de Industrias de Transformación
CCI	Confederación Campesina Independiente (but see pp. 56, 61–62)
CGT	Confederación General de Trabajadores
CIDA	Centro de Investigaciones Agrarias
CNC	Confederación Nacional Campesina
CNIT	Same as CANACINTRA above
CNOP	Confederación Nacional de Organizaciones Populares
CONASUPO	Compañía Nacional de Subsistencias Populares
CONCAMIN	Confederación de Cámaras de Industria
CONCANACO	Confederación de Cámaras Nacionales de Comercio
CONPA	Congreso Permanente Agrario
COPARMEX	Confederación Patronal de la República de México
CROC	Confederación Revolucionaria de Obreros y Campesinos
CROM	Confederación Regional de Obreros Mexicanos
CTM	Confederación de Trabajadores Mexicanos
PAN	Partido de Acción Nacional
PEMEX	Petróleos Mexicanos
PNA	Partido Nacional Agrarista
PNR	Partido Nacional Revolucionario
PRI	Partido Revolucionario Institucional
PRM	Partido de la Revolución Mexicana
UGOCM	Unión General de Obreros y Campesinos de México

Mexican Administrations, 1876-1977

Porfirio Díaz	1876–1911
Francisco I. Madero	1911–1913
Victoriano Huerta	1913–1914
Venustiano Carranza	1914–1920
Alvaro Obregón	1920–1924
Plutarco Elías Calles	1924–1928
Emilio Portes Gil	1928–1929
Pascual Ortiz Rubio	1929–1932
Abelardo Rodríguez	1932–1934
Lázaro Cárdenas	1934–1940
Manuel Ávila Camacho	1940–1946
Miguel Alemán	1946–1952
Adolfo Ruiz Cortines	1952–1958
Adolfo López Mateos	1958–1964
Gustavo Díaz Ordaz	1964–1970
Luis Echeverría Alvarez	1970–1976
José López Portillo	1976–

Index

Other Public Affairs Publications
Sponsored by the
⊖ *Center for Inter-American Relations/New York*

AUG 1 8 1982

Terms of Conflict:
Ideology in Latin American Politics
INTER-AMERICAN POLITICS SERIES, VOLUME 1
Morris J. Blachman and Ronald G. Hellman, editors
Philadelphia: Institute for the Study of Human Issues

The Americas in a Changing World: Including the Report
of the Commission on United States–Latin American Relations
With a Preface by Sol M. Linowitz
New York: Quadrangle/The New York Times Book Company

Latin America: The Search for a New International Role
SERIES IN LATIN AMERICAN INTERNATIONAL AFFAIRS, VOLUME 1
Ronald G. Hellman and H. Jon Rosenbaum, editors
New York: John Wiley and Sons

International Economic Relations of Latin America
SERIES IN LATIN AMERICAN INTERNATIONAL AFFAIRS, VOLUME 2
Joseph Grunwald, editor
Beverly Hills, Calif.: Sage Publications.

The Peruvian Experiment: Continuity and Change Under Military Rule
Abraham F. Lowenthal, editor
Princeton, N.J.: Princeton University Press

3 4 5 6 7 8 9 10 11 12 13 14 15   88 87 86 85 84 83 82 81